Dictionary of

Person-Centred Psychology

Dictionary of
Person-Centred Psychology

Keith Tudor MA, MSc

Temenos, Sheffield

and

Tony Merry MA

University of East London

Consulting Editor: Professor Windy Dryden
Goldsmiths College, University of London

W

WHURR PUBLISHERS

LONDON AND PHILADELPHIA

© 2002 Whurr Publishers Ltd

First published 2002
by Whurr Publishers Ltd
19b Compton Terrace
London N1 2UN, England and
325 Chestnut Street, Philadelphia, PA 19106, USA

British Library Cataloguing in Publication Data
A catalogue record for this book
is available form the British Library

ISBN 1 86156 267 5

Typeset in Garamond by HWA Text and Data Management, Tunbridge Wells

Printed and bound in the UK by Athenaeum Press Ltd, Gateshead, Tyne and Wear

Contents

Preface

The problem with books is that they represent a fixed reality — and one fixed usually a year before the date of publication. The problem with dictionaries is that they imply fixed definitions. In the field of person-centred psychology, based as it is on a belief in the changing and fluid nature of human beings and our phenomenological experience of a changing world, there is a particular irony and tension in writing a book of definitions. From this perspective, given that there is no objective reality or truth, there can be no one defining definition of a word or concept. Indeed, Money (1997) identifies three *modes* of defining: stipulative (prescriptive and authorita-tive), reportive (reflecting common usage) and mythogenic (expressing radical reconceptualizations of concepts); and three *strategies* of defining: using words (verbal), pointing (ostensive) and doing (performative) — the latter echoing Wittengenstein's view/proposition that the meaning of a word is the way in which it is used. Furthermore, combining these modes and strategies yields nine types of def-inition! We have written this dictionary in the spirit of offering definitions in all three *modes*: some, such as the NECESSARY AND SUFFICIENT CONDITIONS and PERSONALITY THEORY, are *stipulative* in that they represent particular formulations or prescrip-tions and carry the authority or at least the influence of the original formulations of the concepts and in doing so we have drawn on Rogers's own definition of certain terms (see Rogers, 1959); most, for example, CONGRUENCE, UNCONDITIONAL POSITIVE REGARD and EMPATHY, are *reportive* in that they draw on common and changing us-age over time, as well as different and differing usages; and some, such as TRANSFER-ENCE (and its COUNTERTHEORY) are *mythogenic* in that they offer non-traditional frames of reference for particular words and concepts, included in which are terms in common usage which hardly need defining (such as EDUCATION) but which have a significance in person-centred psychology in terms of development or application. In terms of Money's categorization, our *strategy* in defining and communicating is, for the present, exclusively *verbal* — it is for the reader and others to point and do!

The person-centred approach (PCA) to psychology and to therapy is both one of the most well-known and most misunderstood and misinterpreted, even by some of its own proponents (see MISCONCEPTIONS OF THE PERSON-CENTRED APPROACH). As Mearns (1997) comments, 'it seems that there is a presumption that simply feeling a philosophical bond with the person-centred approach is sufficient qualification to adopt the label' (p. 192). More strongly, Mearns and Thorne (2000) conclude that:

misconceptions are not always the outcome of ignorance but in some cases, at least, have much deeper roots. It would seem that our approach has the strange capacity to threaten practitioners from other orientations so that they seek refuge in wilful ignorance or in condemnatory dismissiveness (p. x).

In writing this dictionary and offering these types of definitions, we do so in the spirit partly of setting some records straight (e.g. as regards the necessity and sufficiency of the therapeutic conditions) and partly as starting points for developing and encouraging thinking, practice and development in person-centred psychology. Within the PCA there are many debates about theory and practice, terms and meaning — some of which in effect centre on the problem and dangers of definition. In writing the 'definitions' in this dictionary, we are more interested in reflecting such debates and their various strands, rather than defining or having the last or (literally) defining word. Also, as we are interested in dialogue between psychologies in the spirit of mutual respect and understanding, we include a number of entries on other approaches to psychology and 'schools' of therapy, both those with similarities to the PCA and those with significant and important differences from the approach. While we hope that the dictionary will be useful, even influential, the meaning of the words it contains will inevitably change; as the Roman poet Horace put it: 'once released a word flies off without recall' (*Es semel emissum volat inrecovabile verbum*) (Epistolae 18).

This dictionary is also intended as a (re)source book and thus we have included summaries of Carl Rogers' books and his work with clients with whom he worked publicly and/or about whom he wrote (who have individual entries in the dictionary and are summarised in Appendix 1); entries on organizations and networks (the names and addresses of which form Appendix 2); as well as references to relevant books and materials (contained in the extensive list of References). After much debate we decided to refer to influential figures involved in person-centred psychology and its development through their *ideas* and therefore in the substance of relevant definitions, rather than through particular individual biographical entries. This links and locates people with broader developments and avoids the cult of the individual, especially eschewed by the PCA (as well as avoiding the invidiousness of selection and inevitable omission). Readers interested in the person and life of Carl Rogers are referred to and recommended the biography by Kirschenbaum (1979) and to Thorne's (1992) assessment of the man and his work.

Our thanks to Penny Allen, Gay Leah Barfield, Jean Clark and Seni Seneviratne for their contribution to particular entries (INTERPERSONAL PROCESS RECALL, LIVING NOW WORKSHOPS, CROSS-CULTURAL COMMUNICATION WORKSHOPS and WRITING respectively) as well as to friends and colleagues both near and far who have inevitably and richly influenced us and our work. We are particularly indebted to Mike Worrall for his close attention, reading and critique of the text; the responsibility for any lacunae and controversies remain, of course, with us. As ever, our heartfelt thanks and appreciations go to our respective families for tolerating our absences and obsessions.

Conventions used in the dictionary

As in the other books in this series, entries are arranged in alphabetical order. The entry is shown in bold. Cross-references are marked in SMALL CAPITAL LETTERS and occasionally vary from the actual entry, for instance as regards proper names where the entry appears under the second name (e.g. **West, Ellen**) and for ease of reading (for instance a cross reference to REFLECTIVE LISTENING appears under LISTENING, REFLECTIVE); thus, in general we have clustered entries on a subject or theme (e.g. EMPATHY; EMPATHY, ACCURATE; EMPATHY, BLOCKS TO, etc.). The cross-referencing aims to highlight certain entries for further explanation or clarification and to indicate the relation between words and concepts. Italicized words and phrases reflect *emphasis*, non-English words (e.g. *existential angst*), subheadings within an entry, or the titles of books, journals and films. As regards citing and referencing Rogers's extensive writings, where possible we have quoted from and referred to the original version; in some cases we have referred to the edited version in *The Carl Rogers Reader* (Kirschenbaum and Henderson, 1990b).

Although some traditions distinguish between COUNSELLING, PSYCHOTHERAPY and counselling psychology, the person-centred tradition does not; thus, apart from their own entries, we use the generic term 'therapy' within the dictionary to refer to all these forms of psychological healing and helping relationship. The following common abbreviations are used throughout:

client-centred therapy (CCT)
person-centred approach (PCA)
person-centred psychology (PCP)
person-centred therapy (PCT).

In entries in which we refer to 'person' in the singular the discussion may equally be applied to *people*: group, family, community or organization. Although there are separate entries under each of these particular headings, PCP has a wider application than that of the individual (see also note regarding the SELF on p. 125). We generally use 'they' as the generic plural pronoun to stand for s/he; and we leave quotes intact rather than politically 'correcting' them (with the exception of capitalizing certain words for purposes of cross-referencing).

abundancy motive a term associated with the humanistic psychologist Abraham Maslow, meaning a tendency to seek more from life than the satisfaction of NEEDS derived from deficiency; Rogers' idea of the FULLY FUNCTIONING PERSON is related, although this represents the end-point of a process of development rather than the MOTIVATION to fulfil potential (see ACTUALISING TENDENCY).

acceptance the non-judgemental attitude towards another in which the person's WAY OF BEING is accepted as the best that person can be at the present moment in time. Sometimes used as a synonym for UNCONDITIONAL POSITIVE REGARD, in therapy acceptance implies a caring for the client that is unaffected by judgements of the client as a person, although it does not mean remaining uncritical of some aspects of a person's past or even present behaviour. A therapist, for instance, may well not uncritically accept a client's violent BEHAVIOUR. Acceptance, however, as with unconditional positive regard, implies a deeper belief that no matter what a person's destructive behaviour may

have been or is currently, it is a result of psychological DAMAGE. As the possibility still exists for any person to recover from that damage and to repair it, acceptance is directed towards this basic humanness and the capacity, under the right CONDITIONS, for the person to move towards more life-enhancing behaviour and social functioning. Therapists try to create an atmosphere in which clients can explore both positively and negatively viewed aspects of themselves without the fear of (usually negative) evaluations of them(selves) as persons. Positive feelings or self-evaluations by clients are also accepted without moralistic evaluation or affirmation on the part of the therapist. The acceptance of *all* feelings, impulses, etc. offers clients opportunities, perhaps for the first time, to understand themselves fully as they currently are. Rogers said of Virginia Axline (see PLAY THERAPY) that 'I learned courage from her' regarding the therapist's complete acceptance of the client (see Kirschenbaum, 1979, p. 163). Rogers himself tended to equate acceptance with CONFIRMATION although there is some

1

evidence that a few years after his dialogue with Martin Buber (see DIALOGIC; Kirschenbaum and Henderson, 1990a; Anderson and Cissna, 1997) Rogers adopted Buber's term and use of *confirmation* distinct from acceptance (and affirmation) (see Friedman, 1996).

accreditation the process and result of counsellors being furnished with credentials, usually by an external authority or professional organisation such as the BRITISH ASSOCIATION FOR COUNSELLING AND PSYCHOTHERAPY. In a challenging address to the American Psychological Association (APA) in 1973, Rogers asked, among other things, if they (we) dared to do away with professionalism: 'as soon as we set up criteria for certification ... the first and greatest effect is to freeze the profession in a past image. This is an *inevitable* result' (Rogers, 1990d, p. 364). Rogers' regret at his involvement in establishing a board of examiners within the APA is paralleled by Thorne's (1995) more recent concerns about the vicious circle of accountability and the loss of the soul in counselling and the organisation of counselling. In Britain, alternative accreditation procedures are offered by the INDEPENDENT PRACTITIONERS' NETWORK (see REGISTRATION, UNITED KINGDOM COUNCIL FOR PSYCHOTHERAPY and UNITED KINGDOM REGISTER OF COUNSELLORS).

accurate empathy see EMPATHY, ACCURATE.

acquisition of disturbance see PSYCHOLOGICAL DISTURBANCE, ACQUISITION OF.

action research originally developed by Kurt Lewin, research conducted to achieve an understanding of a problem leading to practical applications and solutions. The research carried out by Carl Rogers and his colleagues into the CONDITIONS thought necessary and sufficient for effective psychotherapy could be considered an example of action research. Other examples include the RUST WORKSHOP, and various other attempts at facilitating social change (see HERMENEUTIC and HEURISTIC).

active listening the process of attempting to grasp both the facts (content) and the feelings in what is 'heard' using all the senses. Within the PCA, the term is now almost obsolete, having been replaced by EMPATHIC LISTENING or EMPATHIC UNDERSTANDING.

actualisation the assumed tendency of human beings to strive (though not necessarily CONSCIOUSLY) towards fulfilment of their potential; this concept, found in the work of Goldstein (1940) and Maslow (1943a), is a central tenet of HUMANISTIC PSYCHOLOGY and connotes a more fixed goal and sense of personhood than is found in the ACTUALISING TENDENCY of PCT. Actualisation is not restricted to need or tension reduction, but includes CREATIVITY, learning, and the enhancement of the person as a whole (see FORMATIVE TENDENCY); Heron (1998) identifies this as akin to Aristotle's notion of *entelechy*, the immanent, formative potential of what is actual (see also SELF-ACTUALISATION).

actualising tendency the tendency in all forms of organic life to develop more complex organisation, the fulfilment of potential and, in human beings, the actualisation of the SELF 'in ways which serve to maintain or enhance the *ORGANISM*' (Rogers, 1959, p. 196, our emphasis). In PCP, the actualising tendency is considered to be the sole motivation for human development and behaviour; it is the organism's 'one central source of energy' (Rogers, 1963, p. 6) and forms a POLITICAL process base for HUMAN NATURE, aspiration and action (Rogers, 1978). In a recent article Brodley (1999) discusses and elaborates this concept, identifying a number of its major characteristics: it is individual and universal; holistic; ubiquitous and constant; it changes in TENSION; it is a constructive, directional process which is both organisational and aspirational, towards AUTONOMY; is reflective of pro-social HUMAN NATURE and, in human functioning, is towards constructive human nature — and in this sense is not involved in the development of *all* our potentiality, e.g. towards self-DESTRUCTIVENESS: 'it is clear that the actualising tendency is selective and directional — [thus] a constructive tendency' (Rogers, 1980a, p. 121); finally, reflective CONSCIOUSNESS is a salient human channel of the actualising tendency. The development of the SELF and SELF-CONCEPT is a sub-system of the general actualising tendency, often referred to as SELF-ACTUALISATION, the two terms often being confused by conflation (see entry on self-actualisation for further discussion regarding the distinction between the two terms). In circumstances where experiences of the SELF and experiences of the organism as a whole are not contradictory, actualisation and self-actualisation can proceed harmoniously. Where self and ORGANISMIC EXPERIENCING are in conflict, the actualising tendency can become damaged or frustrated: 'it is clear that it is only the *organism as a whole* which manifests this tendency ... *parts* of the organism — particu-larly those concerned with SELF-PERCEPTION — could fundamentally inhibit or distort the general tendency of the whole organism' (Thorne, 1992, p. 27). Constraints on the actualising tendency arise from the environment in which a person lives (see CONDITIONS OF WORTH). More recently, Mearns and Thorne (2000) warn against naively ignoring the creative tension between the actualising tendency and the person's social context:

there will be times when the pressure of the actualising tendency will inspire a resistance. Such resistance is intimately related both to the actualising tendency and to the person's current existence as a social being. The effect of the resistance serves to maintain a balance which allows for a degree of expression for the actualising tendency while taking care to preserve the viability of the social context within the person's 'life space' ... The forces of social mediation form a coherent and functional part of our existence as social beings, allowing us expression of the actualising tendency but exerting an imperative which cautions against the endangering of the social life space (pp. 182–3).

additive empathy see DEPTH REFLECTION.

adience the movement towards positively valued experiences on the part of the human infant and, indeed, any organism with an internal valuing process (see AVOIDANCE).

adjustment see PSYCHOLOGICAL ADJUSTMENT.

affect attunement a term used particularly in SELF PSYCHOLOGY to describe a distinctive form of affective transaction which originates in the mother/primary carer–child dyad and, later, between therapist and client; it involves the experience of emotional resonance and the recasting of that experience into another form of expression. Stern (1985) distinguishes between affect attunement (occurring largely out of awareness) and EMPATHY (which involves the mediation of cognitive processes) (see EMPATHIC UNDERSTANDING).

affective contact one of three psychological CONTACT FUNCTIONS, identified within PRE-THERAPY as necessary for therapy to begin, consisting of clients' awareness of emotions, moods and feelings (see COMMUNICATIVE CONTACT and REALITY CONTACT).

alienation the feeling of distance or separateness from others. EXISTENTIAL thought includes the situation where a person feels estranged from her/himself. This separation of a person from the 'REAL SELF' is assumed to be a result of conformity with the requirements of others and those of social institutions, resulting in an external LOCUS OF EVALUATION (see CONDITIONS OF WORTH).

analytic psychology an approach to psychology based on the ideas of Carl Jung; several person-centred practitioners write about the similarities between the theories of 'the two Carls' (Thorne, 1998b) as regards the authority of the client, PERSONALITY divisions (persona, and the façade or mask of INCONGRUENCE), the ACTUALISING TENDENCY and individuation (Purton, 1989) and CONSCIOUSNESS (Wijngaarden, 1990).

anchorage the term used by Van Werde (1998) to describe the metaphorical and practical roots by which clients are helped to make and maintain CONTACT. He describes four layers of anchorage which correspond to four kinds of remedial contact: existential contact — the right to exist; PSYCHOLOGICAL CONTACT — the concrete awareness of reality; consolidation and strengthening of the restored CONTACT FUNCTIONS; and cultural contact — the right to cultural identity (see CULTURE).

anger a strong emotional reaction to a feeling of threat, exploitation, being wronged, etc. In many cultures, as anger is often thought of as a 'negative' emotion and therefore socially unacceptable, it can be DENIED to awareness or DISTORTED into a more acceptable emotion, a process which can also be affected by issues of gender. The process of distortion or denial can, however, occur with any emotion or feeling according to an individual's particular CONDITIONS OF WORTH.

'Anger and Hurt' a reference to an anonymous client with whom Rogers conducted two sessions filmed over consecutive days in 1977. Although the two films were entitled 'The right to be desperate' (Whitely, 1977b) and 'Carl Rogers counsels an individual on anger and hurt' (Whitely, 1977a), respectively, the two are commonly known and referred to under the title of the second session, on which there are published commentaries (Brodley, 1996; Menahem, 1996).

anti-oppressive practice practice — usually, though not exclusively, therapeutic practice — which is characterised by an understanding or analysis of OPPRESSION; a view that CULTURE, in its broader definition, is *intentional* (see CULTURAL PSYCHOLOGY); and, from a person-centred perspective, that the (re)discovery and (re)claiming of PER-

SONAL POWER is the most effective way of enhancing the ORGANISM and a genuinely SELF-DETERMINING society and an EMERGING CULTURE.

anxiety a state of tension occurring when an individual dimly perceives INCONGRUENCE within her/himself. When a person has no awareness of incongruence, he or she is open to the possibility of anxiety and disorganisation i.e. VULNERABILITY. Incongruence need not be sharply perceived for it to create anxiety. In therapy, anxiety is often experienced by clients as they become more aware of that part of their experience which is in contradiction to their SELF-CONCEPT (Rogers, 1957). Anxiety is often distinguished from fear because anxiety is usually apparently objectless, whereas fear is usually associated with a known situation, person or event. In EXISTENTIAL PHILOSOPHY anxiety is said to accompany an awareness of the meaninglessness or chaotic nature of the Universe, and is thus considered a result of BEING-IN-THE-WORLD.

apparency the active appearing of the therapist in the therapeutic relationship, a term suggested by G. Thompson (personal communication, 1993) which connotes the positive, intentional and relational quality of TRANSPARENCY in the context of congruence: 'apparency also provides a link between our awareness and living of self and our communicating of that awareness to our client' (Tudor and Worrall, 1994, p. 200).

assessment given that the original uses of assessment lie in 'official' and external valuation (originally for the purposes of taxation), it is perhaps not surprising that PCP and the PCA in general has eschewed the formal psychological assessment — as well as the DIAGNOSIS and pathologising — of clients. Instead, the emphasis in PCP is on making sense of phenomena by understanding the client's subjective view rather than through some so-called 'objective' standpoint of the observer, and on the nature and quality of THERAPEUTIC RELATIONSHIP between therapist and client. Mearns (1997) is particularly strident in his critique of the 'ridiculous' question of assessment, favouring the transfer of resources from employing 'expert' assessors to increased support for counsellors through thorough training and, when necessary, intensive supervision. The PCA thus offers a strong challenge to the conventional view, which informs practice in most counselling agencies, that assessment must be conducted by a 'more experienced' counsellor. While there is broad agreement with Rogers' (1951) critique of the external location and institutional and professional power of diagnosis, there is some debate within PCP about the philosophy, purpose and place of assessment — most of one issue of the *Person-Centered Review* was devoted to a symposium on psychodiagnosis (Cain, 1989). Person-centred practitioners also need to have a clear and coherent response to criticisms, especially from some health authorities, that some counselling training courses do not adequately prepare students for practice as regards the assessment of clients. An alternative to the complete rejection of assessment lies in drawing on theories within PCP which help to *describe* (rather than *prescribe* for) the client and which are consistent with the 'philosophical dedication to the self-authority of the client' (Bozarth, 1991/98a, p. 127) e.g. Rogers' (1961) seven stages of process which, in the spirit he originally intended it, may be viewed as a way of understanding and 'assessing' a client's process of change in therapy — and, *equally*, provides an understanding of the *therapist's* process of change; another example is the assessment of CONTACT FUNCTIONS.

Association for the Development of the Person-Centered Approach (ADPCA) an international, non-profit-making association/community of individuals committed to the development of the PCA, founded in 1986. The Association holds an annual general meeting which takes the form of a community-building event, and publishes a quarterly journal (*THE PERSON-CENTERED JOURNAL*), a quarterly newsletter RENAISSANCE, and a membership directory (see also WORLD ASSOCIATION FOR PERSON-CENTERED COUNSELING AND PSYCHOTHERAPY).

Association for Humanistic Psychology (AHP) formed in the USA in 1961, its early pioneers in HUMANISTIC PSYCHOLOGY included Abraham Maslow, Rollo May, Carl Rogers and Antony Sutich; it produces the *Journal of Humanistic Psychology* (published by Sage).

Association for Humanistic Psychology (Britain) (AHP[B]) the British Association for Humanistic Psychology was formed in 1969 with John Wren-Lewis as its first Chair. The first issue of the British humanistic psychology journal *Self & Society* appeared in March 1973 under the joint editorship of Bob Jones and Vivian Milroy. Contributors to this first issue included John Rowan writing about Maslow and Christopher Ross writing about Rogers. The tone of the first issue of *Self & Society* was highly optimistic and reflected the innovatory nature of much humanistic psychology at the time: workshops were advertised on bio-energetics, ENCOUNTER (ongoing encounter for women, teenage encounter), GESTALT THERAPY and hypnosis. While much of the theory and debates within the AHP(B) are compatible with the philosophy of the PCA, there is not a great presence of person-centred practitioners in the organisation or in the pages of *Self & Society*.

Association of Humanistic Psychology Practitioners (AHPP) an association within AHP(B) comprising a subgroup of practitioners of various applications of humanistic psychology, including psychotherapy, and which is a member and accrediting organisation within the UNITED KINGDOM COUNCIL FOR PSYCHOTHERAPY. Whilst the AHPP recognises a number of categories for full membership (Bodywork Therapist, Gestalt Therapist, Group Psychotherapist, etc.), it does not currently have a specific category of person-centred (psycho)therapists.

attitude disposition, posture, action, mental state or behaviour which, within the PCA, is associated with a way of being (see Rogers, 1980a). The CORE CONDITIONS OF THERAPEUTIC PERSONALITY CHANGE, for instance, are a set of personal attitudes rather than a prescription for therapy or training. Rogers also equates attitudes with the QUALITIES of a person.

attunement see AFFECT ATTUNEMENT, EMPATHIC ATTUNEMENT and EMPATHY.

authenticity see CONGRUENCE.

authority the author of an accepted statement; while most definitions of authority focus on the power or right (derived or delegated) over someone or something, from a person-centred perspective authority is derived from the person her/himself — see EXPERIENCE, which, for Rogers (1961) is the highest authority (see also POLITICS OF THE PERSON-CENTRED APPROACH, SUBJECTIVITY).

autonomous internally directed or self-regulatory; in PCT an autonomous person is one with relatively few CONDITIONS OF WORTH and with an INTERNAL LOCUS OF EVALUATION.

autonomy the state of being AUTONOMOUS, it 'is synonymous with having all experiences available to awareness' (Rogers, 1951, p. 515). Referring also to self-directing, determining and regulating groups, it has a political connotation beyond that of the individual.

autonomy, functional a term proposed by Allport (1961) to account for the observation that behaviour often does not concern itself simply with the satisfaction of primary needs.

avoidance the movement away from negatively valued experiences on the part of the human infant and, indeed, any organism with an internal valuing process; a non-pejorative term in PCP; thus, if a person is avoiding someone or something, it is, at some level, because simply they are valuing or assessing that experience negatively (see ADIENCE).

awareness a subjective or internal state of being conscious of something; the symbolic representation of some portion of our experience. In defining the various forms this awareness takes in varying degrees of sharpness or vividness, Rogers draws on the notion of figure and ground from GESTALT PSYCHOLOGY AND FIELD THEORY. When an EXPERIENCE is available to awareness, it can be symbolised freely, without defensive DISTORTION or DENIAL. For Rogers, awareness is synonymous with CONSCIOUSNESS and SYMBOLISATION. Awareness is a recurring theme in Rogers' writing, and he tends to use the terms 'permitted into awareness', or 'to become aware' where other more traditional writers use the phrase 'to become conscious of something'.

awareness, edge of emotional 'material' (feelings, etc.) of which a person is not fully aware or CONSCIOUS, the term is most closely associated with the work of Eugene Gendlin (1981, 1984) who believed that underlying feelings about an event or experience may be more significant than 'surface' feelings, more easily available. Mearns and Thorne (1988) point out that known feelings are readily available but underlying feelings may conflict with such surface feelings: 'a client may show superficial polite acquiescence towards an event while simultaneously, and not quite consciously, he is seething rebelliously underneath' (p. 48). This concept is important as regards working therapeutically; as Rogers (1966) put it:

> it is not the case that the client-centered therapist responds only to the obvious in the phenomenal world of the client. If that were so, it is doubtful that any movement would ensue in therapy. Indeed, there would be no therapy. Instead, the client-centered therapist aims to dip from the pool of implicit meanings just at the edge of the client's awareness (p. 190).

Mearns and Thorne (1998) echo this: 'simply focusing on the known surface feeling may only be going over old ground, whereas focusing on "the edge" (the FELT SENSE) can be the door to the unknown' (p. 48) and, again, it is Gendlin (1981) who has developed a way of working with this 'edge' (see FOCUSING). More recently, Mearns and Thorne (2000) use the terms 'edge of awareness' and 'SUBCEIVED material' almost synonymously and incorporate both in their expanded concept of SELF. The NON-DIRECTIVE attitude in PCP discourages the therapist from drawing a client's attention to something the therapist regards as out of the client's awareness, though does not necessarily prohibit it. The therapist's level of empathic understanding and sensitivity to the client's experiencing process guides the extent to which feelings or sensations at the edge of awareness are directly referred to by the therapist (see LEVELS OF INTERVENTIVENESS); nevertheless, if a therapist is to work at RELATIONAL DEPTH they need continually to be sensitive to such material, alongside their sensitivity to and understanding of the obvious.

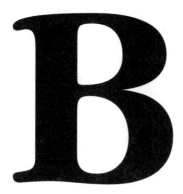

basic encounter group see GROUP, ENCOUNTER.

basic needs see NEEDS, BASIC.

Bebb, Mr Jim one of Rogers' clients, the subject of a major and detailed research analysis involving a battery of research instruments, including Q-SORT cards; described by Rogers (1954a) (see also MRS OAK and Rogers, 1954b) as a 'failure case': in terms of overall ratings the client was considered to be 'near the extreme of highly defensive psychological organization and that in therapy [over nine sessions] he made only slight progress toward real integration' (p. 352). In follow-up interviews the client stated that, while he had gained more respect for his individuality, he had not put into action some of the things he had discovered; there is also some indication that his occasional experiencing of hallucinations had not been addressed, and there is no indication that issues of CULTURE were addressed as such during the course of the therapy (as it emerges that the United States is not 'home' and English is not his mother tongue).

becoming the process (rather than outcome) of human potentiality. Rogers (1961) refers to the process of becoming as one in which people get behind the mask or roles with which we face life, and in which we experience feeling and discover unknown elements of SELF. He goes on to describes the characteristics of the person who emerges from/in this process of becoming a person as: openness to EXPERIENCE, (having) trust in one's ORGANISM, (having) an INTERNAL LOCUS OF EVALUATION, and willingness to be a process. In a sense, according to Rogers, the PCP and EXISTENTIAL philosophy, as human *beings* we are in a constant state of becoming — and thus should perhaps be more accurately referred to as human *becomings*! (see BEING, BELONGING, FULLY FUNCTIONING PERSON and PROCESS).

Becoming Partners: Marriage and Its Alternatives a book by Rogers, published in 1973, written particularly with young people in mind and in an attempt to get *inside* the experience of partnership. Based on interviews and people's own writings in response to Rogers' request, it is a book of its time, place and orientation: it is about the search of men and women in the United States in the early 1970s. Despite these limitations, the book considers different forms of married and co-habiting partnerships, between couples and in collectives i.e. communes, and one cross-cultural marriage between a black man and a white woman (see also GAY AFFIRMATIVE THERAPY).

behaviour the needs-driven and goal-directed attempt/s of the organism to satisfy its needs *as perceived* (see Rogers, 1951). Discrepancies in behaviour arise as a result of INCONGRUENCE between SELF and EXPERIENCE. Behaviour which is consistent with the SELF-CONCEPT is accurately SYMBOLISED and, in turn, maintains, actualises and enhances the self-concept; conversely, behaviour which is inconsistent with the self-concept or which is not ASSIMILATED into the SELF-STRUCTURE is unrecognised (IGNORED), DENIED or perceived in a DISTORTED or selective fashion in such a way to be congruent with the SELF. See also PERSONALITY THEORY.

behavioural science generally, any science that includes the study of the behaviour of organisms, including humans, such as sociology, psychology, anthropology, etc.; sometimes used synonymously with the term social science.

behaviourism the approach to psychology which takes observable, measurable behaviour as its focus for investigation, initially developed by John B. Watson, B.F. Skinner and I.P. Pavlov, and referred to (in retrospect and historically) as the 'second force' in psychology.

being the concept, from EXISTENTIAL philosophy, of the active existence/existing of humankind, which leads to a focus on and acceptance of 'being' in the present (see BEING-IN-THE-WORLD, BECOMING, BELONGING and WAY OF BEING, A).

being-beyond-the-world the EXISTENTIAL idea that humankind has the capacity — and responsibility — to transcend the realities of existence.

being-in-the-world the central EXISTENTIAL notion that humankind's totality is determined by the inevitable phenomena that make up the reality of the present moment, the term is the accepted translation of Heidegger's term *Dasein*.

being received see CONDITION, ASSUMED.

belonging a human NEED for affiliation often achieved through kinship, friends, family and a membership of and/or a sense of COMMUNITY; together with BEING and BECOMING this describes more of the social, relational and INTERSUBJECTIVE nature of the ORGANISM and of humanity and the pro-social nature of the ACTUALISING TENDENCY.

blocks to empathy see EMPATHY, BLOCKS TO.

body reflections see CONTACT REFLECTIONS.

bodywork therapy an approach to therapy deriving from the work of Wilhelm Reich and neo-Reichians; with the exception of a paper by Tophoff (1984) there appears to be little direct connection between this and PCP (see NON-DIRECTIVE APPROACH), although some physical body therapies (such as McTimony chiropractic, sacro-cranial osteopathy and zero balancing) are consistent with the PRINCIPLES OF THE PERSON-CENTRED APPROACH.

boundaries generally and literally, the defined limits to therapy usually concerning agreements about time, frequency, fees (if appropriate), cancellations, etc., sometimes defined in and referred to as a CONTRACT. In his early writing, Rogers (1942) identifies certain limits to action, such as holding to agreed time and safety boundaries, as one of four positive qualities of the THERAPEUTIC RELATIONSHIP. Given the importance of the therapeutic context as a variable which affects the therapeutic process and the willingness of person-centred therapists to offer flexibility alongside consistency to clients, the issue of boundaries is an important one. Mearns and Thorne (2000) discuss boundaries in relation to what they view as a more general drift in the institutionalisation of counselling from functionalism to structuralism i.e. the framing of a 'guideline' as a *prescribed* solution to a situation or perceived problem, observing 'the danger for person-centred practitioners ... [as] that "boundaries" come to be defined "structurally" rather than "functionally"' (p. 48).

breakdown a term used to describe the break in the gestalt of SELF-STRUCTURE which occurs when an organism's process of DEFENCE is unable to operate successfully, i.e. in maintaining the self-structure, and which results in DISORGANISATION.

brief counselling see TIME-LIMITED THERAPY.

British Association for Counselling and Psychotherapy (BACP) (formally the BAC, it added 'psychotherapy' to its title at its annual conference in 2000), founded in 1977, the principal national association for the promotion, organisation and devel-opment of counselling in Britain. Its aims include: the promotion of counselling; increasing the availability of trained and supervised counsellors and to maintain and raise the standards of training and practice, to which end it operates accreditation schemes for individual counsellors, trainers and supervisors; and the representation of counselling nationally and internationally. It produces publications including a monthly *Counselling and Psychotherapy Journal*; has a film and video library; and has developed codes of ethics and professional practice for counsellors, counselling skills, trainers and for the supervision of counsellors. Its membership has grown dramatically over the years and currently stands at nearly 20,000, of which many identify as person-centred; indeed, this is the second most common entry (after psychodynamic) in the BACP's annual *Counselling and Psychotherapy Resources Directory*. For some counsellors, the growth of the BACP has led to a concomitant concern that it is becoming too bureaucratic, rigid and remote from its members. Despite the large membership of person-centred counsellors, neither the BACP's organisation or its codes particularly reflect PCP or the PCA which, together with philosophical concerns about ACCREDITATION and statutory REGISTRATION, has resulted in a number of counsellors looking to other forms of association, organisation and self and peer accreditation (see INDEPENDENT PRACTITIONERS' NETWORK).

British Association for the Person Centred Approach (BAPCA) an association which aims to bring together all interested in the PCA, to act as a forum for discussion, and to increase understanding of the PCA among professionals and lay persons alike. After a number of preliminary meetings, BAPCA held its official inaugural meeting in 1989. The association's membership has grown from around 100 in 1989 to its current 850. It publishes a newsletter and a twice-yearly journal, *Person-Centred Practice*, edited by Tony Merry.

Brown, Jim a client of Rogers with whom he worked for 166 sessions, two sessions each week over two and a half years, in the context of a research project (Rogers, Gendlin, Kiesler and Truax, 1967). Jim Brown (also identified as Mr Vac) was a state hospital inpatient with a diagnosis of 'schizophrenic reaction, simple type'. The published description of the research includes two complete sessions (in the same week) and 15 randomly selected four-minute transcripts from sessions throughout the two and a half years. Rogers (1967a) suggests the crucial turning point of the therapy as (during the second of these two sessions) when the client had deep and irreversible experiencing of feeling. The transcript of the two sessions is reproduced in Farber, Brink and Raskin (1996) with commentaries by Bozarth (1996a) and Greenberg (1996). These particular sessions are notable for their silences (50 and 52 minutes, respectively) and Rogers' use of himself in the therapy (see Baldwin, 1987).

Bryan, Herbert a client of Rogers, a case study of whom was originally published in COUNSELING AND PSYCHOTHERAPY: NEWER CONCEPTS IN PRACTICE (Rogers, 1942), 'the first recorded, fully transcribed and published psychotherapy case in history' (Kirschenbaum and Henderson, 1990b, p. 62). The case of Herbert Bryan, with whom Rogers worked for eight sessions, is presented as an exact transcript so that the reader can follow the moment to moment dialogue between Bryan and Rogers. Included with the transcript is a commentary by Rogers which is disarmingly frank in its open discussion of his own ability as a therapist. For example, at one point (in the first interview) Rogers comments about himself:

> here is the second blunder of the hour. The counselor departs from sound recognition of feeling ... The counselor draws nothing but a confused and somewhat defensive answer ... This indicates how easily the course of constructive therapy can be diverted by errors which may not be recognized as errors at the time (p. 280).

The study also shows Rogers learning from his 'blunders'; as Thorne (1992) comments on another sequence:

> Rogers, with apparently effortless ease, is doing precisely what he criticizes himself for not doing on the other two occasions. He is recognizing feeling in Mr. Bryan and allowing the feeling to be deepened and differentiated. He shows himself as the sensitive companion and not as the somewhat authoritative interrogator (Thorne, 1992, p. 50).

caring used in PCP synonymously with UNCONDITIONAL POSITIVE REGARD (see also PRIZING).

caring, gullible a phrase used by Rogers and Sanford (1984) to describe a caring or UNCONDITIONAL POSITIVE REGARD 'in which clients are accepted as they say they are, not with a lurking suspicion in the therapist's mind that they may, in fact, be otherwise' (p. 1379); as an ATTITUDE it requires GENUINENESS and fosters TRUST.

Carl Ransom Rogers Collection see CARL ROGERS MEMORIAL LIBRARY.

Carl Rogers Dialogues a book, edited by Kirschenbaum and Henderson and published in 1990, comprising the transcripts of five conversations or DIALOGUES between Rogers and leading exponents in a variety of fields (philosophy, theology, psychology, science and education):

- with Martin Buber, philosopher and theologian (see DIALOGIC).
- with Paul Tillich, theologian and author of the influential book *Courage to Be* (Tillich, 1952), with whom Rogers dialogued in 1965 (in what was to be Tillich's last public appearance); the dialogue covered morality, 'the antimoral act being one that contradicts the self-realization of the individual' (Kirschenbaum and Henderson, 1990a, p. 66), the nature of freedom and of 'EVIL', ACCEPTANCE and forgiveness, and the optimal or FULLY FUNCTIONING PERSON.
- with Burrhus Frederic Skinner, the behavioural psychologist, with whom Rogers had three encounters, the last of which, taking place over two days in 1962, was more of a genuine dialogue than the previous ones in which they had each read prepared papers; as expected, this debate centres on behaviour, the choice of values, the evolution of culture, the nature of experience and 'inner life', education and learning theory, and other aspects of BEHAVIOURISM. At one point, Rogers summarises their differences: 'I find myself in ninety percent agreement with all you say about people when you are talking about them from the outside, but I notice you are not willing to get at them from the

13

inside' (Kirschenbaum and Henderson, 1990a, p. 97).

- with Michael Polanyi (see MAN AND THE SCIENCE OF MAN).
- with Gregory Bateson, biologist, anthropologist, psychologist, ethnologist and environmentalist, with whom Rogers dialogued in 1975 principally about the nature of learning.

The book also contains a review and symposium regarding the work of Reinhold Niebuhr, a conservative theologian (though liberal in politics), one of whose books on *The Self and The Drama of History*, Rogers reviewed, a piece which is then discussed by three academics, to whom, in turn, Rogers replies. The book concludes with another of Rogers' reviews, this time of the work of Rollo May, another theologian and humanist, together with their correspondence (originally published in the Journal of Humanistic Psychology).

Carl Rogers Institute of Psychotherapy, Training and Supervision
a part of the CENTER FOR THE STUDIES OF THE PERSON.

Carl Rogers Memorial Library a library containing over 600 papers (articles, chapters, interviews and unpublished manuscripts) as well as non-print media (cassettes, films, etc.), initially collected and arranged by Neil Kandel, the Director of the Library and now incorporated into the Carl Ransom Rogers Collection at the University of California, Santa Barbara (see Appendix 2).

Carl Rogers on Encounter Groups
published in 1970, this small though nonetheless important book brought together Rogers' ideas about ENCOUNTER GROUPS, which he viewed as a 'pro-

foundly significant movement' (p. 169); in the book Rogers discusses GROUP PROCESS, GROUP FACILITATION, the process and effect of change, RESEARCH and areas of application in which the intensive group experience has constructive use.

Carl Rogers on Personal Power: Inner Strength and Its Revolutionary Impact a book by Rogers, published in 1978, setting out the political nature and implications of the PCA on the helping professions, the family and relationships, education and administration. Two key chapters describe the PCA and the OPPRESSED in which Rogers acknowledges the work of Paulo Freire and the PCA in resolving intercultural tensions (see also EDUCATION and CROSS-CULTURAL COMMUNICATION). The remaining chapters focus on the PCA in action, the ACTUALISING TENDENCY as a political base, and the EMERGING PERSON as a new political figure (see QUALITIES). In many ways *On Personal Power* represents Rogers' coming of age politically and his elaboration of the quiet but revolutionary impact of the PCA, its theory, pedagogy (andragogy) and practice (see PERSONAL POWER, POLITICS, THE POLITICS OF THE PERSON-CENTRED APPROACH, POWER).

Carl Rogers Peace Project see INSTITUTE FOR PEACE.

Center for the Studies of the Person
(CSP) founded by Rogers and other colleagues in 1968 as an alternative to the WESTERN BEHAVIORAL SCIENCES INSTITUTE and with which Rogers remained involved until his death in 1989. It currently provides training programmes in psychotherapy and supervision both on site in La Jolla, California and through distance learning, as well as regular workshops and

other projects including a Conflict Transformation Project (see CON-FLICT).

chaos theory chaos is a science of process rather than state, of becoming rather than being' (Gleick, 1987, p. 5) and as such has strong parallels with person-centred philosophy and theory; Sanford (1993) identifies a number of parallels between the new science of chaos theory and the new way of being of PCP and the PCA including: a focus on PROCESS; universality — the more personal is the more general; a movement from closed systems to open systems; the irreversibility of new knowledge and paradigms; and the resonance of the group (see QUANTUM THEORY).

change the process of growing or developing from one level of functioning to another. In PCP, positive change is usually expressed in terms of becoming more FULLY FUNCTIONING and is a result of releasing the potential inherent in the ORGANISM. Rogers' (1957) definition of change included the following elements: change in the personality structure at both surface and deeper levels in a direction which clinicians would agree means greater integration; less internal conflict; more energy utilizable for effective living; and change in behaviour away from behaviours generally regarded as immature and towards behaviours regarded as mature. Rogers coined the term FULLY FUNCTIONING PERSON to describe the characteristics of a person who had become fully ACTUALISED, but he stressed that the PROCESS involved in becoming fully functioning was an ongoing one without an identifiable end point. The full functioning person is a hypothetical construct, rather than a reality. In CCT it is not a function of the therapist to motivate a client towards change, nor is it necessary for the client consciously to motivate her/himself to change; the motivation for change is provided by the ACTUALISING TENDENCY, the organism's tendency to actualise the person's potential, which becomes activated in, for instance, a THERAPEUTIC RELATIONSHIP built on the CORE CONDITIONS or core QUALITIES (see also FLUIDITY, NECESSARY AND SUFFICIENT CONDITIONS OF THERAPEUTIC PERSONALITY CHANGE, SELF-ACTUALISATION).

child development although not widely acknowledged, PCP does have a theory of child development; Rogers (1959) postulates that the human infant has at least six characteristics or attributes:

1. He perceives his *experience* as reality. His *experience* is his reality.

    a. As a consequence he has greater potential *awareness* of what reality is for him than does anyone else, since no one else can completely assume his *internal frame of reference*.

2. He has an inherent tendency toward *actualizing* his organism.

3. He interacts with his reality in terms of his basic *actualizing* tendency. Thus his behaviour is the goal-directed attempt of the organism to satisfy the experienced needs for *actualization* in the reality as *perceived*.

4. In this interaction he behaves as an organised whole, as a gestalt.

5. He engages in an *organismic valuing process*, valuing *experience* with reference to the *actualizing tendency* as a criterion. *Experiences* which are *perceived*

as maintaining or enhancing the organism are valued positively. Those which are *perceived* as negating such maintenance or enhancement are valued negatively.

6. He behaves with adience toward positively valued *experiences* and with avoidance toward those negatively valued' (p. 222, original emphases).

This conceptualisation of child development is *process*-centred rather than task- or achievement-centred. Development is viewed in terms of increasing SELF-AWARENESS, SELF-EXPERIENCE and differentiation from the perceptual field into a fluid concept of self, and predates and is consistent with more recent developmental theorists such as Stern (1985) who emphasise the interpersonal, SUBJECTIVE and INTERSUBJECTIVE world of the infant's experience and domains of relatedness (see SELF PSYCHOLOGY).

client the term originally used by Carl Rogers in 1940, it connoted the newer THERAPEUTIC RELATIONSHIP he promoted; now adopted by many approaches and disciplines similarly concerned to distance themselves from the clinical, medical/psychiatric and orthodox therapeutic models implied in and by the term *patient*; and preferred to patient in PCP to imply a non-pathologising ideology, a more active and involved role on the part of both therapist and client, and greater MUTUALITY.

client-centred therapy the approach developed by Carl Rogers and his colleagues in which the therapist is NON-DIRECTIVE and concentrates on building THERAPEUTIC RELATIONSHIPS based on the six NECESSARY AND SUFFICIENT CONDITIONS OF THERAPEUTIC PERSONAL-ITY CHANGE, which include the three CORE CONDITIONS of CONGRUENCE, UNCONDITIONAL POSITIVE REGARD and EMPATHIC UNDERSTANDING. A fundamental assumption is that the client is best able to solve personal problems her/himself with the therapist acting as an understanding companion rather than interpreter, guide or diagnostician. At one time known as NON-DIRECTIVE THERAPY and, more lately, as PERSON-CENTRED THERAPY, Rogers and Sanford (1984) offer the following definition: 'client-centered therapy is continually developing a way of being with persons that facilitates healthy CHANGE and GROWTH. Its central hypothesis is that persons have within themselves vast resources for self-understanding and for constructive changes in ways of being and behaving and that these resources can best be released and realised in a relationship with certain definable qualities' (p.1374). The distinctive characteristics of client-centred psychotherapy may be summarised:

1. the hypothesis that certain attitudes in therapists constitute key components of the necessary and sufficient conditions of therapeutic effectiveness;

2. a reliance on a GROWTH model of psychotherapy and a rejection of the MEDICAL MODEL;

3. the concept of therapists' functions as those of being immediately present and accessible to clients and of relying on their moment-to-moment EXPERIENCING in their relationships with clients;

4. the intensive and continuing focus on the PHENOMENOLOGICAL world of the client;

5. a developing theory that the THER-APEUTIC PROCESS is marked by a change in the client's manner and immediacy of experiencing with increasing ability to live more fully in the moment;

6. continued stress on the ACTUAL-ISING quality of the human organism as the motivational force in therapy;

7. a concern with the *process* of PER-SONALITY change, rather than with the structure of personality;

8. emphasis on the need for continuing research;

9. the hypothesis that the same principles of psychotherapy apply to all persons;

10. a view of psychotherapy as one specialised example of all constructive interpersonal relationships;

11. a determination to build all theoretical formulations out of the soil of experience, rather than twisting experience to fit a preformed THEORY;

12. a concern with the philosophical issues that derive from the practice of psychotherapy (Rogers and Sanford, 1984);

13. finally, Rogers and Sanford remark that the single element that most sets client-centred psychotherapy apart from many other approaches is 'its insistence that the medical model — involving diagnosis of pathology, specificity of treatment, desirability of cure — is a totally inadequate model for dealing with psychologically distressed or deviant persons' (p. 1374) (see also COUNSELLING, DEVELOPMENT OF THE PERSON-CENTRED APPROACH, PRINCIPLES OF THE PERSON-CENTRED APPROACH).

Client-Centered Therapy: Its Current Practice, Implications and Theory a book written principally by Rogers — with contributions from three of the staff of the UNIVERSITY OF CHICAGO COUNSELING CENTER: on PLAY THERAPY (Elaine Dorfman), group-centred psychotherapy (Nicholas Hobbs) and group-centred leadership and administration (Thomas Gordon) — and published in 1951. Although it is Rogers' fifth book, it is the first with 'client-centered' in the title and in many ways represents his first major exposition of PCT. In Part I Rogers outlines a number of aspects of a current view of client-centred therapy including the attitude and orientation of the counsellor and, significantly, a view of the THERAPEUTIC RELATIONSHIP as experienced by the client. He also confronts questions raised by other viewpoints on TRANSFERENCE and 'transference attitudes', DIAGNOSIS and the applicability of CCT. Part II focuses on applications (as above) and on the TRAINING of counsellors and therapists. The final chapter contains Rogers' theory of personality and behaviour, including his formulation of NINETEEN PROPOSITIONS which outlines and elaborates this theory.

clients, Rogers' Rogers worked for over forty years with clients — from his early days working with children in the 1940s, through his work with psychiatric patients (see JIM BROWN and LORETTA), to the more public 'demonstration' sessions conducted at workshops and conferences. Ten of these sessions are transcribed or summarised in Farber, Brink and Raskin (1996), together with critical commentaries from both within and outside the PCA. While Rogers' work has been (literally) viewed as a model of PCT, there is a problem with the fact that much of his more public work took the form of single (one-off) 'demonstration' sessions. While these often reflect and indeed demonstrate the CONDITIONS and PROCESS of person-centred therapy, they do not represent the long-term therapeutic relationship (Natiello, 1996). Rogers and his colleagues were among the first to record their work with clients (originally phonographically), to transcribe their interactions and to publish both transcripts and commentaries, as a result of which there are a number of published accounts of his work with individual clients. Appendix 1 lists these 'cases', together with references to published transcripts and commentaries, as well as recordings and accounts of Rogers' work in groups.

Clinical Treatment of the Problem Child, The Carl Rogers' first book, published in 1939, focuses (in Part I) on the diagnosis of behaviour problems as ways of understanding the child and, subsequently, on different forms of treatment: a change of environment as a form of treatment (Part II); modifying the environment including the family, the school and other relevant social groups (Part III); and working with the individual child (Part IV). Although clearly focusing on diagnosis and treatment, concepts and practice which Rogers was to later eschew, the book introduces concepts such as ORGANISM, RELATIONSHIP THERAPY and EXPRESSIVE THERAPY which he and others were to develop.

code of ethics a collection or digest of rules and regulations governing ethical practice, for instance in counselling e.g. BAC (1998), based explicitly or, more often, implicitly on ethical and moral principles which, in turn, derive from imperatives from moral philosophy, e.g. 'always tell the truth', 'never lie', 'never breach a person's trust', 'never breach confidentiality'. There is often ambiguity between rules and guidelines in such codes and these are clarified through related codes of practice, by case law and by custom and practice (see Jenkins, 1997). Neither are ethics value-free. It should be noted for instance that the BRITISH ASSOCIATION FOR COUNSELLING and PSYCHOTHERAPY'S codes are not based or centred on PCP and its philosophical principles. It is a useful exercise for practitioners to regularly read the codes of ethics to which they subscribe — especially as it is common for people to subscribe to more than one code, some aspects and clauses of which may be contradictory or mutually exclusive; a further and perhaps more radical exercise is for practitioners to write their own code of ethics and compare their own with standard — and external — codes.

cognition a very general term referring to mental activities such as problem-solving, calculating, intellectual insight, thinking and reasoning.

cognitive dissonance the emotions experienced when two contradictory attitudes or concepts are held simultaneously, or when there is a conflict between behaviour and belief; resolving the conflict is believed to serve as the basis for change in attitudes when beliefs are modified in order to become consistent with behaviour.

cognitive psychology a general approach to psychology which emphasises internal, mental processes and processing, often in terms of mental events, mental representations, beliefs, intentions etc.; Rogers (1961) himself acknowledged his debt to George Kelly and PERSONAL CONSTRUCT PSYCHOLOGY for the term CONSTRUCT and certainly addressed the changes in cognitive processing in his PROCESS CONCEPTION OF PSYCHOTHERAPY; within the PCA there is a tradition (referred to as a 'faction' or a 'wing') of people who, borrowing from cognitive psychology, have developed ways of analysing the therapeutic process as one of integrating information (see Wexler, 1974; Zimring, 1974); within this tradition, authors tend to talk in terms of TECHNIQUES and about EMPATHIC RESPONDING.

collaborative power see POWER.

communication in general, the transmission of something from one place or person to another, but in PCP, communication is much more complex and significant than such a technical definition suggests; Rogers places communication at the heart of person-centred theory, especially as it concerns helping relationships. The communication of EMPATHIC UNDERSTANDING without judgement is the primary therapist activity in CCT but this principle is extended to all other forms of human relationships where CHANGE, personal GROWTH and understanding are key purposes. Clear communication is seen as an outcome of CONGRUENCE or AUTHENTICITY as 'when I am experiencing an attitude of annoyance toward another person but am unaware of it, then my communication contains contradictory messages' (Rogers, 1990e, p. 119). The fact that Rogers saw communication as the prime means by which one person can truly encounter another, and

that positive change and healing can occur as a result is no better illustrated than in his discussion of the case of ELLEN WEST (Rogers, 1980a).

communicative contact one of three psychological CONTACT FUNCTIONS, identified within PRE-THERAPY as necessary for therapy to begin, consisting of clients' communication to others of reality and affect (see AFFECTIVE CONTACT and REALITY CONTACT).

community a group of people settled in one area over a period of time in which each member regards the group as a social unit and shares, to some extent, a feeling of group identity. In applications of the PCA, the term 'community' is often used to refer to an intentional group/groups which come together for a relatively short time-span (anything from a week to a weekend); the purposes of these temporary communities may be, for example, to learn about the people making up the group on a personal level, or to explore aspects of CROSS-CULTURAL COMMUNICATION; in doing so, group facilitators and participants create the CORE CONDITIONS on a much wider scale than is the case in individual CCT. One such temporary person-centred community was the subject of some research reported by Barrett-Lennard (1994). This comprised a community of 136 people, including the ten paid official staff, that came together in the USA during 1976; Barrett-Lennard wrote that its 'major, self-conscious purpose was that of our development as a community, and the learnings that could evolve from this. From another vantage point, our aim was to discover experientially *how to be together* in a way that reflected a broad philosophy, value system, and view of human nature' (p. 71, original emphases). Barrett-Lennard described the event as 'kaleidoscopic, agonizing, exhilarating, frustrating, enlightening, unpredictable, and absorbing' (ibid., p. 71). From his research, which consisted of a mixture of participant observation and questionnaires, and later reflection, Barrett-Lennard developed a theory of community (which he described as a 'first approximation') which consists of the following seven general propositions:

1. An inside view, derived from empathic contact with a cross-section of members absorbed in expressive engagement in their world, and in moments of portrayal and reflection on this engagement, is essential to understanding the nature and identity of a community. The products of this inside view make possible an informed, also necessary 'outside view' by the participant-observer/investigator.

2a. A community forms and evolves as a collective of persons, aware of one another and interconnected in multiple ways. These ways include networks of association among individuals and subgroups, which have reciprocally valued elements for

2b. The more — in both quality and extent — that potential linkages evolve such that community members are 'significant others' in each other's lives, the stronger and more fully formed the community tends to be.

3a. Qualitative development of community tends to build upon itself as in the case where communal life fosters growth processes

among its members and flourishes and evolves through effects of this growth.

3b. When communities satisfy growth or actualisation needs of their own members, beyond a period of initial development, they tend to behave in constructively responsive ways in relation to other communities, organizations, and individuals.

4. Formed communities tend to maintain if not also to enhance themselves; to have a distinctive identity interwoven with the values and self-definition of members; and to satisfy human needs for affiliated BELONGING and presence with others.

5. A well-functioning community is an open system in interface with other systems (especially living systems, and usually including other communities), organically responsive to new external data and to fresh information and initiatives from within, and thus in evolving motion. This motion applies to the scope, subtlety, and wisdom of communal or collective consciousness, and is assisted by an ethic which is at once egalitarian and responsive to the varied, special resources of its members.

6. A poorly functioning or severely threatened community may withdraw and isolate itself, or engage in power manipulation or conflict, in relation to other human collectives. Internally, members are not openly present with one another, and tend to be caught in a personally and communally self-limiting pattern of association. The self-maintaining tendency

may lead to rigidity, and to more concern with image than being; in such circumstances, the ORGANISMIC quality of a well-functioning community recedes or is not present. Extremely faulty attributions may occur in regard to outsiders — individual or collective. The 'community' can become a prison to its members and/or a violent antagonist to its neighbours.

7. A community is an emergent whole with a life of its own which normally it seeks to maintain. In effect, it is an emergent life form, and should not lightly be conceived, aborted, subverted, or destroyed.

Other descriptions, references and research on aspects of person-centred approaches to communities can be found in Rogers (1978); Wood (1984); McIlduff and Coghlan (1991, 1993); MacMillan and Lago (1993) and Merry (1995).

community building the building of intentional communities, based on the work of Scott Peck (1987) and, in many respects, similar to the temporary COMMUNITIES valued, created, developed and studied within the PCA; the Foundation for Community Encouragement, with an international network, fosters the development of communities based on the belief that the mutual caring and creativity engendered within them could help ameliorate some of the conflicts in the world (see Appendix 2).

component factor method a research instrument developed by Rogers during the 1930s to assess the quality of a child's personal and environmental situation; based on eight factors, ratings were designed to indicate whether any factor was either destructive of the child's welfare or contributed to healthy adjustment and behaviour; the eight factors are: quality of family life and influence, the health history or constitution of the child, economic and cultural background and influence, intellectual development, social experience, hereditary factors, education, the degree of the child's self-understanding, self-insight and acceptance of self-responsibility (Rogers, 1939). The method had the advantage of not only assessing the child's current situation, but also suggesting which of the eight factors were changeable; an initial piece of research using this method is reported in Kirschenbaum and Henderson (1990b) in which Bill Kell, a Masters student at Ohio State University, found the rating of self-insight to be most predictive of future behaviour; this result was largely confirmed when the research was later replicated (Rogers, Kell and McNeil, 1948). Rogers now had

> two studies which indicated that the degree of self-understanding, the degree of self-acceptance, the degree to which the child could accept the reality of his or her situation, the degree to which the child was taking responsibility for self — that these factors predicted future behavior (Rogers, cited in Kirschenbaum and Henderson 1990b, p. 208).

Although Rogers was, at first, sceptical of the results of this research, he later began to see the significance of them, especially as the initial results had been largely confirmed by a second study. Without in any way dismissing the influence of the other seven factors, Rogers came to believe that

> rather than feeling that a person is inevitably doomed by unalterable forces which have shaped him, this study suggests that the most potent influence in his future behavior is one which is certainly alterable to some degree without any change in his physical or social heredity or in his present environment. The most powerful determinant would appear to lie in the attitudes of the person himself (ibid., p. 210).

The significance of this research on the development of the PCA is difficult to assess, but it may be more important than has hitherto been realised: within it lies some confirmation that the SELF-CONCEPT and issues concerning SELF-ESTEEM are powerful factors influencing a person's behaviour, and this finds many echoes in Rogers' PERSONALITY THEORY. That the self-concept is open to change through CCT and that this brings about alterations in behaviour, attitudes and self-esteem helps to explain why Rogers did not share the DETERMINISTIC philosophy of either PSYCHO-ANALYSIS or BEHAVIOURISM.

concept the idea of a group of objects sharing common properties, or a general notion such as the *concept* of evolution; in psychology, concepts are usually placed along a spectrum of concreteness–abstractness where a house, for example, is categorised as 'concrete' while 'creativity' is considered abstract and difficult to define in simple terms; SELF-CONCEPT is another example of an abstract concept.

concrete reflections see PRE-THERAPY.

condition, assumed the sixth of Rogers' NECESSARY AND SUFFICIENT CONDITIONS which refers to the client receiving or experiencing the therapist's UNCONDITIONAL POSITIVE REGARD and EMPATHIC UNDERSTANDING ('being received'), which Rogers (1961) regards as the 'assumed condition', although ironically, and with the exception of Watson (1984) and Duncan and Moynihan (1994), perhaps the least regarded or researched of all the necessary and sufficient conditions; Tudor (2000) regards this as *the* 'core' condition.

conditional positive regard the ATTITUDE and situation in which a person receives POSITIVE REGARD in the form of praise or approval, etc. for behaving in ways that are approved of by significant others (see CONDITIONS OF WORTH, UNCONDITIONAL POSITIVE REGARD).

conditioning a set of empirical concepts which in mainstream psychology usually refer to the conditions under which associative learning takes place; in PCP, the term is most often associated with CONDITIONS OF WORTH.

conditions, client's these refer to those of the NECESSARY AND SUFFICIENT CONDITIONS in which the client is required to participate i.e. the (pre-)condition of CONTACT and the condition of client INCONGRUENCE (being vulnerable or anxious), as well as the ASSUMED CONDITION of 'being received' if s/he perceives the therapist's UNCONDITIONAL POSITIVE REGARD or EMPATHIC UNDERSTANDING (see Tudor, 2000); too little is made of that fact that Rogers' (1957, 1959) formulations of this central hypothesis is DIALOGIC and demanding of the client.

conditions, core three of the *six* NECESSARY AND SUFFICIENT CONDITIONS OF

THERAPEUTIC PERSONALITY CHANGE which have become known as the 'core conditions': the therapist is CONGRUENT or integrated in the relationship; the therapist experiences UNCONDITIONAL POSITIVE REGARD for the client; and the therapist experiences an EMPATHIC UNDERSTANDING of the client's internal frame of reference and endeavours to communicate this experience to the client. A common misunderstanding of the PCA (not only from without but also from within) is that the core conditions are necessary and sufficient: they are not and Rogers never claimed that they were — see Tudor (2000) for further discussion of the history of implications of this. One problem with the traditional clustering of these three conditions together is that they are viewed as the same when, in fact, congruence is different (from the other two) in that it is not explicitly required to be perceived by or communicated to the client. Significantly, in his writing Rogers always referred to congruence first as 'genuineness appears to be most basic' (Rogers and Sanford, 1984, p. 1378).

Patterson (2000b) published a review of reviews of the research undertaken into the necessity and sufficiency of empathy, genuineness (congruence), and warmth (unconditional positive regard) in psychotherapeutic relationships, and came to a number of interesting conclusions. He believed that the reviewers he considered did not in many cases come to conclusions that followed from their own summaries of the research; he claimed that many reviewers were biased against recognising the importance of the effectiveness of the core conditions; were biased in their selection of studies to review; applied different standards of critique to studies that were inconsistent with their biases; emphasised or gave greater weight to research that was consistent with their biases; and de-emphasised results that were unacceptable to them when results were positive on some outcome measures but negative on others. Patterson concludes that:

> considering the obstacles to research on the relationship between therapist variables and therapy outcomes, the magnitude of the evidence is nothing short of amazing. There are few things in the field of psychology for which the evidence is so strong. The evidence for the necessity, if not the sufficiency, of the therapist conditions of accurate empathy, respect, or warmth, and therapeutic genuineness is incontrovertible (p. 171).

It should be noted that the core conditions or core QUALITIES to which Rogers referred are viewed as personal qualities, values and attitudes possessed by therapists or other helpers, and *not* as particular techniques, methods or strategies. Equally, these core conditions/qualities are not confined to therapy, but are considered as essential ingredients of all effective relationships e.g. between partners, teachers and students, etc. An excellent discussion, summarising and dealing with misconceptions about the importance of the core conditions, may be found in Mearns and Thorne (2000).

conditions of therapeutic personality change, necessary and sufficient the hypothesised conditions by which the therapist facilitates constructive

PERSONALITY CHANGE: 'for therapy to occur it is necessary that these conditions exist.

1. That two persons are in contact.
2. That the first person, whom we shall term the client, is in a state of INCONGRUENCE, being vulnerable or anxious.
3. That the second person, whom we shall term the therapist, is CONGRUENT in the relationship.
4. That the therapist is experiencing UNCONDITIONAL POSITIVE REGARD toward the client.
5. That the therapist is experiencing an EMPATHIC UNDERSTANDING of the client's INTERNAL FRAME OF REFERENCE.
6. That the client perceives, at least to a minimal degree, conditions 4 and 5, the unconditional positive regard of the therapist for him, and the empathic understanding of the therapist' (Rogers, 1959, p. 213).

In another paper entitled 'The necessary and sufficient conditions of therapeutic personality change' Rogers is explicit: 'no other conditions are necessary. If these six conditions exist, and continue over a period of time, this is sufficient. The process of constructive personality change will follow' (Rogers, 1957, p. 96). This formulation must be viewed in the context of Rogers' (1959) publication, which is a comprehensive presentation of a theory of therapy, personality and interpersonal relationships, as developed in the client-centred framework and which, although *published* two years after the 1957 paper (in 1959) was actually written and completed between 1953 and 1954 *before* the 1957 paper (which was re-

ceived for publication in 1956) (see Rogers, 1957, p. 95, n. 1; Rogers and Hart 1970; Evans, 1975, p. 135) — the delay due to the scale of Sigmund Koch's enterprise in editing a series of volumes on *Psychology: A Study of a Science* and the timescale of publication. Over the years there has been some considerable debate as to the significance of differences in the two statements, especially regarding the term CONTACT (1959 chapter) and *psychological* CONTACT (1957 paper) and the necessity (or otherwise) of the therapist's *communication* of their unconditional positive regard and empathic understanding to the client (1957) or the sufficiency that these attitudes are *perceived* (1959). Considerable light is shed on such debates by the clarification that the more comprehensive formulation takes historical precedence and that the papers were written with different purposes in mind. Notwithstanding such debates, the publication of both papers prompted some controversy and a good deal of research, in the history of which Bozarth (1993) has identified a number of general patterns:

1. 1950–60: Research results, predominantly conducted by investigators from the UNIVERSITY OF CHICAGO, support the hypothesis that the conditions are both necessary and sufficient (e.g. Cartwright, 1957).
2. 1960–70: Research results continue to support the necessity and sufficiency of the conditions. Results summarised by Truax and Mitchell (1971) find that higher levels of the conditions are related to positive outcomes. Cli-

ents with therapists who measure highly on the conditions show greater gains than clients with therapists low in these conditions.

3. 1970–80: Research continues to focus on the relationships between conditions and outcome. Conclusions include that (a) 'More complex relationships exist among therapist, patients and techniques' (Parloff, Waskow and Wolfe, 1978, p. 273); (b) 'Such relationship dimensions are rarely sufficient for patient change' (Gurman, 1977, p. 503); and (c) 'Our conclusion must be that the relationship between the interpersonal skills and client outcome has not been investigated and, consequently, nothing definitive can be said about the relative efficacy of high and low levels of EMPATHY, WARMTH, and GENUINENESS' (Mitchell, Bozarth and Krauft, 1977, p. 488).

4. 1980–87: Research begins to examine aspects of therapy in different ways, and especially the THERAPEUTIC RELATIONSHIP — see Gelso and Carter (1985) who argue that 'the conditions ... are neither necessary nor sufficient although it seems clear that such conditions are facilitative' (p. 220). In an important contribution, Watson (1984) argues that not all six conditions have been adequately studied and that most research focuses on 'THERAPIST-provided CONDITIONS', a theme and critique taken up by Tudor (2000).

Bozarth (1993) concludes that 'the research summaries of the evidence regarding the relationship of the attitudinal qualities to client improvement fundamentally disagree' but goes on to note that 'there is virtually no research that supports the position that the attitudinal qualities are *necessary but not sufficient* for therapeutic personality change' (p. 96). In a novel development, he goes on to speculate whether the CORE CONDITIONS are, in fact, necessary at all. Observing that individuals report significant change and enhanced functioning as a result, for example, 'from experiencing a religious conversion, a sunset, a traumatic experience, and so on' (p. 101), Bozarth concludes

> that the conditions may not necessarily be necessary ... Further consideration of the theoretical underpinnings suggests to me that, rather than conclude the conditions are *necessary but not sufficient*, it is more accurate to conclude that the conditions are *not necessarily necessary, but always sufficient* (p. 102).

Although attention has concentrated on conditions 3 to 6 (above), known generally as the CORE CONDITIONS, some modern developments in person-centred theory have focused on the first condition: that two persons are in psychological contact. Whilst this may seem obvious in therapeutic (and other) situations, it remains a fact that some clients in therapy are unable to form meaningful relationships with their therapists. Examples include people experiencing acute PSYCHOSIS or those in catatonic states. (However much person-centred practitioners dislike labels such as these, they are in common usage and we need to know what they are generally taken to mean; here they are used cautiously.) This phenomenon has been tackled recently by the development of PRE-THERAPY associated with Gary Prouty (e.g. Prouty, 1976, 1990, 1994; Prouty and Cronwal, 1989; and Van Werde, 1998).

The controversy over whether the six conditions described above are both necessary *and* sufficient continues to this day, and may never be finally resolved. Among person-centred practitioners there appear to be two camps emerging: those who believe in the necessary and sufficient argument and those who do not. The former group views the introduction of any techniques or therapist-led interventions (i.e. those that do not emerge from within the client's FRAME OF REFERENCE) as contravening the basic philosophical assumption of the PCA, namely, that trusting totally in the client's ACTUALISING TENDENCY is undermined by the introduction of techniques drawn from other psychotherapeutic traditions. The latter group consider it legitimate to introduce techniques during therapy, viewing them as invitations to clients to explore emotional material in a variety of ways, rather than instructions or manipulations (see LEVELS OF INTERVENTIVENESS). Both groups, however, see the *core conditions* as fundamental to the therapeutic process. The position taken by Rogers in both his 1959 and 1957 statements is, however, that the *six* conditions are necessary and sufficient, although it must be said that this was advanced as a *hypothesis*, rather than as a statement of fact. While most attention has been focused on the meanings of these conditions, Rogers did go on to discuss some implications of this hypothesis which are sometimes overlooked.

For example, Rogers did not believe that the conditions were appropriate with one type of client and that other conditions were necessary for different clients with different needs. He did not believe that the six conditions were necessary only for client-centred therapy and that other conditions were necessary for other kinds of therapy. Indeed his 1957 paper was a statement about therapy and helping relationships in general and may be viewed as an integrative statement (Bozarth, 1996c), while his 1959 paper refers specifically to CCT. His hypothesis was that the conditions applied to any situation in which positive personality change was a goal, including classical psychoanalysis, etc. Rogers (1957) proposed that the variety of techniques common to many forms of psychotherapy (dream analysis, interpretation, etc.) are relatively unimportant except where they serve as means of fulfilling one or other of the six conditions. Even the 'technique' most associated with CCP, i.e. the REFLECTION OF FEELINGS was not considered as essential to successful therapy, except where it acted as a means of the therapist communicating empathy and unconditional positive regard. Feelings could equally be 'reflected' in ways that communicated a lack of empathy. A major purpose for Rogers in offering his hypothesis was to encourage and assist therapists to think critically about their own behaviour, attitudes and experience in terms of those that are essential to psychotherapy and those which may be non-essential or even harmful. Finally,

Rogers' hypothesis extends beyond therapy: the six conditions are obtainable not only in a psychotherapeutic relationship. Rogers believed, for example, that many good friendships fulfil the conditions, but that therapy allows for a heightening of the constructive qualities that exist naturally in some friendships. Rogers also believed that conditions 3, 4 and 5 are 'QUALITIES of experience', acquired by experiential training and not (simply) intellectual functions.

conditions of worth literally, the conditions of worth or value of oneself from the (usually negative) evaluations of significant others in childhood (see EXTERNAL LOCUS OF EVALUATION). Rogers postulated that a function of the ACTUALISING TENDENCY is to differentiate a portion of an individual's experience into an awareness of being and functioning, which awareness he calls SELF-EXPERIENCE; when such a self-experience is evaluated by others as being more or less worthy of POSITIVE REGARD, then SELF-REGARD becomes vulnerable to these external judgements; it is when self-experiences become sought after or avoided because they are more or less deserving of self-regard that the individual is said to have acquired conditions of worth. For instance, an infant feels angry and/or resentful towards a sibling, perhaps for very good reason, and expresses that anger by crying or yelling; if the expression of anger is responded to by a parent or other significant person in the infant's environment with the withdrawal of love (or its threatened withdrawal) as the infant experiences it (e.g. the infant is punished), the infant may develop the condition of worth that it is unaccept-able to feel or express anger; consequently, when a situation is met in the future that is liable to arouse anger or resentment the person may not be able to accept these feelings into awareness because they now threaten the SELF-CONCEPT with its internalised conditions of worth ('I do not feel anger; anger is unacceptable; to feel or express it threatens the continuation of positive regard'). The individual may DENY the feeling altogether or DISTORT it into another feeling that is compatible with the self-concept (e.g. guilt, depression, etc.).

conditions, therapist's these refer to those of the NECESSARY AND SUFFICIENT CONDITIONS offered or embodied by the therapist, i.e. the CORE CONDITIONS (CONGRUENCE, UNCONDITIONAL POSITIVE REGARD, EMPATHIC UNDERSTANDING) as well as the (pre-)condition of CONTACT (see Tudor, 2000).

confidence, unconditional a term, deriving from Tibetan meditation, similar to 'unconditional faith' in another (Rogers, 1961), and which Harman (1990) views as a facilitative precondition for the therapist, viewing it as a *state* of confidence (as distinct from having confidence *in* something) which constitutes a PHENOMENOLOGICAL base for the 'CORE' — or therapist's — CONDITIONS (see OPENNESS, TRUST).

configurations of the self see SELF, CONFIGURATIONS OF.

confirmation ACCEPTANCE OF THE PERSON AS A PROCESS OF BECOMING, a term and use Rogers (1961) adopted from Martin Buber a few years after their dialogue (see DIALOGIC; Kirschenbaum and Henderson, 1990b; Anderson and Cissna, 1997). Distinct from acceptance and the EMPATHIC process of 'entering the client's world', it rests

27

on setting people at a distance and viewing them as independent; this (Buber's) philosophical anthropology emphasises the interhuman and the inbetween (see INTERSUBJECTIVITY); the growth of the SELF is accomplished 'by the confirmation in which one knows oneself to be "made present" in one's uniqueness by another ... the goal is completing distance by relation, and relation here means mutual confirmation, cooperation, and genuine DIALOGUE' (Friedman, 1996, p. 364). Making the other present through 'confirming the other' — and MUTUAL confirmation — means to *imagine* the real and the reality of the person's BECOMING: 'if I accept him as a process of becoming, then I am doing what I can to confirm or make real his potentialities' (Rogers, 1961, p. 55). Rogers distinguishes this kind of confirmation from the operant conditioning of BEHAVIOURISM which confirms the person as an object. Friedman (1996) draws out the distinction between Rogers and Buber on this:

> I do not see in Rogers' statements ... the recognition that confirming you may mean that I do *not* confirm you in some things, precisely because you are not taking a direction. It is not just that I am watching you wrestle with yourself; I am also entering into the wrestling. It is only insofar as you share with me and we struggle together that I can glimpse the person you are to become. (p. 368)

conflict   a situation involving hostile or antagonistic events, motives and behaviours; Rogers himself devoted much of the last few years of his life to working with people in conflict situations, such as in Northern Ireland and Central America. In PCP, the term 'conflict exploration' is generally preferred to 'conflict resolution' or 'conflict management' because no outcome is predicted other than the exploration itself; mutually hostile individuals or groups, it is believed, are more likely to reach some accommodation with each other in an atmosphere of honesty and openness (CONGRUENCE), UNCONDITIONAL POSITIVE REGARD and EMPATHIC UNDERSTANDING, even when these attitudes at first are exhibited only by the FACILITATORS present. Rogers (1965) identifies four elements of conflict:

1. rigidly held conviction and belief by each party (usually 'I am right and you are wrong');
2. breakdown in communication;
3. DISTORTIONS in perceptions; and
4. suspicion and mistrust (see INTERCULTURAL TENSIONS, RUST WORKSHOP, STEEL SHUTTER).

confrontation   literally, the act of facing someone with something, often with the intention of comparison; in therapy this inevitably, therefore, involves the therapist offering their own perceptions of and FRAME OF REFERENCE about behaviour, beliefs, emotions, etc. which differ from those of the client; while some person-centred therapists use confrontation as a way of reflecting a discrepancy or INCONGRUENCE within the, generally it is little used in CCT client: 'accurate empathy results from the client's inner frame of reference alone, while confrontation requires the inner frame of reference of the therapist as well' (Tscheulin, 1990, p. 329) (see NONDIRECTIVE, LEVELS OF INTERVENTIVENESS); developing the hypothesis of client-therapist complementarity, Tscheulin (1990) discusses the effectiveness of confrontation with 'action-centred clients' who, he argues, are less capable than 'self-centred clients' of self-reflection, concluding that a differential approach for these two 'types' of clients engages the therapeutic use of confrontation.

congruence a therapeutic attitude of genuineness or wholeness, first developed in the mid-1950s by practitioners in Atlanta working with Carl Whitaker, later taken up and developed by Rogers who, in coining the term, was inspired by the geometric concept of congruence meaning accordance, agreement or correspondence. There are several elements to the development and meaning of the concept within the PCA:

1. It is a state of integration in which SELF-EXPERIENCES are accurately symbolised and which, if true of all self-experiences all the time, would lead the individual to being a FULLY FUNCTIONING PERSON; more commonly, it is something that, 'at a given moment, one either is or is not' (Brazier, 1993b, p. 4). In his defining formulation of the client-centred framework, Rogers (1959) suggests that OPENNESS TO EXPERIENCE, PSYCHOLOGICAL ADJUSTMENT, EXTENSIONALITY and MATURITY, all derive from the concept of congruence and summarises their relationship to each other and to congruence:

congruence is the term that describes the state. Openness to experience is the way an internally congruent individual meets new experience. Psychological adjustment is congruence as viewed from a social point of view. Extensional is the term which describes the specific types of behavior of a congruent individual. Maturity is a broader term describing the personality characteristics and behavior of a person who is, in general, congruent (Rogers, 1959, p. 207).

2. Some writers distinguish between implicit and explicit congruence (Brazier, 1993b) or inner and outer genuineness (Lietaer, 1993). Citing Rogers (1961) formulation: 'by [congruence] we mean that the feelings the therapist is experiencing are available to him, available to his awareness, and he is able to live these feelings, be them, and able to communicate them if appropriate', Tudor and Worrall (1994) identify four elements: self-awareness, self-awareness in action, communication and appropriateness.

3. It is the first of the CORE CONDITIONS and is a basic requirement of the *therapist*. Significantly, in Rogers' formulations of the NECESSARY AND SUFFICIENT CONDITIONS, it is not something which needs to be communicated explicitly to the client (as does the therapist's UNCONDITIONAL POSITIVE REGARD for and EMPATHIC UNDERSTANDING of the client); as such it is a quiet way of being (at any given moment).

4. In his theory of interpersonal relationships, Rogers (1959) discusses congruent communication (i.e. statements of personal EXPERIENCE) as a pre-requisite of constructive relationships and

essential to the process of improving relationships and of reduction in group conflict.

5. It is often confused with and is not synonymous with honesty, TRANSPARENCY or SELF-DISCLOSURE. Truax and Carkhuff (1967) discriminate between genuineness and self-disclosure and design a measurement scale for facilitative genuineness. Furthermore, Haugh (1998) suggests that genuineness, authenticity, realness and transparency (terms often used synonymously with congruence) are *outcomes* of, rather than definitions of or substitutions for, congruence.

6. Mearns (1996, 1997) discusses stillness and fearlessness as qualities of congruent functioning in working at RELATIONAL DEPTH.

conscientizaçao (conscientisation) a term, originally coined by Paulo Freire, the Brazilian educationalist and revolutionary, which refers to LEARNING to perceive social, political and economic contradictions and, consequently, to take action against the oppressive elements of society — see O'Hara (1989) who compares the ideas of Rogers and Freire (see also FREEDOM TO LEARN).

conscious see CONSCIOUSNESS and UNCONSCIOUS.

consciousness mostly used synonymously with AWARENESS and SYMBOLISATION; reflective consciousness is viewed as a salient human channel of the ACTUALISING TENDENCY. In discussing the phenomena generally referred to as conscious and UNCONSCIOUS, Rogers disassociated himself from agreeing or disagreeing with Freud's conceptions, preferring the view of a range of phenomena: from those in sharp focus in awareness (which he referred to as 'the height of consciousness'); through that material which could be called into consciousness (which Freud referred to as the PRECONSCIOUS and which GESTALT THERAPY refers to as 'the ground' as distinct from 'the figure'); to material which is only dimly perceived (see INCONGRUENCE) and that which is in some way prevented from coming into awareness because it would threaten the person's SELF-CONCEPT (see Evans, 1975). Fromm (1986) summarises this view: 'there is no such thing as "the conscious" and "the unconscious". There are degrees of consciousness-awareness and unconsciousness-awareness' (p. 62).

construct a fixed idea, the basis on which a prediction about the world is made, a term borrowed by Rogers from George Kelly (Kelly, 1955) and used in his seven stages PROCESS CONCEPTION OF PSYCHOTHERAPY in which he refers to constructs as 'the cognitive maps of experience' (Rogers, 1961, p. 157) (see CONSTRUING and PERSONAL CONSTRUCT PSYCHOLOGY).

constructivism a general theory which views PERCEPTION and perceptual experiences as constructed from data signalled by the senses and drawn from memory; in PCP it is the remembered data — themselves constructions from the past — upon which the SYMBOLISATIONS are made, i.e. the basis on which we make sense of things: 'the essence of all constructivist theories is that perceptual experience is viewed as more than a direct response to stimulation' (Reber, 1985, p. 151) — and is contrasted with the notion of *direct* perception (see also POSTMODERNISM).

construing the process of making sense of and thereby predicting our personal worlds (see CONSTRUCT and PERSONAL CONSTRUCT PSYCHOLOGY).

contact synonymous with RELATION-SHIP; in Rogers' (1959) paper it is viewed as the least or minimal experience which could be defined as a relationship, when each person in a relationship makes a PERCEIVED — or SUBCEIVED — difference in the EXPERIENTIAL FIELD of the other and is the first (or pre-condition) of the NECESSARY AND SUFFICIENT CONDITIONS. Rogers (1957) suggests that, alone of the six conditions, it is dichotomous or binary in that it is either present or it is not and, in the sense that one cannot not be in relationship, this is consistent; however, from recent work in the field of PRE-THERAPY and specifically its CONTACT BEHAVIOURS, CONTACT FUNCTIONS and CONTACT REFLECTIONS, it appears more likely that there are describable and definable *degrees* of contact between people; for Mearns (1996, 1997) this is the phenomenological reality for both therapists and clients (see also PSYCHOLOGICAL CONTACT).

contact behaviours specific behaviours measurable so as to illustrate the outcome of PRE-THERAPY, the operationalised aspects of PSYCHOLOGICAL CONTACT and, specifically, the CONTACT FUNCTIONS, thus:

1. Reality contact is operationalised as the client's verbalisations of people, places, things and events.
2. Affective contact (to do with self), is operationalised as the body or facial expressions of affect.
3. Communicative contact (to do with other), is operationalised as the verbalisations of social words or sentences.

(See also CONTACT REFLECTIONS.)

contact functions the three psychological contact functions, internal to the client, and identified within PRE-THERAPY as necessary for therapy to begin:

1. Reality contact is the client's awareness of people, places and objects.
2. Affective contact consists of the client's awareness of emotions, moods and feelings.
3. Communicative contact describes the client's communication of awareness of reality and affect to others.

(See also CONTACT BEHAVIOURS, CONTACT REFLECTIONS.)

contact reflections the five forms of reflections of concrete client behaviour and/or elements from the client's surroundings, identified and developed by Prouty (1976) by which the therapist makes contact with the client and which, indeed, are designed to establish and enhance the client's three CONTACT FUNCTIONS; they take five different forms:

1. Situational Reflections (SR) where people, places and events are referred to, e.g. 'It is raining', 'We are seated by my desk'. Situational reflections are designed to draw attention to the client's present environment.
2. Facial Reflections (FR) reflect the emotion currently observable on the client's face, e.g. 'You look afraid'. The purpose is to help the client become aware of pre-expressive feelings.

31

3. Body Reflections (BR) refer to the client's movements or postures, with the intention to help the client towards an awareness of his or her body, e.g. 'You are sitting up straight', 'Your feet are tapping on the floor'.
4. Word-for-Word Reflections (WWR) are words or sounds that are understandable or seem to have some meaning for the client. They are designed to help clients experience themselves as expressive and/or communicative.
5. Reiterative Reflections (RR) are repetitions of previously successful reflections to strengthen the contact and further the client's experiencing.

For Prouty (1994) these 'counsellor techniques' represent an evolution in the person-centred/experiential method: 'reflection for Rogers embodied the attitude; reflection for Gendlin facilitates the Experiencing process. Reflection for Pre-Therapy develops psychological contact' (p. 37). These 'techniques', however, are not unproblematic as many of the statements cited above represent quasi-objective nominalisations about the other (person, client) and, arguably, are based on a pre-conceived way of being with people (see PRE-THERAPY for further discussion and critique).

contact, levels of the three levels of contact described in PRE-THERAPY (see Prouty, 1976, 1994), comprising: CONTACT REFLECTIONS, CONTACT FUNCTIONS and the CONTACT BEHAVIOURS of clients resulting from the development of contact functions.

contract the bilateral agreement between a helper (therapist) and a person asking for help (client) defining the terms and conditions of their contact and therapeutic work. In describing characteristic steps in the helping process, Rogers (1942) states that 'the helping is usually defined' in terms of defining what (person-centred) therapy is (and what it is not) and of issues of responsibility. Whilst some approaches, such as TRANSACTIONAL ANALYSIS, elaborate the contract into the contractual method of therapy, PCT does not generally emphasise this — although Worrall (1997) explores a PCA to contracting specifically drawing on the six NECESSARY AND SUFFICIENT CONDITIONS as the basis of a necessary contractual framework between client and therapist.

contracting the process of negotiating and agreeing a CONTRACT.

conversation, collaborative a term originally coined by Andersen and Swim (1993) and developed by Hulme (1999) in the context of a discussion about therapeutic responses to MENTAL ILLNESS (see also SCHIZOPHRENIA), arguing that good conversations enable us to 'replace the interrelated forces of fixation with the interrelated forces of flexibility. Drowning, disowning and dogmatism are replaced by reflection, relatedness and relativism' (pp. 168–9); as a process this is similar to CO-OPERATIVE ENQUIRY (see also DIALOGUE, DIALOGIC PSYCHOTHERAPY, INTERSUBJECTIVE).

co-operative enquiry see ENQUIRY, CO-OPERATIVE.

core conditions see CONDITIONS, CORE.

co-transference a term which describes the *mutual* possibility of TRANSFERENCE or TRANSFERENCE ATTITUDES in a therapeutic relationship, i.e. that the therapist equally may 'transfer' projections on to the client.

This term, originating in SELF-PSYCH-OLOGY, acknowledges the responsibility of the therapist and does not carry the same connotation of blame inherent in the term 'countertransference'; co-transference

> better reflects the reality that meaning is being co-created by both subjectivities ... with neither person holding a more objectively 'true' version of reality than the other. It reflects an appreciation of the inevitable, moment-by-moment participation of the therapist's subjective organisation of experience in a system of mutual influence (Sapriel, 1998, p. 42).

Counseling and Psychotherapy: Newer Concepts in Practice

Rogers' second book, published in 1942. Drawing on extensive case material and client interviews, it marks Rogers' move from an initial interest in diagnosis (reflected in his first book on THE CLINICAL TREATMENT OF THE PROBLEM CHILD) to a stronger interest in the PROCESS of counselling and psychotherapy. Part I places counselling in context and introduces 'A Newer Psychotherapy' and contrasts this with older methods of psychotherapy such as exhortation, suggestion, catharsis, advice and interpretation. Part II discusses initial problems faced by the counsellor, the creation of a counselling relationship and introduces Roger's NON-DIRECTIVE approach, while Part III describes the process of counselling itself and includes a chapter devoted to addressing practical questions such as the issue of note-taking during sessions and the effect of charging a fee. Finally, Part IV comprises the first published anno-tated case study of a client, HERBERT BRYAN.

Counseling with Returned Servicemen a short book by Rogers and John L. Wallén, published in 1946 and, essentially, a simplified version of COUNSELING AND PSYCHOTHERAPY for this specific population group.

counselling a general term that covers a number of activities or approaches informed by the many different schools of thought in this area, it usually involves one person (the counsellor) helping another person (the client) to explore and resolve general issues or particular problems in living, utilising first and foremost their own resources: *'effective counselling consists of a definitely structured, permissive relationship which allows the client to gain an understanding of himself to a degree which enables him to take positive steps in the light of his new orientation'* (Rogers, 1942, p. 18, original emphasis). Somewhat confusing (for most definitions of counselling), in some instances it may include the giving of advice, for example in debt or redundancy counselling. In the PCA, no difference is made between the terms and activities of counselling and psychotherapy, with 'therapy' often used as an inclusive, generic description (as in this present volume); *perceived* differences between counselling and psychotherapy, from Rogers' time to the present day, are viewed as historical, political, cultural and organisational (see BRITISH ASSOCIATION FOR COUNSELLING AND PSYCHOTHERAPY, CLIENT-CENTRED THERAPY).

counsellor accreditation see ACCREDITATION.

countertheory of transference see TRANSFERENCE, COUNTERTHEORY OF.

countertransference a psychoanalytic term which incorporates a number of meanings (Sandler, Dare and Holder (1992) identify 11) which focus on the analyst's/therapist's UNCONSCIOUS reactions to the analysand/client. Shlien's (1984) COUNTERTHEORY OF TRANSFERENCE may be applied to countertransference; and the notion of CO-TRANSFERENCE or 'co-transference attitudes' is more consistent with a PCA to this phenomenon in the THERAPEUTIC RELATIONSHIP. In similar vein, Warner (1991) suggests that when the client is intentionally trying to evoke negative feelings in their therapist, these are better understood as 'interpersonal strategies' secondary to the (FRAGILE) PROCESS than as an unconscious defence. Some view CONGRUENCE as the person-centred equivalent of countertransference; this, however, confuses a state and way of being in relationship with the reaction to and in the relationship; in this sense SELF-INVOLVEMENT is more akin to countertransference; Wilkins (1997a) further elaborates the differences as well as the similarities between countertransference and congruence.

creativity based on three 'inner conditions' of openness to experience or EXTENSIONALITY, an INTERNAL LOCUS OF EVALUATION, and an ability to toy with elements and concepts, Rogers (1961) defines the creative process as *'the emergence in action of a novel relational product, growing out of the uniqueness of the individual on the one hand, and the materials, events, people, or circumstances of his life on the other'* (p. 350) and argues that there is a social need for creativity; it depends on a nurturing environment (Rogers, 1980a) and is an outcome of therapy (Rogers, 1959) (see FULLY FUNCTIONING PERSON).

criticisms of the person-centred approach see PERSON-CENTRED APPROACH, CRITICISMS OF.

Cross-Cultural Communication, Center for the Centre, co-founded by Rogers, and directed by Charles 'Chuck' Devonshire, a colleague of Rogers and which gave its name to the sponsorship of international workshops and training programmes conducted by Chuck Devonshire and his colleagues (see CROSS-CULTURAL (COMMUNICATION) WORKSHOPS).

Cross-Cultural (Communication) Workshops international workshops focusing on communication between people from different and, at times, differing, cultures; developing generally from the application of the person-centred approach to wider, social issues, groups and large groups, and specifically from an unstructured large group experience which took place in 1978 in El Escorial, Spain over 12 days involving 128 people from 28 countries, facilitated by Rogers and a group of colleagues mainly from the CENTER FOR THE STUDIES OF THE PERSON. Following this initial workshop, it was decided that further workshops would be organised in Europe and Chuck Devonshire undertook their organisation. Later, Rogers (1991) commented on these cross-cultural workshops as

having a profound international significance. If we are to find in these international groups that it is truly impossible to understand each other — to meet each other as persons — to grasp the significance and meaning of the beliefs of each other, then I suppose there is not much hope for our world. But if it does prove possible genuinely to meet and discover each other as persons, actually to empathise with and understand both the cultural beliefs and political views of each other — then I think that our obscured future may be penetrated with clear rays of light and that we may realistically hope for a better world (p. 40).

Held annually for more than 20 years, these workshops and their (own) culture, as well as the implications for person-centred theory and practice have been well studied and reviewed (see Devonshire, 1991; McIlduff and Coghlan, 1991, 1993; Wood, 1999).

cultural conflict the contention among people or groups of people over contradictory and opposing values or standards (see CULTURAL NORMS); also (and perhaps more subtle) the conflict that occurs, either within a person or between persons, when confronted with two or more cultural VALUES which are, or appear, contradictory but where both are at least partially acceptable as, for example, is commonly experienced in the second generation of immigrants or by incomers to a particular culture or society — the resolution of, or at least communication about, which was the subject and purpose of CROSS-CULTURAL COMMUNICATION WORKSHOPS.

cultural norms the expected standards of behaviour and conduct specified as acceptable and appropriate or simply given within a given culture, including those sanctions which are exercised against a person who violates such standards.

cultural psychology psychology in which CULTURE is made explicit rather than remaining implicit and made *intentional* rather than remaining unintentional or accidental (see Stigler, Shweder and Herdt, 1990); developed (and developing) in response to psychologies which are largely monocultural in their origins and unaware and/or uncritical of this limited, and at times positively imperialist, history (see also ANTI-OPPRESSIVE PRACTICE).

culture defined traditionally in terms of biology and intelligence, broader definitions include ethnographic variables (nationality, ethnicity, language, religion), demographic variables (such as age, gender, place of residence), status variables (social, economic, educational) and affiliation variables (formal as well as informal). Rogers (1951) identifies experiential knowledge of cultural setting and influence as important preparation for the TRAINING therapist; Singh and Tudor (1997) consider culture and cultural variables to be inevitable and frame their discussion of them in the context of Rogers' NECESSARY AND SUFFICIENT CONDITIONS which affect the THERAPEUTIC RELATIONSHIP — and which require further development and study if therapists are to be both intentional and sensitive regarding culture and context.

culture, emerging based on Rogers' (1978) views of PERSONAL POWER, the notion that EMERGING PERSONS would foster a culture which, in ways parallel to the ACTUALISING TENDENCY, is directional and characterised by exciting trends:

- Towards a NON-DEFENSIVE OPENNESS in all INTERPERSONAL RELATIONSHIPS.

- Towards the exploration of the total SELF.
- Towards the PRIZING of individuals.
- Towards human sized groupings.
- Towards a close, respectful, balanced, reciprocal relationship to the natural world (see SUSTAINABLE DEVELOPMENT).
- Towards a quality of personal living, the enhancement of which would provide the criteria whereby we value material goods (and not the other way around).
- Towards a more even distribution of material goods.
- Towards a society with minimal structure.
- Towards leadership as temporary.
- Towards a more genuine and caring concern for those who need help.
- Towards a human conception of SCIENCE.
- Towards CREATIVITY in all fields of human endeavour.

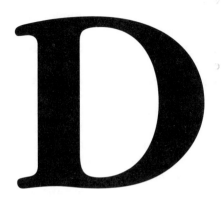

defence in general, any action taken by an organism to protect itself against any real or perceived threat with the goal of maintaining its SELF-STRUCTURE. In PCP, a defence is the means by which anything that is INCONGRUENT with or contrary to the SELF-CONCEPT is prevented from being admitted (in)to AWARENESS. The process of defence is the reaction to THREAT and consists of the selective perception and DISTORTION of experience (see also BEHAVIOUR and INCONGRUENCE). The general consequences of this process are: a rigidity of perception, inaccurate perception of reality and INTENSIONALITY (see Rogers, 1959).

defence mechanism the means by which anything which is inconsistent or threatening to a person's current SELF-CONCEPT is prevented from AWARENESS. The two defence mechanisms postulated and construed in person-centred theory are DENIAL and DISTORTION.

defensiveness the organism's response to experiences perceived or anticipated as threatening, or as INCONGRUENT with the person's current image of her/himself, or of her/himself in relationship to the environment. Such threatening experiences are made temporarily harmless by being distorted or denied to awareness (Rogers, 1951). In person-centred theory INTENSIONALITY describes the characteristics of the behaviour of the individual in a defensive state (Rogers, 1959).

deficiency needs see NEEDS, BASIC.

denial a DEFENCE MECHANISM in which any experience (thought, emotion or behaviour) which is dimly perceived (or subceived) as incongruent with or a threat to a person's SELF-CONCEPT is not admitted to that person's awareness; the existence of the experience is denied in order to preserve the self-structure from threat. It involves the avoidance of conscious recognition of any experience which threatens the current self-concept. There are various forms of denial from the outright denial of experience (of a particular stimulus) to the denial of meaning in communication.

dependence a situation in which a person relies on another for psychological (i.e. emotional) or other kinds of support. The term is most often used to describe a person who has become deeply reliant on at least one other, who shows a lack of self-reliance or autonomy, and experiences an EXTERNAL LOCUS OF EVALUATION.

depth psychology a general term that includes all psychological systems that postulate that explanations for behaviour are to be found in the UNCONSCIOUS. Freudian, Jungian and Kleinian theories are depth psychologies, and the term is sometimes used as a synonym for psychoanalysis.

depth reflection an empathic response made by a therapist (or other helper) to a person that demonstrates understanding and acceptance beyond the current level of the person's AWARENESS. Depth reflections are sometimes thought of as responses that indicate an awareness (on the part of the helper) of underlying feelings, emotions, etc. as well as showing understanding of more obvious, or surface feelings. Some believe that such reflections have an INTUITIVE quality to them, but in any case they are the result of concentrated, accurate listening, and a willingness to engage with a person's total FRAME OF REFERENCE. Sometimes also referred to as additive EMPATHY. Depth reflection needs to be viewed with some caution. First, it should not be a goal for a therapist to achieve depth reflection. Having such a goal might lead the therapist to concentrate more on 'technical expertise' than on achieving any level of EMPATHIC UNDERSTANDING. Second, a therapist who refers to feelings that are not currently within the client's frame of reference runs the risk of directing the client towards considering material for which the client is not prepared and has not chosen. To this extent, such a reflec-

tion could not be considered an example of empathic understanding and would run counter to a fundamental aspect of the person-centred approach: that 'direction' and 'depth' are matters for clients to decide, not therapists (see EMPATHY, EMPATHY SCALE, LEVELS OF INTERVENTIVENESS, NON-DIRECTIVE, REFLECTION OF FEELINGS).

destructiveness, human a term which Rogers discussed in 'A Note on "The Nature of Man"' (Rogers, 1990a) in which he observed that he did not discover 'man' to be well characterised 'in his basic nature as *fundamentally hostile, antisocial, destructive, EVIL*' (p. 403), viewing these as feelings, impulses and desires which, in the context of an accepting, non-threatening (perhaps therapeutic) relationship, tend to 'harmonise into a complex and changing pattern of self-regulation' (p. 405) (see CRITICISMS; Quinn, 1993; Ford, 1994).

determinism the idea that every event has a cause (or causes). In pre-quantum mechanics, it was assumed that if one knew the position and momentum of every particle of matter at any one time, then one would be able to predict their position and momentum at any other point in time. Quantum mechanics, however, advances the idea that levels of cause and effect are probabilistic, so that perfect prediction becomes probabilistic prediction. In psychology the discussion centres on EXISTENTIAL and HUMANISTIC notions of FREE WILL. Rogers took a position that acknowledges both the 'free will' argument and the 'determinism' argument. In other words, as a scientist he believed that valid data could be gathered by studying the objective factors that influence human development and behaviour, but also suggests that these data are most useful only when combined with information from other sources such as subjective experience and EMPATHIC UNDERSTANDING. In the PCA, FULLY FUNCTIONING individuals (theoretically) experience freedom, and their behaviour reflects this. They make choices to behave in ways that are consistent with internal and external stimuli and information:

> however, from a different perspective it can be said that their behavior is *determined* by all the existing factors, since certain behaviors *will* be more satisfying than others. Rogers seems to mean that, at the same time the individual chooses, his or her behavior is being determined by all the relevant conditions that exist ... This individual is free, but he or she *will* take a particular course of action; in the presence of all available stimuli there are definitely certain behaviors that are most productive from *both* subjective and objective points of view. In this case there isn't any contradiction between free will and determinism — in a sense, they coincide (Nye, 1986, p. 103).

In his famous debate with B.F. Skinner, Rogers remarked,

> I am in thorough agreement with Dr. Skinner that, viewed from the external, scientific, objective perspective, man is determined by genetic and cultural influences. I have also said that in an entirely different dimension, such things as freedom and choice are extremely real (Rogers, cited in Kirschen-

baum and Henderson, 1990a, p. 132).

For Rogers, both points of view had their merit: determinism provided a useful perspective in the conduct of scientific enquiry, whereas freedom and free will were vital components in the process of becoming more fully functioning.

development   the process of CHANGE during the lifespan of a person. In PCP, with its emphasis on 'process', the term is usually used in connection with the process of becoming FULLY FUNCTIONING (see also CHILD DEVELOPMENT).

development, sustainable   a view of economic development, influenced by ecological and political perspectives, which echoes Rogers' (1978) views about an EMERGING CULTURE characterised by 'human-sized groupings' (in communities, education and families) and a close(r) relationship to the natural world.

Diabasis   literally meaning 'crossing over', a centre for dealing with acutely schizophrenic young people, founded by John W. Perry and Howard Levine and based on the view that schizophrenic episodes are attempts at growth and self-healing, about which Rogers wrote in his book *Carl Rogers On Personal Power* (Rogers, 1978), citing it as an example of the person-centred approach and its politics in practice.

diagnosis   the identification, classification and description of a disorder, illness or condition from which a person is said to be suffering — and, by implication, the prescription of the 'treatment' and prognosis of its course and ultimate 'cure'. In clinical psychology and psychiatry diagnosis is not a straightforward process and is prone to much misunderstanding and error. Rogers was opposed to the use of diagnostic labels applied to psychological dynamics, calling it unnecessary, unwise and in some ways detrimental (Rogers, 1951). He had two main reasons for taking this attitude:

1. First, he saw the process of diagnosis placing the LOCUS OF EVALUATION in the hands of experts leading to dependency in clients: 'there is a degree of loss of personhood as the individual acquires the belief that only the expert can accurately evaluate him, and that therefore the measure of his personal worth lies in the hands of another' (Rogers, 1951, p. 224).

2. The second objection is that diagnosis has undesirable social and philosophical implications. The responsibility for making decisions about another person's needs, conflicts, and motives, etc. is likely to be accompanied by a degree of control over the person concerned, however well-intentioned: 'the management of the lives of the many by the self-selected few would appear to be the natural consequence' (p. 225).

Rogers thought that making evaluations and diagnoses of clients may be useful only insofar as it provided therapists with a sense of security, and thereby enables them to be more empathic and acceptant of their clients. Shlien (1989) argues that since the primary purpose of diagnosis is to determine treatment and since CCT has only one 'treatment' for all clients, then diagnosis is irrelevant. However, others, such as Schneider and Stiles (1995) see 'countervailing advantages in developing a systematic person-centred diagnostic frame of reference' (p. 67). Given the current predominance of the medical model and that this often influences (even determines) resources, including clients' access to therapy, three approaches regarding diagnosis appear open to the person-centred practitioner/theorist:

1. To eschew diagnosis completely — as represented by Shlien (1989).

2. To understand other systems of psychology and medicine and their approaches to diagnosis, assessment and treatment and to be able to '*translate*' them in person-centred terms — reflected in the approach of Speierer (1990) and some person-centred training courses.

3. To develop a person-centred approach to 'illness', psychodiagnosis and ASSESSMENT, especially as regards INCONGRUENCE and particularly in the context of working with clients who are diagnosed or labelled with medical and/or psychiatric 'illnesses' — this is represented by the work of Fischer (1989), Bohart (1990), Warner (1991, 1998, 2000b), Lambers (1994), Schneider and Stiles (1995), Speierer (1996) and Biermann-Ratjen (1998a).

(See DISSOCIATED PROCESS, FRAGILE PROCESS, NEUROSIS, PERSONALITY DISORDER, PSYCHOPATHOLOGY and PSYCHOSIS.)

dialogic pertaining to the DIALOGUE between people, about which Rogers and Martin Buber, the theologian and philosopher, had a recorded dialogue in 1957, an edited version of which was published in Kirschenbaum and Henderson (1990a) and a complete version more recently published (Anderson and Cissna, 1997), in which they discussed the nature of the 'I—Thou' or 'I—You' relationship which Buber writes about in relation to God (Buber, 1937) and which Rogers was exploring as descriptive of the client–therapist THERAPEUTIC RELATIONSHIP. In the dialogue Buber challenges Rogers on the extent of the reciprocal (MUTUAL) relationship between client and therapist and they discuss the necessity of ACCEPTANCE as the basis of every true existential relationship. Arnett (1989) draws out the differences between Buber's and Rogers' theories and conceptualisations of dialogue and the dialogic, representing them respectively as concerned with: the NARRATIVE, and the between; and the psychological, the internal locus of control and meaning, and CONGRUENCE (see also CONFIRMATION, INTERSUBJECTIVITY; Friedman, 1996).

dialogic psychotherapy   'a psychotherapy of the interhuman' as Hycner (1993) puts it; strongly influenced by Buber's (1937) views on DIALOGUE and the DIALOGIC and by INTERSUBJECTIVITY, dialogic therapy is not identified with a 'School' of therapy, theoretical orientation or technique, it is rather a restatement that the approach and PROCESS of therapy needs to be based on and in dialogue and that the 'goal' of therapy is the enhanced relational ability of the client — summarised by the phrase 'healing through meeting'. The dialogic emphasises the 'between', a perspective from which Hycner (1993) offers a critique of his experience of CCT

and PCT: 'there was so much emphasis on the separate subjective experience of the client and the separate experience of the therapist, that the between was once again slighted. At times, the dialogical seemed more like an afterthought of two separate selves coming together, rather than being an overall comprehensive manner of understanding human existence' (p. 38) (see CONFIRMATION, CRITICISMS OF THE PERSON-CENTRED APPROACH).

dialogue   a conversation between two or more persons which, in the therapeutic context, is emphasised by some therapeutic approaches such as GESTALT THERAPY more than others (see DIALOGIC); Hycner (1993) insists that dialogue 'requires two persons entering into a genuine relationship with each other' (p. 51) (see MUTUALITY); thus it may be viewed both as a *precondition* for therapy (as in Rogers' notion of CONTACT) and *the therapy itself* (see DIALOGIC PSYCHOTHERAPY).

didactic   teaching in the sense of instructing, contrasts with EXPERIENTIAL LEARNING.

differential   incongruence   model (DIM)   a client-centred model of disorder developed by Speierer (1996), according to which 'client-centered therapy is the treatment of incongruence' (p. 300). As with the American Psychiatric Association's (1994) *Diagnostic and Statistical Manual of Mental Disorders* (DSM-IV) the DIM is a multi-axial model comprising five dimensions:

1. Conditions of health, including social environmental conditions affecting health and disorder.

2. Relevant psychopathogenic features of the SELF, including basic human needs, the actualising tendency, and a person's 'liability' for self-incongruence.

3a. The 'congruence theory' of health, including the concept of the FULLY FUNCTIONING PERSON.

3b. The 'incongruence theory' of health.

4. Pyschopathological developments and disorders.

5. Disorders according to a diagnostic system — Speierer refers to the World Health Organization's (1991) International Classification of Diseases (ICD-10).

differentiation the process whereby a portion of the individual's experience becomes symbolised (see SYMBOLISATION) in an awareness of being and of functioning as a separate being/person; one part of the ACTUALISING TENDENCY and central to the development of the SELF.

directive therapy forms of psychotherapy in which clients are directed, even exhorted, to change in certain aspects that may be selected by the therapist usually after a process of discussion and negotiation with the client concerned; examples include some forms of behavioural therapy, rational emotive behaviour therapy, and hypnotherapy; PCT is not a directive therapy (see NON-DIRECTIVE THERAPY).

disease model see MEDICAL MODEL.

disorganisation the state resulting from a BREAKDOWN in which 'the organism behaves at times in ways which are openly consistent with experiences which have hitherto been distorted or denied to awareness' (Rogers, 1959, p. 229).

dissociated process one of the three styles of process, along with FRAGILE and PSYCHOTIC, which Warner (1998) identifies; commonly referred to as 'dissociative identity disorder' (see, for instance, APA, 1994) and often linked to an original severe trauma, it manifests in extremes of altered perceptions and dissociated 'parts' of the personality; Warner and her colleagues are developing ways of working with clients which acknowledge and convey an empathic understanding of all such 'parts' (see also RECOVERED MEMORY and CONFIGURATIONS OF SELF).

distortion a DEFENCE MECHANISM in which an experience (thought, emotion, behaviour) which is incongruent with or threatening to the current SELF-CONCEPT, together with its internalised CONDITIONS OF WORTH, is not admitted to AWARENESS; instead, the feeling may be changed into something more acceptable and thus in accord with the self-concept, e.g. anger may be experienced as guilt:

> perceptual distortion takes place whenever an incongruent experience is allowed into conscious awareness but only in a form that is in harmony with the person's current self-concept. The virtuous man, for instance, might permit himself to experience hostility but would distort this as a justifiable reaction to wickedness in others: for him his hostility would be rationalized into righteous indignation (Thorne, 1996a, p. 128).

(See also PSYCHOLOGICAL DISTURBANCE, ACQUISITION OF.)

disturbance see PSYCHOLOGICAL DISTURBANCE, ACQUISITION OF.

disturbance, acquisition of see PSY-
CHOLOGICAL DISTURBANCE, ACQUISITION
OF.

disturbance, perpetuation of see PSY-
CHOLOGICAL DISTURBANCE, PERPETUA-
TION OF.

dreams imaginary sense impression in
sleep, generally classified in PCP under the domain of INTUITION. As Rogers (1957) saw no therapeutic value in
the interpretative analysis of dreams
(along with analysis of the transference, hypnosis, interpretation of life-
style, suggestion etc.), dreams and
dreaming have been a neglected area
in PCP. However in a later article Rogers (1990d) tackles the question 'Dare
we develop a human science?' in
which he argues for a psychological
science,

> based upon understanding the
> PHENOMENOLOGICAL world of man,
> as well as his external behaviour
> and reactions. This trend towards
> convergent lines of confirmation
> has been evident in research in psy-
> chotherapy. It also shows up dra-
> matically in the increasingly
> sophisticated work on dreams by
> numerous investigators, tying
> together the completely subjective
> irrational dream world of the indi-
> vidual with his responses on vari-
> ous electronic measuring devices.
> Here, indeed, one of the most an-
> cient subjective realities — the

dream — is linked to the most
modern technology (p. 360).

In an earlier article, again discussing
the behavioural sciences, Rogers
(1968) had remarked, 'it is deeply em-
bedded in most behavioral scientists
that we "ought" to be concerned only
with the observable in behavior. Until
recently, this has tended to inhibit
work on dreams, on fantasy, on creative thinking' (p. 71). Despite his evident interest in dreams as part of the
individual's subjective world, Rogers
did not devote any time to developing
a way of working with dreams that
would be consistent with general person-centred principles. In a rare article on the subject Jennings (1986)
takes up the challenge of developing
the PCA in a way which facilitates the
client's 'exclusive capacity' in understanding their own dreams which includes a number of 'experiential
techniques'; Gendlin (1986) also
writes about the body as interpreter
of dreams; and Finke (1990) and
Vossen (1990) develop CCT with
dreams.

drives, primary those drives which
arise from an intrinsic physiological
characteristic of an ORGANISM, a concept used in psychology which is similar to MOTIVATION in PCP (and distinct
from secondary or acquired drives
whose motivating properties are
learned).

eclectic literally, the borrowing from various sources; in ancient times, philosophers who selected doctrines from different schools; in psychology, the denotation is similar, that is, of selecting what is considered to be the best from a number of approaches — a process which begs the question of the criteria for such selection. In the therapeutic sphere the word connotes a complex debate (see also INTEGRATIVE). Subscribing to the PHILOSOPHY, PRINCIPLES, general and specific theories of the PCA, person-centred therapists are not eclectic; at the same time, there still exists a debate among person-centred practitioners concerning how far it is possible and legitimate to borrow, incorporate or integrate techniques and methods derived from other systems into CCT and still remain faithful to the fundamental assumptions of the PCA (see Hutterer, 1993; Sanders, 2000). Some take the view that *any* technique or method derived from other approaches *always* violates reliance on the client's ACTUALISING TENDENCY; others believe that it is possible to remain firmly within the parameters of the approach whilst using TECHNIQUES or EXPERIMENTS (see GESTALT THERAPY) that are more often associated with art therapy (see EXPRESSIVE THERAPY) or PSYCHODRAMA (see also EXPERIENTIAL, INTERNATIONAL CONFERENCE ON CLIENT-CENTERED AND EXPERIENTIAL PSYCHOTHERAPY).

ecopsychology an approach to psychology which, with its roots in deep ecology and as developed by the Norwegian ecophilosopher Arne Ness, dissolves the (essentialist) boundaries between the SELF and the world, and demands a CONGRUENCE between self and nature, an expansion of notions of self and 'self-realisation', and which ultimately shifts the focus of therapy from the individual and even the GROUP or COMMUNITY to the planet; the tension between ecopsychology and CCT is explored by Neville (1999).

edge of awareness see AWARENESS, EDGE OF.

education, person-centred approach to consistent with its PHILOSOPHY and PRINCIPLES the PCA in education gives primacy to the ACTUALISING TENDENCY of the student/trainee in negotiating their learning, asserts the necessity and sufficiency of the THERAPEUTIC CONDITIONS in the context of their translation and application to the learning environment, and gives primacy to the NON-DIRECTIVE attitude at least in the content of education. This represents a radical shift in educational philosophy and practice which is antithetical to concepts of education which create a dependent relationship between 'expert' teacher and ignorant student, which are curriculum led, and which seek to 'ambush' the student through formal examination. Rogers' ideas on education (see especially Rogers, 1969, 1983) are essentially an application of the PCA; they also have resonances with the work of others regarding how children learn — and fail (Holt, 1967b, 1967a respectively), on free schools (e.g. Neil, 1968) and on deschooling (Illich, 1973), as well as the work of Paulo Freire, an educator and revolutionary who worked with illiterate Brazilian peasants before being 'encouraged' to leave the country following a military junta. Rogers (1978) acknowledges the similarities between his and Freire's (1967/76, 1972) ideas on education as:

• both are subversive of authoritarian structures;

• both are statements about change in power relationships — in breaking the vertical, top-down 'banking' concept of education (see also TRAINING);

• both propose a dialogical problem-posing (as distinct from problem-solving) education; and

• both view this type of educational work as representing a new factor in wider, social change and development.

(See also LEARNING.)

Eigenwelt see EXISTENTIAL THERAPY.

emerging culture see CULTURE, EMERGING.

emerging person see PERSON, EMERGING.

emotions feelings or affective states; Rogers thought of emotions as falling primarily into two groups: 'unpleasant and/or excited feelings, and calm and/or satisfied emotions. The first group tends to accompany the seeking effort of the ORGANISM, and the second to accompany satisfaction of the need, the consummatory experience' (Rogers, 1951, p. 493). Unpleasant and/or excited emotions, except when experienced to an excessive degree, appear to have an integrating and concentrating effect, rather than having a disintegrating effect and 'the intensity of the emotional reaction appears to vary according to the perceived relationship of the behavior to the maintenance and enhancement of the organism' (ibid., p. 493) (see also FEELING, NINETEEN PROPOSITIONS).

empathetic the adjectival form of the noun EMPATHY; although linguistically correct (and parallel to sympathetic) it is less commonly used than the term EMPATHIC.

empathic the more commonly used adjective from the noun EMPATHY.

empathic attunement a term sometimes (although confusingly) used synonymously with EMPATHY; more accurately there is a distinction between AFFECT ATTUNEMENT and the cognitive processes involved in empathy.

empathic resonation see EMPATHY CYCLE.

empathic responding a term used particularly by those within PCP who draw on COGNITIVE PSYCHOLOGY 'to stress the fact that [empathy] is not merely an attitude but a consistent style of behaviors given as responses to the client' (Wexler, 1974, p. 96); in this tradition, an empathic response is much more deliberate and organised:

> when it is optimal, *an empathic response is a structure or group of structures that more fully captures, and better organizes, the meaning of the information in the field that the client is processing than had the structure(s) the client had generated himself* (ibid., p. 97).

(See also EVOCATIVE REFLECTION, REFLECTION OF FEELINGS.)

empathic understanding a term used synonymously with EMPATHY and generally more often used by Rogers in his writings on the subject; it carries the connotation that empathy is (only) a cognitive process, a notion which Greenberg and Elliot (1997) expand, identifying four forms of empathic responding in addition to understanding: evocation, exploration, conjecture and INTERPRETATION. The term includes both empathy as an experience of the therapist and its subsequent communication. It can be difficult for a client to experience the therapist's empathy unless it is communicated in some form; the communication of empathic understanding allowing the opportunity for the client to correct inaccuracies of 'understanding'. In a discussion of the difference between AFFECT ATTUNEMENT and empathy, Stern (1985) identifies four distinct and probably sequential cognitive process to empathy: '(1) the resonance of feeling state; (2) the abstraction of empathic knowledge from the experience of emotional res-

onance; (3) the integration of abstracted empathic knowledge into an empathic response; and (4) a transient role identification' (p. 145). The process of therapy can, through appropriate resonance, response and checking out of understanding by the therapist, be(come) a genuine DIALOGUE in which client and therapist engage in a search for deeper levels of understanding of the client's experiencing process and INTERNAL FRAME OF REFERENCE.

empathy the therapist's experiencing of an accurate understanding of the client's awareness and experience, a state whereby the therapist 'perceive[s] the INTERNAL FRAME OF REFERENCE of another with accuracy, and with the emotional components and meanings which pertain thereto, as if one were the other person, but without ever losing the "as if" condition' (Rogers, 1959, p. 210). This distinguishes empathy as a state or way of being from the technique of REFLECTIVE LISTENING with which empathy is sometimes confused and equated; empathy is rather 'a qualitative and holistic experience of the therapist' (Bozarth, 1984, p. 65). In the first (historically) of his two seminal formulations of the NECESSARY AND SUFFICIENT CONDITIONS Rogers (1959) implies that it is enough that the therapist is experiencing an empathic understanding of the client's internal frame of reference and that the client perceives this in some way. In the second formulation of the theory (Rogers, 1957), he states that the therapist both experiences empathic understanding and endeavours to communicate this experience (and understanding) to the client. Although empathy is most commonly communicated verbally, non-verbal responses are also forms of empathic expression and communication. Recent discussions (e.g. Barrett-Lennard, 1997; Myers, 1999) have focused on empathy as an aspect of 'the between', the interpersonal ENCOUNTER (see DIALOGIC, INTERSUBJECTIVE) which highlights the co-creative and reflective nature of empathy. Whilst empathy is central to PCP and the PCA, especially in the attitude of the therapist and the conditions of therapy, it is not the sole preserve of this approach and is the subject of much discussion within psychoanalytic circles and, more recently, SELF-PSYCHOLOGY and is associated with the work of Heinz Kohut (see EMPATHIC ATTUNEMENT). It is unfortunate, however, that while Rogers' work and writing on the subject predates Kohut's and, indeed, Rogers (1986c) wrote an article considering the dissimilarities and differences between himself and Kohut (and Erickson), Kohut himself appears to ignore the work of Rogers and others on empathy. A recent volume (Bohart and Greenberg, 1997) brings together client-centred, experiential and psychoanalytic perspectives in reconsidering empathy.

empathy, accurate a term coined by Truax and Carkhuff (1967) to describe the highest — that is, the most accurate — level of 'unerring' therapist response to a client; while used by some within the approach, Truax and Carkhuff themselves acknowledged that this notion 'contains elements of the psychoanalytic view of moment-to-moment diagnostic accuracy' (p. 43).

empathy, blocks to the interference(s) with a listener's ability to enter a talker's FRAME OF REFERENCE and understand something of their experience; they take a variety of forms, for example, thoughts may occur to the listener who then pays more attention to them than to listening to and attempting to understand the talker; everyday distractions, such as noise or uncomfortable surroundings may also interfere with the listening process, as can internal states such as hunger or feeling ill. Less obvious blocks to EMPATHY include:

- *Being defensive*, whereby the listener feels under some kind of threat, or is feeling judged or evaluated.

- *Being over-sympathetic*, whereby feelings of wanting to 'rescue' the talker, solve the problem for them, or reassure them, lead the listener to abandon the talker's INTERNAL FRAME OF REFERENCE; alternatively, the listener's sympathetic feelings may become quite overwhelming, as a result of which the listener begins to attend more to their own feelings than those of the talker.

- *Feeling dislike*, whereby the listener's feelings of antipathy for the talker make it impossible to listen without judgement.

- *Identifying*, whereby the talker reminds the listener of similar events or feelings that have occurred in the listener's life; this can lead to listeners assuming that they know how the talker feels and what these events or feelings mean to them.

- *Feeling shocked or embarrassed*, whereby the talker says something that conflicts with one or more of the listener's VALUES, or refers to thoughts, feelings or situations with which the listener is uncomfortable.

- *Rehearsing a response*, whereby the listener is engaged more with thinking about a reply, or refuting an argument, etc. than with concentrating on understanding the talker.
- *Focusing on the content* of what is what said, the story, etc., rather than on the person.
- *Therapist (*UNCONSCIOUS*) prejudice*, whereby judgements, out of awareness, and emanating from learned messages which signify only conditional acceptance or even rejection, contaminate empathic understanding.

Fairhurst (1999) reports her research into factors identified as blocks to empathy, categorising them as to do with the therapeutic relationship (time, connectedness, differences, etc.), those within the therapeutic relationship involving both therapist and client (identification, prejudice, etc.) and those factors external to the therapeutic relationship (environmental, organisational and so on (see also COUNTERTRANSFERENCE).

empathy, client most discussion of empathy focuses on the empathy of the therapist, overlooking the important factor of a client's empathy for and understanding of themselves; also, empathy begets empathy: in the group context, Giesekus and Mente (1986) observe the client's empathy for others as the most important therapeutic factor in therapy groups — and the basis for group cohesion.

empathy cycle a cycle, identified by Barrett-Lennard (1981), comprising three distinct phases of empathy: Phase 1, the listener's emergent recognition of the other person's experiencing (empathic resonation); Phase 2, the communicative expression of this awareness (expressed empathy); and Phase 3, the awareness on the part of the recipient of being so understood (received empathy) (compare with Stern's (1985) cognitive processes of empathy, see EMPATHIC UNDERSTANDING).

empathy, idiosyncratic a term coined by Bozarth (1984) to reflect empathy as a way of being which is unique and idiosyncratic to the therapist, the client and to their particular experiencing of each other; idiosyncratic empathy emphasises: '(1) the TRANSPARENCY of the therapist in relationship to the other person; (2) the person-to-person encounter in the relationship; and (3) the INTUITION of the therapist' (Bozarth, 1984, p. 69).

empathy, kinds of a five-level evolutionary model of empathy, based on the work of the 'cultural philosopher' Jean Gebser who suggested that the evolution of human consciousness has evolved through five stages: the archaic, the magical, the mythical, the mental-rational and the integral (where each previous evolution is present in some form); Neville (1996) relates each evolution to a kind of empathy.

empathy 'lab' (laboratory) a training/learning exercise conducted in groups of three and designed to offer an experience of empathy and to focus on trainees' ability to respond with empathic understanding to a client's process of self-exploration and expression (possibly originating with Charles 'Chuck' Devonshire and described in Mearns, 1997; and Merry, 1999).

empathy, levels of a scale, developed by Truax and Carkhuff (originally in

1961 and published in 1967) which distinguished originally nine levels of empathy: from no apparent awareness of even the most conspicuous of client's feelings (which, by definition, it appears hard to conceive as empathy) through to the highest level of ACCURATE EMPATHY.

empathy, self- 'the attitude of compassion and curiosity regarding one's own experience that enables one to be simultaneously conscious of feelings and detached from them' (Snyder, 1994, p. 97), a concept further explored by Barrett-Lennard (1997).

encounter literally a 'meeting', sometimes defined as 'face to face' or 'in conflict' and a form of group (see ENCOUNTER GROUP). As Schmid (1998a) points out: 'the word meaning points to the "against", indicating *vis-à-vis*; as well as resistance' (p. 75). Arguing that the relational aspect of the PCA was developed after most of Rogers' original theoretical statements, Schmid goes on to reconceptualise the meaning of 'en-counter' in terms of philosophy, DIALOGICAL anthropology, theology and personality development, arguing that 'each encounter involves *meeting reality* and *being touched* by the essence of the *opposite*' (p. 81).

encounter group see GROUP, ENCOUNTER.

enquiry, co-operative 'two or more people researching a topic through their own experience of it, using a series of cycles in which they move between this experience and reflecting together on it ... it is a vision of persons in reciprocal relation' (Heron, 1996, p. 1) (see COLLABORATIVE CONVERSATION, DIALOGIC, HEURISTIC and RESEARCH).

entropy a measure of the energy present in a system that is unavailable for doing work; more generally, a term used to describe the tendency of any system (including the universe as a whole) to progress towards eventual disintegration; important in PCP because of Rogers' (1980a) observation that even in the context of an entropic universe, organisms (and other systems) strive to maintain INTEGRATION, GROWTH and development (see FORMATIVE TENDENCY, SYNTROPY).

environment literally and originally (from the Old French) *encircle*, thus: that which surrounds; this general meaning invites many uses in many spheres and this is no less true in psychology in general and in PCP. When not qualified, it is taken as standing for the total surroundings of an ORGANISM and carries a connotation of influence and reminds us of the significance of the context of environment on BEHAVIOUR, CONDITIONING, CONDITIONS OF WORTH, PERSONALITY, THERAPY, RELATIONSHIPS, etc.

ethics the science of morals (see CODE OF ETHICS).

evaluation the act of evaluating (see EXTERNAL LOCUS OF EVALUATION, INTERNAL LOCUS OF EVALUATION and ORGANISMIC VALUING PROCESS).

evil the antithesis of good and the subject of an exchange of open, published letters between Rogers and Rollo May, the American theologian, counsellor, minister and psychologist (see Kirschenbaum and Henderson, 1990a), in which Rogers maintained that 'evil', that is, 'DESTRUCTIVE, cruel, malevolent behavior' (Kirschenbaum and Henderson, 1990a, p. 237), is not inherent in HUMAN NATURE but rather the product of cultural influences which may warp the human ORGANISM

49

and of the individual's choice. In response to May's critique (that humans have *both* constructive and destructive inherent impulses), Rogers asserts the constructive and pro-social nature of the ACTUALISING TENDENCY; what is generally thought of and referred to as 'evil' is, more accurately, an outward expression of a person's internal estrangement between the actualising tendency and their drive to SELF-ACTUALISATION; as Rogers (1951) puts it: 'behavior is then often best described as meeting the needs of the self, sometimes as against the needs of the organism' (p. 493). More recently, in the context of a discussion of two opposing views of 'evil' (Mearns and Thorne, 2000), Mearns offers a secular and (by his own admission) 'disparaging' definition of evil: 'a hypothetical construct used to describe someone whom we fear and whom we do not understand' (p. 59). In the face of human tragedy, a diagnosis of evil is all too common and easy; moreover, it individualises the problem or issue, rather than focusing on the causes and situation of estrangement and ALIENATION.

evocative reflection   see REFLECTION, EVOCATIVE.

existentialism   a philosophy which emphasises the contrast between human existence and that of natural objects. Founded by the Danish philosopher Sören Kierkegaard in reaction to the idealism of Hegel, key concepts include: the distinction between God and 'man' and the inexplicability and absurdity of our relations with God; and the importance of voluntarism, FREE WILL, individuality, SUBJECTIVITY (rather than 'objective' science) and personal responsibility and decision-making in a world without reason or purpose. In an interview with Evans (1975), Rogers identifies himself less with the despairing existentialists such as Sartre as with Kierkegaard and Buber (see DIALOGIC), and more with the more positive and optimistic American existentialism and praises Rollo May for his presentation and interpretation of existentialism (above those of his European counterparts). The PCA is strongly influenced by existential thought in that, like PHENOMENOLOGY, it is concerned with how individuals construe meaning from experience (see also PERSONAL CONSTRUCT PSYCHOLOGY), and that we behave in ways that match our subjective awareness of ourselves and our surroundings: 'objective reality', even if it exists, does not determine our behaviour as much as our perceptions of that 'reality' (see NINETEEN PROPOSITIONS OF PERSONALITY AND BEHAVIOUR). The PCA views individual members of humankind as having at least some significant freedom of choice and free will; exercising such freedom to choose in the face of the unknown is often accompanied by fear or EXISTENTIAL ANXIETY. Although *influenced* by existentialism (see, for instance COMPONENT FACTOR METHOD), CCT is not viewed or categorised as an EXISTENTIAL THERAPY (see also HUMANISM).

existential anxiety   the ANXIETY (*angst*) which arises from the sense of impermanence, uncertainty and insignificance of being human. As there is no essential self, we are in a permanent state of process or 'being process' (Rogers, 1961) which, whilst being CONGRUENT, also entails anxiety or INCONGRUENCE at an existential dimension (see BEING, BECOMING and BELONGING).

existential living   the concept that people can live, fully open to their EX-PERIENCE and without defensiveness, in a way in which each moment is new; the self and personality then emerge from the experience (rather than experience being translated to fit a pre-conceived self-structure; it involves 'an absence of rigidity, of tight organization, of the imposition of structure on experience. It means instead a maximum of adaptability, a discovery of structure in experience, a flowing, changing organization of self and personality' (Rogers, 1961, p. 189). Along with an increasing OPEN-NESS TO EXPERIENCE and an increasing TRUST in the ORGANISM, it is one of the characteristics of the FULLY FUNC-TIONING PERSON.

existential therapy   a therapeutic approach concerned primarily with understanding people's position in the world and what it means to be human (see van Deurzen-Smith, 1996). Existentialism distinguishes four basic dimensions or spheres of human existence, all of which are appropriate foci for therapy:

- The physical dimension or *Umwelt* (the literal translation from the German is *self-world*), that is, how we relate to our physical world, including our body and physical surroundings.
- The social dimension or *Mitwelt*: our relationships with others, including our response to the context in which we live (class, culture, etc.).
- The psychological dimension or *EIGENWELT*: our relationship with ourselves and our personal worlds.

- The spiritual dimension or *Über-welt*: how we relate to the unknown and unknowable, and to the meaning we make of life.

Singh and Tudor (1997) apply these dimensions in extending EMPATHIC responses in PCT.

experience   (noun) any event through which one has lived and the learning gained from it: 'all that is present in immediate awareness or consciousness ... [including] memory and past experience ... events of which the individual is unaware, as well as all the phenomena which are conscious' (Rogers, 1959, p. 197). Rogers placed a high premium on the validity of personal experience: '*experience is, for me, the highest authority* ... Neither the Bible nor the prophets — neither Freud nor research — neither the revelations of God nor man — can take precedence over my own direct experience' (Rogers, 1961, pp. 23–4). Dolliver (1995) points out the parallels with Martin Luther's declaration who, as Rogers described in a university course paper, 'dared to set the authority of his own reason and his own clear conscience above any other' (quoted in Kirschenbaum, 1979, p. 33). However, Rogers also remarked that, 'my experience is not authoritative because it is infallible. It is the basis of authority because it can always be checked in new primary ways. In this way its frequent error or fallibility is always open to correction' (Rogers, 1961, p. 24) (see SUBJECTIVITY). Rogers' strong leanings towards science and testing for validity in experience was revealed by the further comment:

thus I have come to see both scientific research and the process of theory construction as being aimed toward the inward ordering of significant experience. RESEARCH is the persistent, disciplined effort to make sense and order out of the phenomena of subjective experience (p. 24).

Charges that Rogers was 'unscientific' in his approach to the study of humankind are easily dispensed with by reference to this and many other similar statements.

experience (verb) 'to receive in the organism the impact of the sensory or physiological events which are happening at this moment' (Rogers, 1959, p. 197).

experience, immediate a distinction has been made between immediate and mediate experience: immediate experience consists of pure and momentary elements of perception; mediate experiences consist of inferences drawn from previous experience; for example, when looking at a colour photograph of a relative, if you see a shape or shapes with various colours and shadings, you are introspecting on an immediate experience; if you see your relative you are introspecting on a mediate experience. This distinction becomes important in the PCA as Rogers (1961) argues that if an individual, in a given moment, was

entirely CONGRUENT, his actual physiological experience being accurately represented in his awareness, and his communication being accurately congruent with his awareness, then his communication could never contain an expression of external fact. If he was congruent he could not say, 'That rock is hard', 'He is stupid', 'You are bad', or 'She is intelligent'. The reason for this is that we never experience such facts. Accurate awareness of experience would always be expressed as feelings, perceptions, meanings from an INTERNAL FRAME OF REFERENCE ... if the person is thoroughly congruent then it is clear that all of his communication would necessarily be put in a context of personal perception (p. 341).

experiencing a central concept in PCT and defined by Rogers (1980a): 'when a hitherto repressed feeling is fully and acceptably experienced in awareness during the therapeutic relationship, there is not only a definitely felt psychological shift, but also a concomitant psychological change, as a new state of INSIGHT is achieved' (p. 132).

experiential freedom see FREEDOM.

experiential learning see LEARNING.

experiential field see PHENOMENAL FIELD.

experiential therapy a form of therapy, developed in part out of CCT and in particular from the work of Gendlin (1964, 1981) and others; the principal departure from CCT and PCP is that therapeutic change in experiential theory is the result of a specific process of experiencing, based on FOCUSING which, in turn, requires the therapist to direct the client towards the focused experiencing process; another difference centres on the issue of trust in the whole person (CCT), as distinct from trust in the client's experiencing process (experiential therapy). Although both traditions share a triennial conference (see IN-TERNATIONAL CONFERENCE ON CLIENT-CENTERED AND EXPERIENTIAL PSYCHO-THERAPY), within the person-centred movement, experiential therapy 'is variously seen an extension of client-centred therapy, or an emergent departure with its own separate identity' (Barrett-Lennard, 1998, p. 348, n.) (see also Brodley, 1990).

experiment more often associated with GESTALT THERAPY, there is some evidence that Rogers used this as a suggestion, although always tentatively and, according to Villas-Boas Bowen (1986) 'gingerly'.

expressed empathy see EMPATHY CYCLE.

expressive therapy a therapeutic development from the PCA which uses expressive arts such as art, drama, music and movement, etc. as ways to experience feelings. Founded by Natalie Rogers, she refers to the core of training in this approach as 'the creative connection' (N. Rogers, 1993), through which expression via one medium stimulates and nurtures expression in other media, although therapists using this approach are careful not to direct or persuade clients into trying out forms of expression if they are unwilling to do so. However, clients who have difficulty expressing themselves verbally may find new ways of self-expression, and therapists in TRAINING may benefit from the personal growth nurtured through experimenting with the expressive arts. The PCA (along with other 'talking therapies' which rely on words as medium) has been the subject of some criticism for appealing only to the articulate middle classes and 'it is somehow appropriate that his [Rogers'] daughter should be chiefly in-strumental in the training of person-centred therapists for whom verbalization is the least preferred mode of expression' (Thorne, 1992, p. 96). Equally, expressive therapy has attracted some criticism for encouraging a directive attitude in therapists and is certainly as (if not more) influenced by GESTALT THERAPY as it is PCT. It is, nevertheless, generally based on the same philosophical assumptions as the PCA, that is, a belief in the ACTU-ALISING TENDENCY, and the importance of the CORE CONDITIONS of therapeutic growth (see Appendix 2).

Expressive Therapy Institute, Person-Centered founded in 1983 by Natalie Rogers, an Institute running programmes for professionals seeking training in the expressive arts and for anyone aspiring to a higher sense of self and CREATIVITY (see Appendix 2); a European Institute ran in Britain for ten years between 1990 and 2000.

extensional a term which describes the specific, expansive types of behaviour and understanding of someone who is CONGRUENT; in his THEORY OF INTER-PERSONAL RELATIONSHIP, Rogers (1959) describes a person who is increasingly able to be congruent and not vulnerable in the area of COMMUNICATION as able to perceive the response of others in an accurate and *extensional* manner.

extensionality a term, which Rogers took from general semantics, to describe when a person reacts to or perceives their experience in limited, differentiated terms; the opposite of INTENSIONALITY, the features may be characterised as: 'to be aware of the space-time anchorage of facts, to be dominated by facts, not by concepts, to evaluate in multiple ways, to be aware of different levels of abstraction, to test his inferences and abstractions against reality' (Rogers, 1959, pp. 206–7). While intensionality describes the characteristics of the behaviour of an individual in a defensive state, extensionality describes the specific types of behaviour of a CONGRUENT person.

external frame of reference   see FRAME OF REFERENCE, EXTERNAL.

external locus of evaluation   see LOCUS OF EVALUATION, EXTERNAL.

facial reflections see CONTACT REFLEC-
TIONS.

facilitative attitude see ATTITUDE and
FACILITATOR.

facilitator one who facilitates, a term
generally preferred in the PCA to that
of 'leader' or 'conductor', especially
in the context of GROUP THERAPY and
LEARNING; in addition to holding the
PHILOSOPHY and PRINCIPLES of the PCA,
some of the characteristics of an
effective facilitator are, in terms of AT-
TITUDE, being genuinely free of a desire to control the outcome; in terms
of BELIEF, respecting the capacity of
the GROUP to deal with its own problems; and, in terms of SKILLS, skills in
releasing individual expression (see
Rogers, 1978). Rogers (1983) describes the best facilitator in the
words of the Chinese philosopher Lao
Tse:

A leader is best
When people barely know he
exists,
Not so good when people obey
and acclaim him,
Worst when they despise him.

But of a good leader, who talks
little,
When his work is done, his aim
fulfilled,
They will say 'We did this
ourselves'.

facilitation literally, the act or process
of rendering easier or helping forward; see FACILITATOR.

Facilitator Development Institute an
international person-centred training
programme initially developed in the
1970s by Charles 'Chuck' Devonshire
as one of the activities of the centre
for CROSS-CULTURAL COMMUNICATION,
run in a number of countries in Europe, and which led to the establishment of a number of independent
training courses and organisations in
several countries (for further history
of which see Barrett-Lennard, 1998).
The Facilitator Development Institute
in Britain was founded in 1974 by
Elke Lambers, Dave Mearns and Brian
Thorne (see Mearns and Lambers,
1976) and became the umbrella for
biannual training workshops which
took place between 1975 and 1995

(for a history of which see Barkham, 1999).

false memory see MEMORY, RECOVERED.

family-centred therapy the specific application of person-centred philosophy, theory and practice to family therapy, the family being the context for the interdependence of its individual members (see Anderson, Cain and Ellinwood, 1989; Gaylin, 1990, 1993; O'Leary, 1999).

family concept an analogue to the SELF and IDEAL SELF concept and, Gaylin (1990) argues, primary to and subsuming of the SELF CONCEPT.

fee the charge a therapist makes for their service, predominantly in the context of the private practice of therapy; Rogers (1942) discusses issues in charging a fee which are of therapeutic value, including the encouragement of client responsibility, motivation and independence but also emphasises the need for the fee to be 'genuinely adjusted to the economic resources of the client' (p. 245); more recently, the meaning of money in therapy and the setting, changing and payment of fees are discussed by Tudor (1998) and money in relation to collusion, competition and co-operation by Tudor and Worrall (in press).

feedback giving information, usually about performance, often in the context of TRAINING: 'improved information has more potential than anything else ... for the creating of more competence in the day-to-day management of performance' (Gilbert, 1978, p. 175); as with MODELLING, it derives from BEHAVIOURISM and, in its common confirmatory, corrective or motivating forms is a kind of operant conditioning; almost universally and uncritically employed in the training of counsellors and psychotherapists. Facilitating the practitioner in making sense of their practice, for example through the use of INTERPERSONAL PROCESS RECALL is more compatible with the philosophy of the PCA than the traditional offering of 'feedback' from an EXTERNAL LOCUS OF EVALUATION.

feeling 'an emotionally tinged experience, together with its personal meaning' (Rogers, 1959, p. 198); this essentially experiential and phenomenological definition provides the basis for EMPATHIC UNDERSTANDING of the individual's FRAME OF REFERENCE about their feelings and their associated meanings which are most likely to be different from that of the observer or therapist, e.g. one person's disappointment may be another's anger.

felt sense the region lying between what is known and what lies just on the EDGE OF AWARENESS or just out of awareness, a term coined by Gendlin (1981); FOCUSING on the felt sense can be the 'door to the unknown' (Mearns and Thorne, 1988, p. 48) (see PRECONSCIOUS, SUBCEIVED, UNCONSCIOUS).

field theory the view, developed by Lewin (1952) and taken up particularly by GESTALT THERAPY, that psychological relationships may — and, indeed, can only — be studied and understood in terms of their surrounding 'field': 'only the interplay of organism and environment ... constitutes the psychological situation, not the organism and environment taken separately' (Perls, Hefferline and Goodman, 1951/73, p. 19). Given Rogers' definition of AWARENESS, and the belief of the PCA that people are essentially social animals (see PERSON and SOCIETY) and its emphasis on GROUP, it is perhaps surprising that field theory is not more figural in the theoretical ground of PCP.

fixity   a state of rigidity in both PERSON-ALITY and PROCESS (CONCEPTION OF PSY-CHOTHERAPY) (see Rogers, 1961) where all the elements (FEELINGS, EXPERIENCE, COMMUNICATION, etc.) are separately discernible and understandable; the opposite of FLUIDITY; echoing this view, Hulme (1999) discusses fixity as an aspect of experience in the context of mental illness.

fluidity   a state and WAY OF BEING which Rogers (1961) describes in his PROCESS CONCEPTION OF PSYCHOTHERAPY as at the opposite end of a continuum from FIXITY:

> in the new experiencing with immediacy ... feeling and cognition interpenetrate, SELF is subjectively present in the experience, volition is simply the subjective following of a harmonious balance of organismic direction ... [at which point] the person becomes a unity of flow, of motion ... he has become an integrated process of changingness (p. 158).

See also FULLY FUNCTIONING PERSON.

focusing   a process of directing attention to or focusing on feelings or sensations not directly articulated or discriminated, a term and a process associated with the work of Eugene Gendlin and his colleagues (see Gendlin, 1961, 1981, 1984). The process of focusing involves attention to felt but non-verbal sensations leading to more easily recognised and, therefore, more easily verbalised feelings and sensations; new insights and meanings may then follow, with feelings becoming more clearly differentiated and understood; over time, feel-ings and sensations which originally were only vaguely experienced evolve until they are more fully experienced, and their implications for other aspects of the client's life begin to become apparent.   Barrett-Lennard (1998) describes Gendlin's works as pointing to

> an implicit, pre-conceptual level of inner life process, seen as the primary substrate of experience. This includes unarticulated bodily felt processes, 'gut reactions' for which words have not formed, images without clear shape, unlabelled *sensed* emotions and energies, and implicit connections not yet born in symbols (p. 85).

(See also Gendlin, 1986.) There is some debate within the person-centred community about the extent to which focusing runs counter to important PRINCIPLES OF THE PERSON-CENTRED APPROACH, including that of the NON-DIRECTIVE stance of the therapist; as Barrett-Lennard (1998) remarks: 'a further implied CONDITION [of this theory] is an active willingness to guide the other person in the focusing mode' (p. 86) (see also EXPERIENTIAL THERAPY, INTERNATIONAL CONFERENCE ON CLIENT-CENTERED AND EXPERIENTIAL PSYCHOTHERAPY).

formative tendency   the directional tendency towards increased order and interrelated complexity found in nature from micro-organisms through crystals and in stellar space (see Rogers, 1980a); SYNTROPY rather than ENTROPY (the tendency towards deterioration and disorder), it supports the notion of the interconnectedness of all things and is reflected in the universality of the ACTUALISING TEN-

DENCY in humans. Rogers (1980) viewed this tendency as 'a base upon which we could begin to build a theory for humanistic psychology. It definitely forms a base for the person-centered approach' (p. 133); echoing Rogers, though taking this further, Ellingham (2000) argues that the formative tendency 'constitutes a base upon which we can build a theory for psychology as a whole, i.e. a genuine scientific paradigm' (p. 2).

Forum, The see INTERNATIONAL FORUM ON THE PERSON-CENTERED APPROACH.

fragile process one of three processes (along with DISSOCIATED PROCESS and PSYCHOTIC PROCESS) which Warner (1991, 1998) identifies as often challenging to therapists, and characterised as experiencing core issues at very high or very low levels of intensity. Empathy is often the only response clients operating with this process can accept without feeling traumatised or disconnected from their experience and, according to Warner (1991), effective therapy with such clients involves 'the kind of empathic holding that was missing in the client's early childhood experiences (p. 49). Many clients operating with fragile process are diagnosed traditionally as having PERSONALITY DISORDERS (often, borderline, narcissistic or schizoid).

frame of reference the subjective and unique way in which someone understands the others and the world by 'framing' (as in a window) their perceptions: 'an organised pattern of perceptions of self and self-in-relationship to others and to the environment' (Rogers, 1951, p. 191). Used somewhat similarly in TRANSACTIONAL ANALYSIS to describe the overall structural and functional matrix of the personality.

frame of reference, internal everything in the realm of EXPERIENCE, including sensations, perceptions, meanings and memories, available to AWARENESS of a person at a particular time: the subjective world of a person that can be fully known only to that person, and only partially by any other. In the NINETEEN PROPOSITIONS Rogers (1951) writes:

> our knowledge of the person's frame of reference depends primarily upon communication of one sort or another from the individual. Hence only in clouded fashion can we see the world of experience as it appears to the individual (p. 495)

> [however] it is possible to achieve, to some extent, the other person's frame of reference, because many of the perceptual objects — self, parents, teachers, employers, and so on — have counterparts in our own PERCEPTUAL FIELD, and practically all the attitudes towards these perceptual objects — such as fear, anger, annoyance, love, jealousy, satisfaction — have been present in our own world of experience (ibid., pp. 495–6).

It is difficult to overstate the importance and centrality of this term within PCP. PCT relies on close attention being paid by the therapist to understanding the client's internal frame of reference, a disciplined form of EMPATHIC UNDERSTANDING. Rogers remarks that the client-centred emphasis on the client's internal frame of reference has led us to feel that here is a way of viewing experience which is much closer to the basic laws of personality process and behaviour. Not only does there result a more vivid understanding of the meaning of behavior, but the opportunities for new learning are maximized when we approach the individual without a preconceived set of categories which we expect him to fit (pp. 496–7).

This stands in marked contrast to other forms of psychotherapy in which attempts are made to understand clients against a background of preconceived diagnostic constructs (see PHENOMENOLOGY; Patterson, 2000d).

frame of reference, external   everything in the realm of experience, etc. of an(other), that is, an external person, including their perceptions of and about others. Introjected CONDITIONS OF WORTH are, by definition, originally located in an external frame of reference, usually of a significant other. When the SELF-CONCEPT is threatened, a person may look to and even seek opinions, judgements and evaluations from an external source; in this way the other person's (i.e. external) frame of reference becomes internalised and may dominate or even replace the subject's own internal frame of reference.

freedom   described by Rogers (1983) (with reference to Victor Frankl) as being able to choose one's own ATTITUDES in any given set of circumstances: 'it is the discovery of meaning from within oneself ... that comes from listening sensitively and openly to the complexities of what one is experiencing. It is the burden of being

responsible for the self one chooses to be' (p. 276) and, once experienced, is irreversible (see Rogers, 1978) (see also EXISTENTIALISM); it is thus a subjective, personal and experiential sense of freedom; psychological freedom is one of the external conditions which foster CREATIVITY (see PSYCHOLOGICAL SAFETY; Rogers, 1961).

Freedom to Learn   a book written by Rogers in 1969, a thoroughly revised version of which was published in 1983 under the title *Freedom to Learn for the 80's*. One of the differences between the two editions is, as Rogers himself points out, that in the intervening years there was more research and more 'hard evidence' to support the theories outlined in the original and elaborated with examples and experience in the later edition. Rogers (1983) identifies the aims of the book — and, indeed, the aim of a more human EDUCATION — as (typically) being a movement:

*   towards a climate of TRUST in the classroom;
*   towards a participatory mode of decision-making in all aspects of learning by all participants;
*   towards helping students PRIZE themselves;
*   towards developing excitement and curiosity in intellectual and emotional discovery;
*   towards developing in teachers the ATTITUDES in FACILITATING learning and helping them grow as persons.

The 1983 edition is divided into seven sections which cover: the external forces and circumstances which determine the activities of the teaching profession; a number of stories and examples of freedom to learn under the title 'Responsible Freedom in the Classroom'; a section for the teacher on innovation, facilitation and relationship, including issues of POWER and the politics of education; on research which confirms the value of person-centred attitudes; followed by a section on failures in such experiments; a section on philosophy, values and humanness; and a final section on the advantages of the PCA to education as well as comments on the resistance to change. Nearly twenty years later, the principles and practice are as relevant as ever — even more so in a political climate of 'schooling' (as distinct from education), including in the TRAINING of counsellors, psychotherapists and counselling psychologists, which is largely defensive, protective and curriculum-led.

free will   the general term used to describe the philosophical position that a person's behaviour is under the control of that individual. The alternative position, DETERMINISM, assumes that all behaviour results from causes of which the person might be unaware;

the 'free will versus determinism' argument featured in the debate between Rogers and B.F. Skinner (see Kirschenbaum and Henderson, 1990a), in which Skinner remarked,

> there is reasonable certainty, on the basis of evidence available now, that the extent to which a person enjoys music, or art or literature, or the extent to which a person continues to work with a high level of interest in a given field — these things can be traced to lucky histories of reinforcement (Skinner quoted in Kirschenbaum and Henderson, 1990a, p. 98).

A basic tenet of PCP is that free will, or freedom of choice does exist, and is indicated by the EXISTENTIAL nature of much of Rogers' writing (see RANKIAN THERAPY).

fully functioning person, the
   see PERSON, FULLY FUNCTIONING.
functional relationships
   see RELATIONSHIPS, FUNCTIONAL.

G, Ms a demonstration client of Carl Rogers, filmed in 1983 during a training workshop, remarkable as an example of Rogers' ability to co-create an atmosphere of genuine empathic understanding and sensitivity in a short time (30 minutes), a full transcript of which is reproduced in Merry (1995).

gay affirmative therapy refers to therapy based on 'a special range of psychological knowledge which challenges the traditional view that homosexual desire and fixed homosexual orientations are pathological' (Maylon, 1982, p. 69) (see also Davies and Neal, 1996). While challenging traditional views and an anti-institutional attitude or QUALITY is very much a part of the tradition of PCP and the PCA (see Rogers, 1978), the notion of affirmation is more controversial. Person-centred practitioners tend towards being 'im'-personal (see THERAPEUTIC RELATIONSHIP) and to a radical neutrality in which all aspects of a person are ACCEPTED (or CONFIRMED) rather than 'affirming' any one aspect or even the whole aspect of a person, however they define themselves. Ex-

amining the necessity and sufficiency of Rogers' therapeutic conditions, Davies, one of the authors of *Pink Therapy* (Davies and Neal, 1996) discusses the relationship between gay affirmative therapy and the PCA (Davies, 1998).

gender 'kinds', corresponding (more or less) to distinctions of sex, in relation to which Wolter-Gustafson (1999) suggests that Rogers' theory is radically liberating because, consistent with a PHENOMENOLOGICAL attitude, the person her/himself is recognised to be the expert on her/his experience, and that PCP holds an open attitude to changing constructions of the SELF which emerge; furthermore, Natiello (1999b) argues that the PCA offers a solution to gender splitting between male and female, especially in daring to be CONGRUENT (see also Natiello (1999a).

genuineness see CONGRUENCE.

Gestalt a German term which is generally translated as 'configuration', it usually refers to unified or completed wholes or structures that cannot be understood simply by an analysis of the various parts of which they consist. Rogers uses the term several times in his PERSONALITY THEORY to refer to the wholeness of the SELF-STRUCTURE (Rogers, 1951) and in his defining formulation of the client-centred framework (Rogers, 1959).

gestalt therapy the therapy based on the notion of GESTALT and the perceptual principle of making wholes, with roots in FIELD THEORY and HOLISM or mind–body unity; Rogers (1951) acknowledges his indebtedness to gestalt psychology especially 'its emphasis upon the wholeness and interrelatedness of the cluster of phenomena which we think of as the individual' (p. 4); philosophically and theoretically, possibly the closest to the PCA of other humanistic psychologies and therapies (see also and compare EXISTENTIAL THERAPY, PERSONAL CONSTRUCT PSYCHOLOGY and TRANSACTIONAL ANALYSIS); there are a number of papers on the similarities between and even possible syntheses of gestalt and the PCA (see Cochrane and Holloway, 1974; O'Hara, 1984; O'Leary, 1997).

ghosting empathising or taking an empathic stance with an absent family member or partner (Gaylin, 1993).

Gloria a client with whom Rogers conducted a single session filmed interview in 1964 which was followed by her working with Fritz Perls (to demonstrate GESTALT THERAPY) and Albert Ellis (rational-emotive therapy) (Shostrom, 1965). Each session is preceded by the therapist outlining his respective theory and followed by his reflections on the session. The transcript of Rogers' session is reproduced in Rogers and Wood (1974) and there are a number of commentaries and articles about his work with Gloria (Rogers, 1984; Weinrach,

1990; Thorne, 1992; Zimring, 1996). Possibly the most famous client in the history of psychotherapy through her introduction by means of these three films to generations of training therapists, Gloria subsequently attended workshops and corresponded with Rogers until her death from cancer.

goodness the quality or condition of being good (a term of general or indefinite commendation); PCP is often criticised for its view of the inherent goodness of HUMAN NATURE (see CRITICISMS OF THE PERSON-CENTRED APPROACH); this criticism confuses person-centred views on the *constructive nature* of the ACTUALISING TENDENCY (see also the FORMATIVE TENDENCY) (as distinct from destructive forces — see ENTROPY and SYNTROPY) with an overly positive and naive *evaluation* of human nature, behaviour, society, etc. — which is not inherent in the theory or practice of PCP or the PCA (see EVIL). Ironically, such criticisms are examples of an EXTERNAL LOCUS OF EVALUATION of the approach itself by those who misunderstand the nature and importance of the INTERNAL (organismic) VALUING PROCESS which, of course, may be applied to a system or an approach as much as an individual.

good life, the 'the process of movement in a direction which the human organism selects when it is inwardly free to move in any direction, and the general qualities of this selected direction appear to have a certain universality' (Rogers, 1961, p. 187) (see also FULLY FUNCTIONING PERSON).

group development the notion of stages of group development is at odds with the approach of PCP to the descriptive (rather than prescriptive) study of human phenomena. Yalom

(1995) challenges what he views as confusion about group development and observes: 'each group is, at the same time, like *all groups, some groups, and no other group!* ' (p. 306); this said, Yalom accepts — and argues — that there are modest advantages to group therapists having some broad schema of a group's development. In his book *Encounter Groups*, and on the basis of his observations, Rogers (1970) describes the following patterns in the process of ENCOUNTER GROUPS, 'roughly in sequential order' (p. 22):

1. milling around;
2. resistance to personal expression or exploration;
3. description of past feelings;
4. expression of negative feelings;
5. expression and exploration of personally meaningful material;
6. the expression of immediate interpersonal feelings in the group;
7. the development of a healing capacity in the group;
8. self-acceptance and the beginning of change;
9. the cracking of façades;
10. the individual receives feedback;
11. confrontation;
12. the helping relationship outside the group sessions;
13. the basic encounter;
14. the expression of positive feelings and closeness;
15. behaviour changes in the group.

Barrett-Lennard (1979) suggests that this formulation may be summarised in three phases:

1. engagement;
2. trust and process development;
3. encounter and change.

In the context of the large group in counselling training, Mearns (1997) posits four stages:

Stage 1 Polite tolerance;
Stage 2 Confusion and disorientation;
Stage 3 Glimpsing the potential;
Stage 4 Valuing and working in the open process.

Rogers (1970) also observed six stages in the development of individuals in such groups:

Stage 1 Communication is predominantly about matters external to the group; personal feelings are not expressed; close relationships between group members are thought of as dangerous.
Stage 2 People are remote from their subjective experience, and feelings remain unowned and external; expression is about non-self topics; there may be some recognition of inner conflict, but only tentatively.
Stage 3 Feelings that are not actually present in the 'here and now' are described, but are often characterised as unacceptable; there may be some communication about the self, but usually as a reflected object existing primarily in others; there is the beginning of a recognition that problems exist inside the person rather than externally.
Stage 4 Intense feelings are described, but are not present in the moment; there is a recognition that denied feelings may break through into the present, and this is seen as an unwelcome possibility; expression of self-responsibility for problems increases; there is an occasional willingness to

relate to others in the group on a more emotional basis.

Stage 5 Feelings are fully expressed as they are experienced in the present moment, and are owned and accepted; previously denied feelings begin to 'bubble through' into awareness; there is an expressed desire to be the 'real me', and the person has a definite feeling of responsibility for the problems and conflicts existing internally.

Stage 6 Immediate feelings are no longer denied, feared or struggled against; this experiencing is often a dramatic release for the individual; there is complete acceptance that feelings provide useful referents for gaining insight into a person's life; individuals risk themselves in relating directly to others.

group dynamics   originally, the 'qualities' of the group (Lewin, 1952); more generally, any and all of the interactions or intragroup processes which take place within the context of a group.

group, encounter   a small, intentional group designed to focus on the interpersonal relationships among participants, the word 'ENCOUNTER' implying deeper, more personal meetings between people in an atmosphere where TRUST and understanding are highly valued qualities. A central concept of encounter is that of IDENTITY which has both an inner aspect, including the rules we have which govern us (often introjected CONDITIONS OF WORTH), as well as an outer expression of this — which expression may be facilitated by being in an encounter group. Thus, goals are often ex-pressed in terms of the achievement of open, honest communication among members and the dissolving of defences and barriers to communication. While the first mention of encounter goes back to a series of poetic writings published by Jacob Moreno in 1914, the two major influences on encounter were Schutz (1973), who came from a psychoanalytic tradition and, from within the humanistic tradition, Rogers (1970/73). Schutz, who joined the staff of the Esalen Institute in California in 1967, developed what became referred to as an 'open encounter model' of group. Drawing on the work of Reich and neo-Reichians, Schutz prioritised the somatic in his analysis that body tensions are and represent blocks against feelings. In open encounter the group leader brings the client's awareness to bear on their body and encourages them to express their feelings in the form of some physical activity such as pushing against or falling back on others. Applying his research and ideas about the facilitative conditions for change, and favouring a more participative approach on the part of the facilitator, Rogers developed the basic encounter group in which interaction is largely verbal, with people commonly seated in a circle. In an encounter group the role of FACILITATOR is important. In person-centred encounter groups, facilitators:

- by definition, aim to make communication among group members as easy as possible;
- are, themselves, willing to be open, CONGRUENT (or integrated) and NON-DEFENSIVE;
- attempt to contribute to the development of trust and openness in

the group by responding to individual members with UNCONDITIONAL POSITIVE REGARD and EMPATHY, especially if they have not been responded to by other participants — and, therefore, do not direct or 'lead' the group;

- attend to the maintenance needs of the group such as time boundaries, breaks and so on;
- address the fact that as facilitators they have — or are perceived to have — more POWER than the participants. In principle, this concern is similar to that of the therapist in one-to-one therapy and the response is the same: to behave in such a way that they do not take power away from the participants.

There is sometimes confusion about the differences between an encounter group and a therapy group. Rogers and Sanford (1984) made a useful distinction: 'if persons come together because they are seeking help with serious problems, it is termed group therapy; if their purpose is to enrich and enhance their own development, it may be called an encounter group; but the process is much the same' (p. 1386). Rogers (1970/73 viewed the encounter group as a significant invention, one of the most important implications of which is that it helps the individual adapt to CHANGE:

in the troubled future that lies ahead of us, the trend towards the intensive group experience is related to deep and significant issues having to do with change ... in persons, in institutions, in our urban and cultural alienation, in racial tensions, in our international fric-

tions, in our philosophies, our values, our image of man himself. It is a profoundly significant movement. (p. 169)

(For further reading on encounter see Merry, 1995; Yalom, 1995; and Tudor, 1999a.)

group facilitator literally a person who FACILITATES a group.

group, large there is no precise definition of the large group or the smaller, 'median' group, although some practitioners and authors cite numbers from 30 to 300 participants (the democratic forums in ancient Greece involved 2,000 people!). The theory and practice of the large therapeutic group has been strongly influenced by PSYCHOANALYTIC ideas (see Kreeger, 1975); within the person-centred tradition, the first large group — community for learning — took place in 1973 and the PCA now draws on considerable experience and research into the phenomenon of the large group and its association with COMMUNITY (see, for instance, Bozarth, 1981; Wood, 1984, 1999):

what a person-centred approach taught us about community was that a large group, in a creative state, can resolve crises, find solutions to complex problems, intelligently co-ordinate its activities without plans, legislation, or parliamentary procedures, and even transform its culture in a compassionate and efficient process that involves, respects, and benefits each of its members and itself (Wood, 1984, p. 311).

group therapy distinguished from ENCOUNTER GROUP as being a forum to which people come if they are seeking help with serious problems (as distinct from personal development) (Rogers and Sanford, 1984).

growth progress towards physical and psychological development; movement towards enhanced functioning; in the PCA growth is often used synonymously with constructive PERSONALITY CHANGE (see also INTEGRATION).

growth principle the view — and principle — that growth is inevitable; PCP regards GROWTH as a process occurring throughout life and, as with CHANGE, a continuing process prompted by the ORGANISM'S ACTUALISING TENDENCY. PCP does not regard the PERSON as attaining a fixed or static state, however desirable (see SELF-ACTUALISATION), instead viewing the person as continually developing in response to EXPERIENCE. While growth, DEVELOPMENT and change are ubiquitous, the *direction* of growth may be thwarted by experiences of negative REGARD from others (see PSYCHOLOGICAL DISTURBANCE); experiences of relationships rich in the CONDITIONS of growth are regarded as a means of re-establishing a constructive direction for change and growth.

gullible caring see CARING, GULLIBLE.

healing the process of becoming whole, the effect — both in PROCESS and OUTCOME — of THERAPY.

helping relationship a phrase used in a generic sense to refer to those relationships which may be personal (neighbour) or professional (teacher, nurse but not necessarily a therapist), characterised by the FACILITATIVE CONDITIONS and which are, thereby, helpful.

helping relationship, characteristics of see THERAPEUTIC RELATIONSHIP.

here-and-now a phrase, commonly used in GESTALT THERAPY, to emphasise the existential present moment in space (location) and time, and the AWARE participation in the present.

hermeneutic deriving from the Greek word for interpreter, the theory of interpretation and, importantly, understanding of the significance of human actions and utterances; in order to do this, the researchers/interpreters must immerse themselves in the history, customs, values, beliefs, symbols and expression of the subject of enquiry (see RESEARCH).

heuristic a philosophical and conceptual orientation which gives rise to a method of inquiry and RESEARCH based on proceeding towards an unknown goal by incremental exploration, that is, building upon what is known; it is a highly personal, self-searching, intuitive and reflective method/process of research which is very compatible with the PCA (see also SCIENCE); therapy *as* heuristic inquiry is explored by O'Hara (1986).

holding 1. (literal) physical, embracing contact between two people, developed from PLAY THERAPY and explored as a therapeutic option for parents of severely disturbed children by Lindt (1988), it requires 'persistent, intensive cherishing, which provides safety and abreaction, (p. 229); also used in SHARING LIFE THERAPY and in reparative therapeutic work with adults; controversial in that it is open to misinterpretation and abuse (see TOUCH).

2. (metaphorical) used originally to describe the necessary 'total environmental provision' in child development and, later, a therapeutic environment which is experienced as 'holding' for the client (see Winnicott, 1960/85).

67

holism a general term applied to philosophical and psychological approaches, such as PCP, which focus on the whole (and WHOLENESS of the) living organism. According to Reber (1985), 'the basic axiom of a holist position is that a complex phenomenon cannot be understood by an analysis of the constituent parts alone' (p. 325). Drawing on the work of Friedlaender (1918) and Smuts (1926), GESTALT PSYCHOLOGY especially has advanced the holistic (sometimes, playfully, 'whole-istic') approach of mind–body unity and embracing complexity and conflict (see also CHAOS THEORY and POSTMODERNISM).

human destructiveness see DESTRUCTIVENESS, HUMAN.

humanism originally concerned with the belief in the humanity of Jesus of Nazareth, humanism encompasses a number of fields of religion, philosophy, pure and social sciences and psychology concerned with the study of human affairs (see HUMANISTIC PSYCHOLOGY). It was significant for the later development of his ideas that Rogers' first graduate training was at the liberal Union Theological Seminary in New York and that he was attracted to and encouraged in unorthodox thinking.

humanistic psychology an approach to psychology sometimes referred to as the 'third force' (a phrase originally coined by Abraham Maslow describing developments after PSYCHOANALYSIS and BEHAVIOURISM); philosophically influenced by ideas and concepts within EXISTENTIALISM and PHENOMENOLOGY, it is concerned with issues such as CREATIVITY, BEING and BECOMING, individuality, meaning, love, and ways of living which are both individually enhancing and socially constructive. Humanistic psychology generally takes a positive, optimistic stance on questions of HUMAN NATURE, in contrast to the more pessimistic view adopted by Freud and many of his followers. At its heart lies the assumption that there exists in all forms of life a tendency towards more complex organisation, the fulfilment of potential and the actualisation of the 'self', the process of becoming all of which we are capable; both Maslow and Rogers referred to this as the ACTUALISING TENDENCY, although they differed in exactly how this tendency is manifest.

There is, too, a political dimension to humanistic psychology in that it challenges existing POWER structures in society wherever they tend to overpower rather than enable people; this political dimension is based on a set of assumptions about human nature which are very different from those underpinning most modern institutions: where tradition tells us that people are best kept under control and denied freedom of expression and action, humanistic psychology argues for liberation, more open decision-making and a sharing of power and control. For a good introduction to humanistic psychology see Rowan (1988, 1994) and for a more recent exposition of core beliefs see the Association of Humanistic Psychology Practitioners (1998). Maslow is generally credited with providing the initiative that eventually led to the establishment of humanistic psychology, and in 1957 he and Antony Sutich agreed to launch a new journal, the *Journal of Humanistic Psychology* which first appeared in 1961. The American ASSOCIATION

FOR HUMANISTIC PSYCHOLOGY was formed two years later in 1963.

An important landmark in the development of humanistic psychology was the opening in 1962 of the Esalen Institute in Big Sur, California. This was the first of the so-called 'growth centres' dedicated to furthering what had become known as the HUMAN POTENTIAL MOVEMENT. Esalen became extremely popular, partly perhaps because of its luxurious surroundings and spectacular scenery, and was visited by most of the leading figures in humanistic psychology, including Rogers and Fritz Perls, the founder of GESTALT THERAPY, many of whom ran workshops and gave talks there. It became the model for other growth centres in America, and was the inspiration behind more modest British attempts to establish similar places, such as Kaleidoscope and Quaesitor in London. Although PCT is often viewed as a humanistic psychology and conceptually located within this 'third force', as Mearns and Thorne (2000) point out, 'the governing feature of person-centred therapy (PCT) is not its "humanistic" orientation but its forsaking of mystique and other "powerful" behaviours of therapists. In this regard many humanistic therapies are as different from PCT as PSYCHOANALYSIS' (p. 27).

human nature   described in PCP as 'positive, forward-moving, constructive, realistic, trustworthy' (Rogers, 1990a, p. 403), and equated with the characteristics of the HUMAN ORGANISM; Rogers continues: 'to be a human being is to enter into the complex process of being one of the most widely sensitive, responsive, creative, and adaptive creatures on this planet' (ibid., 1990a, p. 405); those general QUALITIES of humans that differentiate us from other species. All approaches to counselling and psychotherapy have an explicit or implicit theory of human nature that attempts to explain what makes people the way we are, why we believe in the ways we do, and what our inherent characteristics might be. In contrast to some other approaches (see BEHAVIOURIAL and PSYCHOANALYTIC), the PCA generally emphasises a constructive stance on human nature, a view which is often characterised as overly optimistic and naive (see GOODNESS, CRITICISMS OF THE PERSON-CENTRED APPROACH). The PCA stresses that humans are constantly 'in PROCESS' and FLUID rather than static or FIXED, and that people are *not only* deficiency-motivated but also motivated by the tendency for GROWTH, DEVELOPMENT and enhancement (for further discussion on which see Merry, 1999).

humanness   a word which refers to and highlights the universality of human nature.

human organism   see ORGANISM, HUMAN.

human science   see SCIENCE.

hypothesis   a proposition, supposition or conjecture put forward to account for known facts, a form which Rogers often used in his writings, perhaps most famously in his proposition regarding the NECESSARY AND SUFFICIENT CONDITIONS (Rogers, 1957, 1959). Such construction concerning RESEARCH carries both a certain humility as well as an openness, epitomised in one of his papers:

the statement which follows is not offered with any assurance to its correctness, but with the expectation that it will have the value of any THEORY, namely that it states or implies a series of hypotheses which are open to proof or dis-proof, thereby clarifying and extending our knowledge of the field (Rogers, 1957, p. 95–6).

iatrogenic disorder a disorder, illness or disease (dis-ease) produced by the effects of treatment of an existing disorder. In medicine, this includes hospital-generated infections and diseases, the consequences of so-called 'side effects' of medication, and dependency on drugs prescribed to treat, say, depression or anxiety. Examples of iatrogenesis in psychotherapy include the creation of over-dependency on the therapist to solve problems (whereas the desired effect is for the client to become AUTONOMOUS, and the 'side effects' of certain techniques (especially in forms of regressive therapy). In the field of education and training, educational iatrogenesis is created by the imposition of external (national) curricula and evaluation, the 'banking' concept and paradigm of EDUCATION and the related and widespread notion of the expert trainer (sometimes guru), and the undemocratic and/or inaccessible structures of school, training institute, etc.

ideal self see SELF, IDEAL.

identification the process whereby a person attributes to her/himself, either with or without awareness, the characteristics of another person; in psychoanalysis, such identification might be explained as TRANSFERENCE, especially if it were UNCONSCIOUS; in CCT, identification needs to be clearly distinguished from EMPATHY: the EMPATHIC UNDERSTANDING response to a client shows that the therapist understands the client from the client's perspective or FRAME OF REFERENCE, with an 'as if' quality to it, that is, the therapist understands 'as if' s/he were the client. To identify with the client means that the therapist becomes unable to distinguish between the client's experiencing of a particular phenomenon, and the therapist's experiencing of the same or similar phenomena — and, therefore, not separate enough to be helpful or useful (see Rogers, 1958/90e).

identity the way in which people define themselves in relation to others, a definition or definitions which include a range of factors such as age, CLASS, CULTURE, disability, ethnicity, race (see Carter, 1995), SEXUALITY, etc. and referred to as 'personal identity'; also a person's sense of BELONGING TO

71

a certain social group which, together with the emotional and value significance of such membership, forms our 'social identity' (Tajfel, 1972); in PCP, identity is inextricably linked to PHENOMENOLOGICAL notions of the SELF (see also SELF-CONCEPT, SELF IDEAL etc.) and of self *in context*.

idiosyncratic empathy see EMPATHY, IDIOSYNCRATIC.

ignoration the act of ignoring and one of the three ways in which the individual responds to and processes experience (we refer to the noun form of the verb 'to ignore' to echo the related terms SYMBOLISATION, DENIAL and DISTORTION) (see NINETEEN PROPOSITIONS); Rogers (1951) argues that we ignore experiences because

> they are irrelevant to the SELF-STRUCTURE ... they exist in the ground of my phenomenal field, but [since] they do not reinforce or contradict my concept of self, [and] they meet no need related to the self, they are ignored (p. 503).

See also PRECONSCIOUS.

immediate experience see EXPERIENCE, IMMEDIATE.

incongruence the discrepancy between the actual experience and the self-picture of the individual insofar as it represents that experience (Rogers, 1957). Two examples of incongruence were given by Rogers in his 1957 paper: the first concerned a student experiencing, at an ORGANISMIC level, a fear of examinations since these may demonstrate a fundamental inadequacy in him; however, the student's fear of inadequacy is not consistent with his SELF-CONCEPT so this experience becomes DISTORTED in his awareness into a fear of climbing stairs in the building in which examinations take place, developing, perhaps, into a fear of stairs in any building; there is, therefore, a discrepancy between the experienced meaning of the situation and the symbolic representation of the experience in AWARENESS in such a way as not to conflict with the self-concept. The second example is of a mother who becomes ill whenever her son makes plans to leave home; her need is to maintain her only source of satisfaction, but to admit this into awareness would be inconsistent with the picture she has of herself as a good mother; illness, however, is consistent with the self-concept so the experience is symbolised in this distorted fashion. Incongruence develops and is maintained by the person through their selective PERCEPTION of EXPERIENCE on the basis of CONDITIONS OF WORTH.

In effect, Rogers identifies three process elements of incongruence: a general and generalised VULNERABILITY, a dimly perceived tension or ANXIETY, and a sharp awareness of incongruence; Singh and Tudor (1997) identify and elaborate these elements as regards cultural conditions of therapy. In recent years, incongruence has become the basis for a person-centred theory of illness and PSYCHOPATHOLOGY (see Speierer, 1990, 1996 and DIFFERENTIAL INCONGRUENCE MODEL). As a concept incongruence is generally viewed in *intra*psychic terms; it is equally applicable to the *extra*psychic, relational, INTERSUBJECTIVE sphere; as Brazier (1993c) reminds us that: 'clients ... are incongruent precisely in the extent to which self-preoccupation has distracted them from the world of others to whom they need to attend' (pp. 88–9). Moreover, beyond the individual, their (individual) experience and self-picture, it may also be applied more widely to group and organisational experiences and 'self', i.e. group/organisational concept.

incongruence, therapist's since it is one of the CORE CONDITIONS of effective therapy that therapists are CONGRUENT in their relationships with clients, an incongruent therapist would be unable to satisfy this condition and to this extent therapy would be ineffective. However, Rogers remarks that it is neither necessary nor possible for a person to exhibit total congruence in every aspect of their lives; instead, it is sufficient that therapists are accurately themselves during the time they spend with their clients, even if this means 'being themselves' in ways that are not generally regarded in therapy as being ideal; for example, therapists who fear a client or who, from time to time, are distracted by their own inner processes, would not be ineffective if they were AWARE of these feelings, i.e. they are able to admit them to themselves (Rogers, 1957). There is, therefore, a clear implication in person-centred theory that therapists should become as self-aware as possible; whilst Rogers stopped short at insisting that person-centred therapists *should* have their own therapy in an effort to minimise incongruence, it does appear incongruent and against the ethos of MUTUALITY for therapists to avoid finding ways of attending to their own PERSONAL DEVELOPMENT which may include PERSONAL THERAPY (see also TRAINING THERAPY).

independence the opposite of dependence and in PCP akin to FREEDOM as expressed personally, e.g. individually, and politically, e.g. as nations (see Rogers, 1960).

Independent Practitioners' Network (IPN) a response to the increasing professionalisation of counselling, based on a horizontal and multi-centred (rather than vertical/pyramidal) structure and favouring diversity and ecological complexity; the IPN comprises groups of therapists involved in mutual and peer assessment who agree to 'stand by' each other's work, to take responsibility for supporting each other's good practice and to address any problems, conflicts and complaints; membership of the IPN is open only to such groups or 'cells', although interested individuals may attend and have equal footing at regional and national meetings; a minimum of five practitioners form a cell which, formulates its own CODE OF ETHICS and practice and which then links up with at least one other cell in the network, the two groups, in turn, agreeing to stand by each other's work. In many ways the IPN is a more direct and personal form of organising: 'each practitioner's integrity is bound with that of their colleagues' (Totton, 1997, p. 289) (see also ACCREDITATION and REGISTRATION); this, together with a structure based on autonomous self-responsible actions and pluralistic consensus, rather than representative but distant democracy and decision-making, is entirely compatible with the PCA.

individual see HUMAN ORGANISM.

individuation a term used in Jungian (analytic) psychology to describe the process of BECOMING an individual who is AWARE of their individuality, akin to MATURITY.

infant/s see CHILD DEVELOPMENT.

73

innate pertaining to that which is natural or inherent to an ORGANISM (see also HUMAN NATURE).

insight the (often sudden) understanding of one's emotional or psychological situation or condition of which one was previously unaware; Rogers (1942/90f), gives the example of Mr. B.:

> MR. B.: In the last analysis it comes down to this, that I enjoy the neurotic symptoms more, but respect them less.
>
> Counsellor: Yes, that's a good way of ...
>
> MR. B.: Or to use other words, I suppose I'm beginning to value self-respect more now, otherwise I wouldn't give a damn (p. 213).

The insight described by Mr. B is followed by his genuine indecision about whether he wants to be neurotic or healthy, to stay as he is or to grow; at first, Mr. B had wanted his therapist to 'cure' him, but he comes to the insight that he has to take responsibility for himself by searching for healthy situations and entering into them.

instinct an INNATE impulse or response (also viewed as a tendency or disposition), characterised by being unlearned, complex and (disputably) inherited (see also HUMAN NATURE, ORGANISM).

Institute for Peace originally named the Carl Rogers Peace Project and founded in 1984 by Rogers and Gay Leah Swenson (later Barfield), a project of the CENTER FOR STUDIES OF THE PERSON, and instrumental in convening the RUST WORKSHOP; renamed after Rogers' death in 1989 (see Rogers and Barfield, 1984).

insurance, professional indemnity a form of (perceived) security for therapists against liability (accident, false information, etc.) and possible litigation (thus legal costs) which, commonly, is a requirement of membership or association with a professional body and, increasingly, of supervised practice and employment, for a critique of which see Mearns (1993).

integration 1. a state of personality and being in which 'all the sensory and visceral experiences are available to awareness through accurate symbolization, and organizable into one system which is internally consistent and which is, or is related to, the structure of the self' (Rogers, 1951, pp. 513–14); a term often used synonymously with CONGRUENCE (see also INDEPENDENCE, MATURITY and WHOLENESS).

2. a term used to describe the making up of a whole by adding together or combining in some way the separate parts or elements of different psychological theories (see INTEGRATING).

integrating a process of integration which usually implies or, arguably, requires an organised and organising meta-system by which the integration is described and makes sense; Bozarth (1996c) argues that Rogers' (1957) statement of the NECESSARY AND SUFFICIENT CONDITIONS OF THERAPY is an integrative statement in that it relates to theoretical investigations of therapy *generically*.

integrative a state of personal (or professional) INTEGRATION or CONGRUENCE.

integrative impressions a term coined by Villas-Boas Bowen (1986) to describe a type of EMPATHIC response which enables clients 'to integrate fragmented and confusing parts of their experience into a higher order of coherence and understanding' (p. 303), reflective and facilitative of ORGANISMIC ORGANISATION and enabling of personal reorganisation, they may comprise a REFLECTION OF FEELINGS, the identification of underlying issues, the creation of metaphors or the use of EXPERIMENTS (see also INTUITION).

integrative therapy a description of psychological, therapeutic and/or professional identity by which a therapist describes themselves in terms of theoretical orientation, it is very much of the *zeitgeist* with increasing numbers of counsellors and psychotherapists defining themselves as 'integrative'; however, this in itself does not describe the INTEGRATING principle (CONDITIONS, THERAPEUTIC RELATIONSHIP, etc.) and thus often offers definition only by substitution.

intensionality a type of DEFENCE, when a person perceives their experience in absolute, unconditional and overgeneralised terms and confuses fact and evaluation, without reference to any anchor or reality-testing in terms of space or time; whilst DENIAL and DISTORTION are defence mechanisms, intensionality describes the characteristics of the BEHAVIOUR of an individual in a defensive state (see Rogers, 1959).

intentionality see CULTURAL PSYCHOLOGY.

intercultural tensions the tension (stress, pressure, anxiety) which arises between cultures and between people of different and, at times, differing cultures (see CROSS CULTURAL COMMUNICATION WORKSHOPS, CULTURAL CONFLICT, RUST WORKSHOP).

internal frame of reference see FRAME OF REFERENCE.

internal locus of evaluation see LOCUS OF EVALUATION.

International Conference on Client-Centered and Experiential Psychotherapy first held in 1988 and now a triennial event taking place in different countries, with published papers from the conferences on both client-centred and experiential psychotherapy and the interface between the two fields. The respective conference publications are a rich source of theory and practice in PCP and PCT: from Leuven, Holland 1988 (Lietaer, Rombauts and Van Balen, 1990); Stirling, Scotland 1991 (Brazier, 1993b); Gmunden, Austria 1994 (Hutterer, Pawlowsky, Schmid and Stipsits, 1996); Lisbon, Portugal 1997 (Marques-Teixeira and Antones, 2000); and Chicago 2000 (Watson, Warner and Goldman, in preparation). The fact that the title of these conferences includes 'experiential' reflects Eugene Gendlin's usage of the term (see EXPERIENTIAL, FOCUSING, PROCESS CONCEPTION OF PSYCHOTHERAPY); (sometimes referred to as the 'scientific conference' to distinguish it from the INTERNATIONAL FORUM ON THE PERSON-CENTERED APPROACH).

International Forum on the Person-Centered Approach a biennial forum, the first of which was organised by Alberto Segrera in honour of Rogers' 80th birthday in 1982 and held in Oaxtapec, Mexico; papers were invited and collected (Segrera, 1984) though not formally presented, the form of this and subsequent Forums being unstructured, with the programme, structure and dialogue

75

emerging from the process of the large group; subsequent Forums have been held in Norwich, England (1984), La Jolla, USA (1986), Rio de Janeiro, Brazil (1989), Tscherschelling, Holland (1992), Thessaloniki, Greece (1995), Johannesburg, South Africa (1998) and Ako City, Japan (2001) (see Appendix 2).

international relations   one of the many and perhaps the most public of applications of the PCA, to the improvement of which Rogers himself devoted much of the work of the later years of his life (see INTERCULTURAL TENSIONS, RUST WORKSHOP).

interpersonal process recall   (IPR)   a self-reflective process of learning about interpersonal communication and therapeutic practice, developed by Norman Kagan and his colleagues at Michigan State University in the early 1960s and taught by Kagan (until his death in 1994) through experiential workshops held around the world. IPR is a particular method of recalling and learning about our own process in interpersonal communication; it is a process of self-discovery rather than a skill; a way of creating space in the belief that each individual is a unique authority about her/himself and knows best about the meaning of their own experience. It is based in the knowledge that at any moment in time we are experiencing a multitude of feelings, thoughts and sensations, of which we are not usually aware and do not have time to process, but which subtly affect the way we behave, react and interact. If we can find a safe way to bring this information into conscious awareness and examine it in a non-judgemental spirit of enquiry, then it can provide us with useful information about our own interactions,

our mode of behaving in certain situations, the way we perceive others and the way they may perceive us.

In IPR, using the playback of tape-recorded sessions, the 'recaller' (therapist) retains control of the process and the learning is theirs; the 'inquirer' (colleague/supervisor) aims to help the recaller to stay in the moment of the original interaction and to focus minutely on what was going on in their own process at that time, 'back then'; the inquirer's role, then, is to facilitate the recaller's self-learning — it is not to guide, criticise or judge (see Clarke, 1997 for further details of the process). IPR may also be conducted with the other participant on the tape (client, supervisee, etc.); through this mutual recall, both parties may gain insight into the effect they were having on the other person in the original interaction. IPR is non-threatening and as such minimises both the negative power dynamics between people as well as the destructive, internal 'critical-self' voice — both of which can be present in supervision; it can be particularly helpful as a method for the trainee therapist to review their tape recordings of sessions; as Kagan often put it:

> what we learn through intrinsic motivation, we don't need external nagging to maintain. In order to learn well we need to address our own anxieties. Skills are easily learned and as easily forgotten (or denied) if they put us into situations where we feel uncomfortable (personal notes from workshop presentations).

In this sense the approach and logic of IPR is consistent with the principles and practice of the PCA; indeed Clarke (1997) suggests that, despite it being highly structured, 'it has a clear affinity with the person-centred approach to therapy and education, and might be described as aimed at developing the "internal supervisor"' (p. 94) (see CO-OPERATIVE ENQUIRY, SUPERVISION). Although primarily used in counselling and psychotherapy, IPR has also been found to be helpful in other fields such as education and in the training of other helping professions including medicine (PA).

interpersonal relationships see RELATIONSHIPS, INTERPERSONAL.

interpersonal therapy the form of therapy (and psychiatry) associated with the work of Harry Stack Sullivan who, with other neo-Freudians, viewed humans as social beings and focused in their work on the effects of the individual's social and cultural life on their inner life and hence on interpersonal relationships; Rogers (1951) acknowledges the contribution of Sullivan and others (such as Karen Horney) to the development of PSYCHOANALYTIC thinking and their 'threads of interconnectedness' with CCT; Rogers uses the phrase 'interpersonal relationships' in various formulations of his theory, although there is no evidence that he intended any particular association by this with Sullivan's theories.

interspace the space between a couple or between and among a family which the therapist may reflect back to the couple or family (see Gaylin, 1993).

intersubjectivity the notion that SUBJECTIVE phenomena are or may be assumed to be experienced by others; it follows, therefore, that the focus of human enquiry (including psychology and therapy) is (a) on the other

and (b) on the 'inbetween'; in respect of the former, Brazier (1993c) argues that 'the natural functioning of the person is other-oriented and not self-oriented' (p. 84) or, put another way, 'human subjectivity is necessarily directed towards alterity' (Crossley, 1996, p. 11); regarding the inbetween or 'the between' see DIALOGIC, DIALOGIC PSYCHOTHERAPY, DIALOGUE and MUTUALITY.

intervention style, group therapist a set of nine scales divided into four umbrella sections, developed from a cluster and factor analysis by Lietaer and Dierick (1996) which are proposed as a summary of styles of interventions made by group therapists:

A Facilitating the experiential process
Scale 1 Deepening individual exploration
Scale 2 Stimulating interpersonal communication
B Personal presence
Scale 3 Personal commitment and support
Scale 4 Give personal here-and-now feedback
C Meaning attribution
Scale 5 Providing individual insight
Scale 6 Clarification of interactions and group process
Scale 7 Psychodynamic interpretation
D Executive function
Scale 8 Direction, advice and procedures
Scale 9 Process rules and evaluation.

This is useful in a number of respects: it accords with factors found by Lieberman, Yalom and Miles (1973) i.e. emotional stimulation, caring, meaning attribution and executive function; it elaborates and develops our understanding of group therapists' style of interventions across different orientations in which we may discern some similarities and commonalities between the PCA and other more analytic approaches, for instance in meaning attribution; and, finally, this research is especially important in offering the person-centred group therapist a view that intervention and structure do not necessarily equate with direction (see Coghlan and McIlduff, 1990).

interventiveness 'the degree to which a therapist brings in material from outside the client's frame of reference and the degree to which this is done from a stance of authority or expertise' (Warner, 2000a , p. 31).

interventiveness, levels of a five-level framework developed by Warner (2000a) to characterise therapist responses and styles:

Level 1 The therapist's pure intuitive contact (a largely hypothetical level).

Level 2 The therapist's conveying of their understanding of the client's INTERNAL FRAME OF REFERENCE.

Level 3 The therapist brings material into the therapeutic relationship in ways which foster client choice.

Level 4 The therapist brings material into the therapeutic relationship from their own frame of reference, from a position of authority or expertise.

Level 5 The therapist brings material into the therapeutic relationship that is outside the client's frame of reference, and in such a way that the client is unaware of both the intervention/s and the therapist's purpose or motivation.

These levels may be applied to all therapies and help to define and distinguish the person-centred practitio-

ner from more DIRECTIVE and interpretive therapists; and may equally be applied to supervisors' responses and styles. Given the universality of the NECESSARY AND SUFFICIENT CONDITIONS, they are relevant to therapy and therapies at all five levels; nevertheless, Warner suggests that there is a fundamental dividing line between levels 3 and 4 between the more client-directed therapies which focus on the nature of the client's process (Levels 1–3) and more authoritative therapies (Levels 4 and 5). Warner also suggests that 'there are very real dangers in trying to mix interventions and theories at different levels of intervention, since these therapies are grounded in quite different types of THERAPEUTIC RELATIONSHIP' (p. 34).

introjection the process where beliefs, evaluations, VALUES and attitudes of another person (usually someone of significance such as a parent) are taken up by an individual and become part of that individual's means of coping with life experiences; in PCP it is the introjection of values and, most significantly, CONDITIONS OF WORTH which are often responsible for the ACQUISITION OF DISTURBANCE and the PERPETUATION OF DISTURBANCE; once such attitudes, beliefs, etc. have become incorporated into the personality, i.e. internalised, they can lead to the development of a negative SELF-CONCEPT.

intuition 'the process of instantaneously coming to direct knowledge without inference or reasoning' (Villas-Boas Bowen, 1986, p. 300); the ability of the therapist to be close to their intuitive self was a characteristic which Rogers (1986a) acknowledged as requiring further investigative research (see also UNCONSCIOUS).

Jan a client with whom Rogers conducted one of his last demonstration therapy sessions in 1986 and written up by Rogers (1986a) who, in his own reflections on the session, appears excited to have caught an 'intuitive response' which Thorne (1992) links to Rogers' interest in the quality of 'PRESENCE', particularly in his later years.

Jill a client with whom Rogers conducted a demonstration therapy session in 1983; it is transcribed in Farber, Brink and Raskin (1996). As Villas-Boas Bowen (1996) observes in her commentary on the case, in addition to his deep empathy, unwavering respect for Jill's autonomy and ability to access the subceived level of awareness, two changes are evident in Rogers' work with this client:

first, he uses a much broader array of techniques ... he uses interpretation; he uses the client's body cues to bring her to the here and now; he uses metaphors, humors her, and exaggerates and repeats her self-deprecating comments to accentuate their absurdity and promote greater accuracy in her self evaluations. Second, he allows himself to be directive ... he introduces topics, he breaks silences (p. 85).

Ultimately, Villas-Boas Bowen views these observed changes in Rogers as reflective of his increasing trust in the client, including their SELF-DETERMINATION and SELF-REGULATION and, as a result, being 'less at the mercy of the therapist's influence' (p. 94).

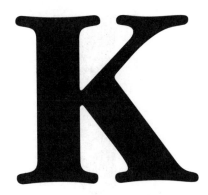

knowledge   a personal knowing which, for Rogers (1968), was clearly based on the SUBJECTIVE: 'I *experience*; in this experiencing, I *exist*; in thus existing, I in some sense *know*, I have a "felt assurance". All knowledge, including all SCIENTIFIC knowledge, is a vast inverted pyramid resting on this tiny, personal, subjective base' (p. 60).

leadership see FACILITATION.

learning the action of the subject of 'being educated' or 'being taught' which, from a person-centred perspective, is based on insatiable curiosity to absorb knowledge and implies an active participation on the part of the learner/student/trainee; Rogers clearly favoured *experiential* learning which, literally, involves learning from our experience and experiencing and, per se, has personal meaning and relevance (see EDUCATION, FREEDOM TO LEARN; Rogers, 1969, 1983; Merry, 1995, 1999).

levels of interventiveness see INTERVENTIVENESS, LEVELS OF.

listening, reflective the therapeutic technique of listening by means of reflecting back to the client what has been said or heard. In developing this, Rogers was influenced by the work of Otto Rank, who originally taught therapists to 'listen' for feelings through discerning the patterns in what clients say. It is often confused and equated with EMPATHY (see also REFLECTING).

Living Now Workshops established by Gay Leah Barfield, annual workshops which ran between 1977 and 1998, to which participants came from all over the globe; the difference between these and other person-centred ENCOUNTER events was (1) that they had a central theme each year, usually focusing on social, political, racial, gender, spirituality and peace issues related to current events; (2) that, along with Carl Rogers, they had invited guest speakers (such as Ram Dass, Elizabeth Kübler-Ross) to address the particular theme; and (3) that it was pre-structured with a clear design to each day: with a general, open community meeting, guest speaker session, small encounter groups facilitated by a female/male staff team in each group, yoga and Tai Chi and open time; many of the staff also worked on the CARL ROGERS INSTITUTE FOR PEACE. Further, periodic workshops are planned (see Appendix 2).

locus of evaluation the source of evidence of VALUES and ORGANISMIC VALUING PROCESS.

locus of evaluation, external describes the source of evidence of values as being external to the individual, using another person/other people, most commonly initially parents, parent figures and/or 'significant others'. In this case, the judgement of other/s as to the value of an experience or object becomes the principal criterion of value for the individual. When the external evaluation concerns the individual/SELF, such judgements form CONDITIONS OF WORTH.

locus of evaluation, internal

describes the source of evidence of values as within the individual her/himself, i.e. that the individual is at the centre of her/his ORGANISMIC VALUING PROCESS.

Loretta   a client of Rogers with whom he conducted a single, demonstration session during a four-day workshop held by the American Academy of Psychotherapists (AAP) in 1958 (AAP, 1958). Loretta, a state hospital inpatient and diagnosed as a paranoid schizophrenic, had been interviewed by Albert Ellis the previous day and by Richard Felder earlier the same day. It is an unusual piece of work in being one of the few verbatim recordings of a therapeutic interview within a specific (indeed, any) therapeutic orientation with a diagnosed psychotic patient and in many ways is a single clinical test of Rogers' hypothesis that the approach could work with such a diagnosed client group, a hypothesis he

and others went on to test (Rogers, Gendlin, Kiesler and Truax, 1967) (see THERAPEUTIC RELATIONSHIP AND ITS IMPACT). The transcript is reproduced in Farber, Brink and Raskin (1996) with a commentary by Raskin (1996b).

Louise   a client with whom Rogers conducted a demonstration therapy session in 1986 in the context of an Expressive Therapy Training Programme event (see also MARY), its transcript is published in Farber, Brink and Raskin (1996). In her commentary on both cases Natiello (1996) suggests that Rogers departed from his own way of doing therapy 'perhaps in order to accommodate the kind of therapeutic processes used in the training program he was visiting' (p. 126), although she draws a distinction between the two, viewing his work with Louise as directive and, indeed, redirective, with the result that Rogers does not achieve the RELATIONAL DEPTH usually evident in his work.

love   originally and sometimes used synonymously with UNCONDITIONAL POSITIVE REGARD, Brazier (1993c) explores this as *the* NECESSARY CONDITION and, following Fromm (1962), the primacy of the human need to love (as distinct from the need to be loved).

maladjustment (see PSYCHOLOGICAL MALADJUSTMENT).

Man and the Science of Man a book, co-authored by William Coulson and Rogers (Coulson and Rogers, 1968), based on the contributions to a five-day conference on the same subject held in July 1966 at San Diego State University during which Rogers had a recorded and televised dialogue with Michael Polanyi, a chemist, social scientist and philosopher, with whom Rogers had come into contact during 1962/63 when he spent a year as a Fellow at the Center for Advanced Study in the Behavioral Sciences at Stanford; the exchange focused on the difference between knowledge and science, the nature and place of science in the community and in culture, and the contribution of science to an understanding of 'man' (see CARL ROGERS DIALOGUES; Kirschenbaum and Henderson, 1990a).

Mark a client of Rogers with whom he conducted a single demonstration session in front of a small study group of professionals in 1982. Rogers (1986d) wrote it up, publishing the transcript together with his own reaction and excerpts from a subsequent correspondence with Mark. It is reproduced in Farber, Brink and Raskin (1996) with commentaries by Seeman (1996) and Hayes and Goldfried (1996). During the interview, subtitled 'The Dilemmas of a South African White', Mark moves from seeing the dilemmas as primarily external (the system, etc.) to a (more) painful position in which he accepts the conflict and confusion within himself.

Mary a client with whom Rogers conducted a demonstration therapy session in 1986 in the context of an Expressive Therapy Training Programme event (see also LOUISE), its transcript is published in Farber, Brink and Raskin (1996). In her commentary on both cases Natiello (1996) suggests that Rogers departed from his own way of doing therapy 'perhaps in order to accommodate the kind of therapeutic processes used in the training program he was visiting' (p. 126), although she draws a distinction between the two, viewing his work with Mary as reflecting the positive effect of Rogers' artistry, variety and the increasing scope of his responses in this limited context.

mass society originally a sociological theory which describes a loss of individuality and identification with society as a whole (the mass) and most succinctly summarised in the concept of ALIENATION; perhaps the most famous example of which in the psychological field is Reich's (1933/75) study of fascism; Homans (1974) discusses Rogers' psychology in relation to a number of theories of mass society and concludes that:

> Rogers' description of PSYCHOLOGICAL MALADJUSTMENT (concept of CONDITIONS OF WORTH) assumes and depends upon the view of social reality highlighted by the theory of mass society. However ... his psychology (concept of the ORGANISMIC VALUING PROCESS) [also] attempts to overcome the effects of mass society ... It is as though Rogerian man had been designed exactly for the purpose of living successfully in a mass society (pp. 335–6).

mature the mature person, according to Rogers (1959), displays the following characteristics: the capacity to perceive realistically and in an EXTENSIONAL manner; a lack of defensiveness; responsibility for one's difference from others and one's own behaviour; ability to evaluate experience in terms of the evidence of one's own senses and ability to change the evaluation of experience only on the basis of new evidence; acceptance of others as unique individuals different from oneself; and an ability to prize oneself and others (see FULLY FUNC-

TIONING PERSON). 'Maturity is a broader term [than extensional] describing the personality characteristics and behavior of a person who is, in general, congruent' (Rogers, 1959, p. 207).

maturity see MATURE.

Measuring Personality Adjustment in Children Nine to Thirteen Years of Age Rogers' doctoral thesis, undertaken at Teachers College, New York and completed in 1931, in which he attempted to reconcile the tension between two forces and influences: measurement and statistics he was being taught at the College, and the emphasis on emotions and personality dynamics which he experienced in his work as a Fellow at the Institute for Child Guidance, also in New York.

median group see GROUP, LARGE.

medical model an approach to psychological disturbance and 'illness', based on DIAGNOSIS→TREATMENT→CURE, in which it is assumed that the person is sick and in need of expert (allopathic medical) treatment and that this treatment effects the necessary cure — and that any unwanted effects of treatment are 'side effects' (see IATROGENESIS); clinically contrasting with homeopathy and, philosophically, in direct contrast to the PCA which as a HUMANISTIC psychology is based on a 'growth model' of DEVELOPMENT (see also PSYCHOPATHOLOGY).

meeting see ENCOUNTER.

memory 1. the mental function of retaining information after the original stimuli are no longer present,

2. 'the hypothesised "storage system" in the mind/brain that holds this information' (Reber, 1985, p. 429).

memory, recovered that part of our memory or memories which is/are recovered or regained usually in the course of therapy; specifically and controversially, this refers to the situation in which clients (some estimates suggest up to 30% of all clients in therapy) who have no memory of abuse prior to therapy regain such memories during therapy; this is the subject of much debate about the nature of memory, cognition, repression and suggestion — for an introduction to which see Goodrich and Bekerian (2000), debates made more acute by the fact that some clients have subsequently accused parents/carers of abuse, some of whom, in turn, have brought actions against therapists for inducing 'false' memories in their clients. As PCP and the PCA takes a PHENOMENOLOGICAL view of EXPERIENCE, memories are not subject to external (e)valuation 'true' or 'false', rather to the client's INTERNAL VALUING PROCESS; secondly, person-centred practitioners are somewhat protected from 'false' accusations by the PRINCIPLES OF THE PERSON-CENTRED APPROACH, in particular the primacy of the ACTUALISING TENDENCY and the NON-DIRECTIVE attitude (see Sanders, 2000); practitioners should nevertheless be especially alert to their own process (reinforcing the necessity of PERSONAL DEVELOPMENT and PERSONAL THERAPY) and to the possibility of the *unknowing* induction of 'false' memories (Lindsay and Read, 1994).

mental health   see PSYCHOSANOLOGY.

mental ill-health
see PSYCHOSANOLOGY.

mental illness   see PSYCHOPATHOLOGY.

metaskills   the skills of the therapist/facilitator which underlie specific response skills, a concept coined and developed by Mindell (1992), akin to Rogers' ATTITUDINAL QUALITIES of the

therapist (see PROCESS-ORIENTED PSYCHOLOGY).

ministry   the concept in Quakerism of speaking of something for no apparent reason which West (1998) likens to Rogers' concept of PRESENCE (see also INTUITION).

misconceptions of the person-centred approach   see PERSON-CENTRED APPROACH, MISCONCEPTIONS OF.

modelling   a technique, with its origins (like FEEDBACK) in the BEHAVIOURIST tradition of psychology, whereby a person, usually a trainer, teacher or person in authority, demonstrates something by doing, thereby and *with the intention* of 'portraying' (see PORTRAYAL) or 'modelling' what to do or how to be — with the implication that the student learns by copying (see EDUCATION and LEARNING). Taking issue with the view that staff in person-centred GROUPS model facilitative behaviour, Wood (1995) comments that

to 'model facilitative behavior' — that is, to encourage a group participant to mimic the behavior of someone in authority — is operant conditioning. It is diametrically opposite to the person-centred approach which would be more interested in participants discovering their own 'WAY OF BEING' (p. 3).

Fairhurst and Merry (1999) are equally sceptical about this and draw a useful distinction between modelling and internalising 'qualities and attitudes to the extent that they are natural and genuine for us' (p. 60) — a way of being which, of course, has an impact on the phenomenal field experienced by the student/supervisee who may internalise some of those qualities and attitudes *for them-*

selves in an INTERNAL VALUING PROCESS.

moment of movement an immediate experience of SELF-ACCEPTANCE and integration occurring during therapy or, of course, in other situations; typically, such moments have the following characteristics: they are immediate and consist of total experiences, not thoughts or intellectual understandings; they are new in that, while they may have been experienced before (at least, in part), never completely or with awareness matching physiological reactions; they are self-accepting in that they are owned as a part of the SELF; and they are integrated:

> I see successful therapy as being a large number of such units, in which an increasing number of the facets of EXPERIENCE which the CLIENT previously has been unable to accept as integrated parts of his self, are so experienced. Thus one way of putting this is that experiences which have hitherto been denied into awareness are now experienced in awareness as well as viscerally or organically. Another way of putting it is that the client is able to experience in an integrated way, an increasing proportion of his life, and to own that life as his own (Rogers, 1956, p. 6).

morphic tendency see SYNTROPY.

motivation the intervening process or internal state of the ORGANISM concerned with or having the quality of movement, the substratum of which, for Rogers (1978) is the organismic tendency towards fulfilment or ACTUALISATION (see also ACTUALISING TENDENCY, ADIENCE and AVOIDANCE);

similar to the concept of PRIMARY DRIVES; in reviewing and elaborating a unitary theory of motivation, Patterson (1964/2000a) makes the point that 'there is no such thing as lack of or absence of motivation. To be alive is to be motivated, to be unmotivated is to be dead. Thus we cannot say that a client is unmotivated' (p. 16). In discussing the problem of the 'unmotivated' client, Rogers (1962/67b) notes:

> the absence of conscious motivation constitutes a really profound problem in psychotherapy ... There is a great difference between working with the consciously motivated client, whether neurotic, or psychotic, and working with the person who has no such conscious motivation, whether that person is normal, neurotic or psychotic ... working with a lack of conscious motivation in the individual is more difficult than working with the problem of psychosis (pp. 183–4).

See also RESISTANCE.

Mun, Miss a client with whom Rogers worked in a filmed demonstration over a number of sessions in 1955 (Rogers and Segel, 1955a) which is notable for its early emphasis on EMPATHY.

mutuality the concept that there is, in this context, some reciprocity in the relationship between therapist and client, teacher and student, etc. as regards understanding, POWER and HUMANITY; although an integral part of the philosophy of the PCA and PCP, there is surprisingly little in the literature on it. Mearns (1994) describes mutuality as 'where the counsellor and client understand each other across different levels of perspective' (p. 6); Natiello (1990) talks in terms of an equality of power in relationship, describing co-operative or 'COLLABORATIVE POWER'; Merry (1999) regards some degree of mutuality as characteristic of effective therapy relationships: 'there is a sense that the two people are mutually engaged in exploring meanings and working towards understanding. In successful counselling relationships, mutuality can develop into an intimate and close sharing of thoughts, emotions and experiences' (p. 67).

mystical see PRESENCE and SPIRITUAL.

necessary and sufficient conditions of therapeutic personality change, the see CONDITIONS OF PERSONALITY CHANGE, NECESSARY AND SUFFICIENT.

need a fundamental necessity of life.

needs, basic refers to that part of Maslow's (1943a, 1943b) theory of motivation and personality in which primary or basic needs are *physiological*, e.g. water, food, avoidance of pain, etc., while other needs such as for security and SELF-ESTEEM are *psychological*; also referred to as 'deficiency needs' since a person who by definition is deficient in these needs will actively seek to satisfy them.

needs, hierarchy of a hierarchical need system, postulated by Maslow, comprising: physiological needs (water, food, etc.), safety (freedom from threat, security, etc.), belongingness and love (affiliation, ACCEPTANCE, etc.), esteem (achievement, PRIZING, etc.), cognitive (knowledge, understanding, curiosity, etc.), aesthetic (order, beauty, art, etc.), and self-actualisation (self-fulfilment, etc.). Although Maslow conceptualised this hierarchy as universal and invariant, this is disputed, particularly from different cultural perspectives.

Network of the European Associations for Person-Centred and Experiential Psychotherapy and Counselling (NEAPCEPC) the origins of this network which, to date, comprises 21 member associations, including the BRITISH ASSOCIATION FOR THE PERSON-CENTRED APPROACH and Person-Centred Therapy — Scotland, and which is a member of the European Association for Psychotherapy and of the WORLD ASSOCIATION FOR PERSON-CENTRED AND EXPERIENTIAL PSYCHOTHERAPY AND COUNSELLING lie in meetings of the boards of German-speaking associations (meeting in the early 1980s) which then became more international; the motivation for a Europe-wide network included: supporting those associations which are not yet recognised in their own countries or where the PCA is not legally (or politically) recognised as a 'legitimate' method of therapy or 'psychotherapy' (e.g. in Germany); and participating in the process of detailed regulations for a European Certificate for Psychotherapy; the

Network was formally founded at a meeting in Luxembourg, 25–27 September 1998 (see Appendix 2).

neurosis in person-centred terms, a vulnerable SELF-CONCEPT developed over time as a result of early CONDITIONS OF WORTH which then becomes fixed and restimulated in response to similar or new perceived THREATS (see also PSYCHOSIS).

neutrality, the rule of an analytic attitude and value comprising: a caring commitment to the client, a respect for client AUTONOMY, and a devotion to the pursuit of truth (Dorpat, 1985), similar to Rogers' (1951) view of the therapist–client relationship as *impersonal* in its independence, absence of external evaluations and its consistent acceptance (see THERAPEUTIC RELATIONSHIP).

nineteen propositions (of a theory of personality and behaviour), the see PERSONALITY AND BEHAVIOUR, THE NINETEEN PROPOSITIONS (OF A THEORY OF).

non-directive approach based on a belief in the ACTUALISING TENDENCY and historically used synonymously with CLIENT-CENTRED THERAPY, this describes the ATTITUDE and role (and *not* the behaviour) of the therapist/educator/facilitator, and distinguishes CCT and PCT from more analytic and directive approaches — see Snyder (1945) whose investigation into non-directive psychotherapy influenced Rogers' thinking, and Raskin (1948) on the development of non-directive therapy. For Brodley (1999), it concerns the therapist's intentions and awareness of how their behaviour may be perceived and experienced by clients, and is part of the essential meaning of the CORE CONDITIONS: 'the concept of nondirectivity comes into existence *within the meaning* of these therapeutic attitudes' (p. 79). Non-directiveness, for Merry (1999), refers to

a general non-authoritarian attitude maintained by a counsellor whose intention is empathically to understand a client's subjective experience. It refers also to the theory that the actualising tendency can be fostered in a relationship of particular qualities, and that whilst the general direction of that tendency is regarded as constructive and creative, its particular characteristics in any one person cannot be predicted, and should not be controlled or directed (pp. 75–6).

Patterson (2000c) reviews and takes issue with recent discussions of directiveness–non-directiveness in the person-centred literature and distinguishes this from the (more relevant) issue of the *influence* the therapist has and its consistency with the PHILOSOPHY OF THE PERSON-CENTRED APPROACH and, from this, restates the centrality of the NECESSARY AND SUFFICIENT CONDITIONS OF THERAPY in providing the conditions for client self-discovery (see also LEVELS OF INTERVENTIVENESS).

Oak, Mrs a client of Rogers and the subject of a major and detailed research analysis involving a battery of research instruments, including Q-SORT cards — see Rogers (1954b) who felt that 'a significant degree of reorganization of attitudes and personality had taken place' (p. 261), a feeling certainly borne out by the research (see MR BEBB).

Ohio State University where Rogers was appointed a full professor in 1939 and where he worked until 1944; his graduate students included Virginia Axline who went on to develop PLAY THERAPY (see Axline, 1964); Arthur Combs, later a pioneer in humanistic education and whose work was cited by Rogers (1951); Thomas Gordon and Nicholas Hobbes who later contributed chapters in *Client-Centered Therapy* (Gordon, 1951; Hobbs, 1951); and William Snyder whose investigation into NON-DIRECTIVE psychotherapy (Snyder, 1945) was one of the first doctoral theses to be completed under Rogers' supervision.

On Becoming a Person published in 1961, the second of Rogers' books, which outlined the fundamental philosophy, theory and practice of the approach (see *Client-Centered Therapy* and *A Way Of Being*); it comprises seven parts which range from the personal, through philosophy and research to the implications of the PCA for living; both huge in its scope and eminently readable, it appeals to professional and lay audiences alike. It contains key concepts of, and ideas within, the approach, including: the characteristics of a helping relationship (see THERAPEUTIC RELATIONSHIP), a PROCESS CONCEPTION OF PSYCHOTHERAPY, the FULLY FUNCTIONING PERSON, three chapters on RESEARCH, and a critique of BEHAVIOURISM.

On Encounter Groups see CARL ROGERS ON ENCOUNTER GROUPS.

openness to experience the way a congruent individual meets new experience, one of the characteristics of the EMERGING PERSON (see Rogers, 1961) and the EMERGING CULTURE (Rogers, 1978) and the subject of some further conceptualisation and research by Pearson (1974), who defined and described such openness as 'a three phase assimilation process serving both informational and identity functions' (p. 140) and comprising phases of attention-recognition, reaction and exploration-closure.

oppression the action of oppressing (pressing injuriously) or condition of being or feeling oppressed, the tyrannical exercise of POWER; in his understanding of oppression, Rogers (1978) draws heavily on the work of Paulo Freire (1972) (see CONSCIENTIZAÇAO, EDUCATION, FREEDOM TO LEARN) and identifies the importance of a change in POWER relationships and the significance of problem-posing (for instance in education) for developing a pedagogy of the oppressed and for facilitating (revolutionary) social change and development. In working with oppressed groups or groups of oppressed people, Rogers (1978) suggests (in his familiar 'if–then' formulation) that if a person with FACILITATIVE ATTITUDES gains entry to the group, then a process will result which, in effect, is ANTI-OPPRESSIVE and pro PERSONAL POWER and is characterised by:

- the expression of long-suppressed, mostly negative, hostile and bitter feelings;
- recognition of the individual's uniqueness and strengths and the development of mutual trust;
- the defusion of the most irrational feelings and the clarification and strengthening of feelings based on experiences common to the group;
- the growth of self and group confidence;
- the movement towards innovative, responsible, even revolution-

ary steps, taken in an atmosphere of realism;
- leadership is multiplied (shared), action taken is constructive, and individuals feel supported in taking action even when high risk is involved.

See also CULTURAL CONFLICT, RUST WORKSHOP, STEEL SHUTTER.

organisation a complex system of parts that are functional, distinguishable (in terms of structure), interrelated and co-ordinated — which applies to the ORGANISM, individual, small and large GROUPS as well as sophisticated political, industrial, commercial and multinational organisations and societies. Rogers (1970/73) described the group as 'like an organism' (having a sense of its own direction) and this is equally applicable to organisations: 'organizations are living systems. They too are intelligent, creative, adaptive, self-organizing, meaning-seeking' (Wheatley and Kellner-Rogers, 1996, p. 3). Comparatively little work has been published on the application of PCP to organisations and organisational development, although it appears implicit in much of the literature; there are similarities, for instance, between the PCA to LEARNING and Senge's (1990) concept of the emergent organisation as a 'learning organisation'; Coghlan and McIlduff (1999) explore the person-centred contribution to four levels of organisational behaviour (the individual, team, interdepartmental and the organisation itself) (see also Lloyd Valentine, 2000; and EMERGING CULTURE).

organism generally 'any living thing', a term used by Rogers to denote both the HUMAN ORGANISM and, synonymously, the individual, but also as a wider referent to the human species and beyond that to all organic life, including GROUPS and ORGANISATIONS; Rogers' use of the concept 'organism' derives both from a unified concept of human motivation and from a focus on the human species and in this sense it may be more accurate to talk about a 'people-centred' or even 'species-centred approach'. As formulated in his THEORY OF PERSONALITY AND BEHAVIOUR (Rogers, 1951), the human species (as with other species) 'has one basic tendency and striving — to actualize, maintain, and enhance the experiencing organism' (p. 487) and continues: 'it seems entirely possible that all organic and psychological needs may be described as partial aspects of this one fundamental need ... the words used are an attempt to describe the observed directional force in organic life' (pp. 487–8). In his reading of Rogers, Barrett-Lennard (1998) identifies a further five properties of the organism:

1. *The organism behaves as an organised whole* — 'the organism reacts to the field as it is experienced and perceived ... [and which] is, for the individual, "reality"' (Rogers, 1951, p. 484); Barrett-Lennard (1998) describes the organism as 'a purposeful, open system, in particularly active interchange with its environment' (p. 75).

2. *The human organism interacts with perceived 'outer' and 'inner' reality in the service of the actualizing tendency*, which emphasises its FORMATIVE and DIALOGIC nature.

3. Through healthy development, human beings engage in an *organismic valuing process* (see CHILD DEVELOPMENT).

4. *Differentiation is an important effect of the actualising tendency*, such differentiation of the organism's experience being symbolised in an awareness of being, i.e. 'self-experience'.

5. *The organism is always in motion* reflecting the ubiquitous nature of CHANGE.

In their major work on theories of personality Hall and Lindzey (1957) associated Rogers with organismic theory and in many ways the PCA may be considered an *organismic* psychology (as distinct from a SELF-PSYCHOLOGY). Rogers' use of the term 'organism' both as a biological referent and as an analogy is both useful and problematic: it is useful in moving on from earlier more mechanistic theories (with mechanical analogies), in encouraging interconnectedness and (unwittingly as far as Rogers was concerned) in its philosophical staying power, for instance, in relation to social constructivism and postmodernism; it is problematic, however, in that, from a systems perspective, the organism both echoes and reinforces survival and homeostasis; furthermore, 'the organismic analogy encourages the view that it is the environment which influences and the system which responds' (Burrell and Morgan, 1979, p. 64). Such passivity on the part of the organism contradicts much of Rogers' work, for instance, on PERSONAL POWER (Rogers, 1978) and on the pro-social and pro-active nature of the ACTUALISING TENDENCY.

organism, human synonymous with the individual, and having, according to Rogers (1959), essentially two characteristics or capacities:

1. the capacity to EXPERIENCE in AWARENESS the incongruencies between her/his SELF-CONCEPT and her/his total experience, which is the factor or process in her/his PSYCHOLOGICAL MALADJUSTMENT;

2. the capacity — and, indeed, the tendency — 'to reorganize his *self-concept* in such a way so as to make it more *congruent* with the totality of his *experience*' (p. 221), thus moving towards PSYCHOLOGICAL ADJUSTMENT.

Rogers suggests that these capacities and this ACTUALISING TENDENCY are, especially when latent (as distinct from evident), released or enacted in any interpersonal (HELPING) RELATIONSHIP in which the CORE CONDITIONS are present and are communicated to the individual.

organismic integration a core construct identified by Seeman (1984) in the study of effective (FULLY) FUNCTIONING: *organismic* suggests 'a pervasive phenomenon that includes all of a person's behavioral subsystems: biochemical, physiological, perceptual, cognitive, and interpersonal ... [while] integration indicates a transactional process that blends these subsystem behaviors in ways which are congruent, harmonious and adaptive' (p. 146).

organismic self see SELF, ORGANISMIC.

organismic self-regulation the fluent exchange with and adjustment to the environment, one of the characteristics of the ORGANISM.

organismic valuing process
see VALUING PROCESS, ORGANISMIC.

outcomes of therapy the observed results of the therapeutic process. Rogers (1959) did not make a clear distinction between process and outcome, but did hypothesise that certain changes of a relatively permanent nature were likely to result from successful client-centred therapy:

1. The client is more CONGRUENT, OPEN TO EXPERIENCE and less DEFENSIVE.

2. S/he is more realistic, objective and EXTENSIONAL in their perceptions.

3. S/he is more effective in problem-solving.

4. S/he is more psychologically adjusted.

5. S/he is less vulnerable to threat as a result of increasing congruence between SELF and EXPERIENCE.

6. The perception of the IDEAL SELF is more realistic and achievable.

7. The self is more congruent with the ideal self.

8.. Tensions of all kinds, including physiological and psychological tension and ANXIETY, is reduced.

9. S/he has an increased level of positive SELF-REGARD.

10. The LOCUS OF EVALUATION is more internal, and the client is more confident, self-directing, with values determined by an ORGANISMIC VALUING PROCESS.

11. Others are perceived more realistically and accurately.

12. There is a higher degree of ACCEPTANCE of others.

13. Behaviour changes so that more behaviour is owned as belonging to the self, and less disowned and felt to be 'not myself'. Behaviour is perceived as being more under the person's control.

14. Behaviour is experienced by others as more socialised and mature.
15. Behaviour becomes more creative, more EXISTENTIAL and immediate, and more fully expressive of the person's own VALUES and purposes.

P

parallel process   the notion, originally developed by Ekstein and Wallerstein (1958) and commonly referred to in the SUPERVISION of therapeutic practice, that the process between client and therapist *influences* the supervisory relationship; later, Doerhman (1976) demonstrated that themes can pass both ways, i.e. from supervision to therapy as well as from therapy to supervision. In these ways the supervisory process — and relationship — is reflective of *and in this sense is parallel to* the therapeutic process and relationship. While the paralleling in supervision of the therapeutic process and, similarly (although hopefully less common), in therapy of the supervisory process, is a powerful narrative in supervision, the phenomenon of influence (and especially of determination) is debatable and there are criticisms of the concept (e.g. Feltham and Dryden, 1994). Mothersole (1999) suggests the following 'broad encompassing definition':

> parallel process is the reflection of aspects of the client/psychothera-pist dyad and the supervisee/supervisor dyad in each other. As such, parallels will always have some implication, however tentative, for all individuals in these dyads. It involves reciprocal and/or complementary roles and may involve shifts in these roles. Such roles are based on the involvement of aspects of the internal world of participants acting in a way that is currently out of awareness. In this sense, [parallel process] is an interpersonal process with major intrapsychic aspects (p. 119).

This definition avoids the unacceptable (and magical) determinism, grandiosity and blame inherent in interpretations of parallel process and consequent diagnostic assumptions made by supervisors in the absence of the therapist's client.

perceive   see PERCEPTION.

perception   'a hypothesis or prognosis for action which comes into being in awareness when stimuli impinge on the organism' (Rogers, 1959, p. 199); perception is thus almost synonymous with awareness, with perception being the more specific term relating to the importance of the (usually external) stimulus; while our perceptions and SYMBOLISATIONS change, there is a sense in which perception is based on consensual REALITY (see SUBCEPTION).

perceptual field the reality to which a person reacts: 'I do not react to some absolute reality, but to my perception of this reality' (Rogers, 1951, p. 484). The second of the NINETEEN PROPOSITIONS which outline Rogers' theory of personality develops this point further: Rogers takes the EXISTENTIAL position that it is not 'objective reality' which determines a person's BEHAVIOUR (even if such a reality exists), but a person's *perception* of reality, a perception that is open to change; he gives the example of a person whose perception is that a parent is a domineering individual and, as far as this person is concerned, this perception constitutes reality for him or her; if, later, this perception changes so that the parent is viewed as a pathetic individual attempting to maintain his status, then this will constitute the person's new 'reality'.

perpetuation of disturbance see PSYCHOLOGICAL DISTURBANCE, PERPETUATION OF.

person although the person is central to PCP and PCT, Rogers does not explicitly define the term in his writing; Schmid (1998b) reports asking Rogers about the definitions of the expressions 'organism, 'self' and 'person' and receiving the reply:

> I use the term organism for the biological entity. The actualising tendency exists in the biological human organism. I use the term self when I am referring to the concept a person has of himself, the way he views himself, his perceptions of his qualities and so on ... I use the term person in a more general sense to indicate each individual (p. 47)

from which Schmid argues that 'person' is a superordinate concept. Schmid (1998b) traces two philosophical conceptions of the person: the individualistic and the relationalist. He argues that Rogers' (1961, 1969) concept of the FULLY FUNCTIONING PERSON is influenced by an individualistic view of the person; when, however, Rogers talks about the *characteristics* of the fully functioning person: openness to experience; the ability to live in the present and be attentive to each moment; trust in organismic experiencing (Rogers, 1961), i.e. when he describes the *process* of being and becoming a person, this sounds more relational and more applicable to diverse cultures which understand 'experience' and experiencing in various ways. In later writings, when Rogers discusses 'the EMERGING PERSON' (Rogers, 1978) and 'the person of tomorrow' (Rogers, 1980a) he emphasises the relational nature and aspirations of the person, person-to-person, in group and community, even (and latterly) especially across divides and conflicts.

personal construct see CONSTRUCT.

personal construct psychology a psychological model of human beings, developed by George Kelly, which posits that we are continually seeking to make sense of our worlds through interpretation, anticipation and experimentation (see CONSTRUCT and CONSTRUING). In 1956 Rogers had written a review of Kelly's work under the title 'intellectualized psychotherapy' (Rogers, 1956a); he nevertheless borrowed the concept of PERSONAL CONSTRUCT ('Kelly's useful term', Rogers, 1961), using it in his seven stages PROCESS CONCEPTION OF PSYCHOTHERAPY. The assumptions — or postulates — on which personal construct psychology is based are similar to and compatible with PCP and the PCA in a number of respects:

- Regarding REALITY — both are based on the notion that people each live in a personal world and make sense of it by applying personal constructs to it which we have created in the past.
- Regarding EXPERIENCING — both are theories of human experiencing: 'our construing of the world *is* what we are experiencing' (Fransella and Dalton, 1990, p. 10) parallels 'the organism reacts to the field as it is experienced and perceived. This perceptual field is, for the individual, "reality"' (Rogers, 1951, p. 484).
- Regarding the optimal or the FULLY FUNCTIONING PERSON — both have a similar image; within personal construct psychology it is described as: forging our own destiny, being in motion and construing the world in such a way that predictions are validated; within person-centred psychology as: increasing OPENNESS to experience, increasing EXISTENTIAL LIVING and increasing TRUST in our ORGANISM.
- Regarding behaviour — we create and apply personal constructs (mini theories) and *predict* the result of action; we then behave 'as if' that action will result; thus behaviour is the experiment — which is similar to the notion in PCP that BEHAVIOUR is needs-driven and goal-directed; also, both differ from BEHAVIOURISM, in postulating/believing that humans act upon the world rather than (simply) respond to it: we act, we create (and can re-create) our own lives, we inquire and we move (we are in motion) and we change — and hence the notion, in personal construct psychology of 'man' as incipient scientist.
- Regarding diagnosis — both are critical of traditional, medical/psychiatric models; in personal construct psychology illness is a construct, and the use of the medical model as hampering our understanding of people; Kelly conceptualised 'psychological disturbance' in terms of functioning: a disorder is '*any personal construction which is used repeatedly in spite of consistent invalidation*' (Fransella and Dalton, 1990, p. 12) (see DIAGNOSIS).
- Regarding CHANGE — both view this as a process; within personal construct psychology, through experience and learning, choice, transitions, reconstruing experience and cycles of change, experience, creativity and decision-making.

For his part, Kelly (1955/63), while recognising certain similarities between the two theories, viewed personal construct psychology as rooted in *psychological* postulates (as distinct from CCT's *philosophical* convictions).

personal development an essential aspect of TRAINING in PCP and PCT and, generally, takes place and is fostered in the training group (as distinct from individual personal therapy away from training): 'personal development for professional working is so crucial to the person-centred approach that it cannot be left to the vagaries of individual therapy' (Mearns, 1994, p. 35) (see PERSONAL THERAPY and TRAINING THERAPY).

personality and behaviour, the nineteen propositions (of a theory of) the group of statements which, together, constitute a PERSON-CENTRED THEORY OF PERSONALITY AND BEHAVIOUR, to which Rogers devoted a chapter in *Client-Centered Therapy* (Rogers, 1951). In this, Rogers acknowledges a number of influences, including Goldstein (1940), Angyal (1941), Maslow (1943a, 1943b), Lecky (1945), Sullivan (1945) and Snygg and Combs (1949). In his conclusion, Rogers makes the following statement:

> this theory is basically PHENOMENO-LOGICAL in character, and relies heavily on the concept of the SELF as an explanatory construct. It pictures the end-point of personality development as being a basic CONGRUENCE between the PHENOMENAL FIELD of EXPERIENCE and the conceptual structure of the self — a situation which, if achieved, would represent freedom from internal strain and ANXIETY, and freedom from potential strain; which would represent the maximum in realistically oriented adaptation; which would mean the establishment of an individualised value system having considerable identity with the value system of any other equally well-adjusted member of the human race (p. 532).

A detailed discussion of the nineteen propositions may be found in Rogers (1951); here the propositions are summarised in their original sequence:

1. Every individual exists in a continually changing world of EXPERIENCE of which s/he is the centre.

2. The ORGANISM reacts to the field as it is experienced and perceived. This perceptual field is, for the individual, 'reality'.

3. The organism reacts as an organised whole to this phenomenal field.

4. The organism has one basic tendency and striving — to actualise, maintain, and enhance the experiencing organism.

5. BEHAVIOUR is basically the goal-directed attempt of the organism to satisfy its needs as experienced, in the field as perceived.

6. EMOTION accompanies and in general facilitates such goal-directed behaviour, the kind of emotion being related to the seeking versus the consummatory aspects of the behaviour, and the intensity of the emotion being related to the perceived significance of the behaviour for the maintenance and enhancement of the organism.

7. The best vantage point for understanding behaviour is from the INTERNAL FRAME OF REFERENCE of the individual her/himself.

8. A portion of the total perceptual field gradually becomes differentiated as the SELF.

9. As a result of interaction with the environment, and particularly as a result of evaluational interaction with others, the structure of

self is formed — an organised, fluid, but consistent conceptual pattern of perceptions of characteristics and relationships of the 'I' or the 'me', together with VALUES attached to these concepts.

10. The values attached to experiences, and the values which are a part of the self-structure, in some instances are values experienced directly by the organism, and in some instances are values introjected or taken over from others, but in distorted fashion, *as if* they had been experienced directly.

11. As experiences occur in the life of the individual, they are either (a) SYMBOLISED, perceived, and organised into some relationship to the self, (b) IGNORED because there is no perceived relationship to the self-structure, (c) DENIED symbolisation or given a distorted symbolisation because the experience is inconsistent with the structure of the self.

12. Most of the ways of behaving which are adopted by the organism are those which are consistent with the concept of the self.

13. Behaviour may, in some instances, be brought about by organic experiences and needs which have not been symbolised. Such behaviour may be inconsistent with the structure of the self, but in such instances the behaviour is not 'owned' by the individual.

14. PSYCHOLOGICAL MALADJUSTMENT exists when the organism denies to awareness significant sensory and visceral experiences, which consequently are not symbolised and organised into the gestalt of the SELF-STRUCTURE. When this exists, there is a basic or potential psychological TENSION.

15. PSYCHOLOGICAL ADJUSTMENT exists when the concept of the self is such that all the sensory and visceral experiences of the organism are, or may be, assimilated on a symbolic level into a consistent relationship with the concept of self.

16. Any experience which is inconsistent with the organisation or structure of self may be perceived as a THREAT, and the more of these perceptions there are, the more rigidly the self-structure is organised to maintain itself.

17. Under certain conditions, involving primarily complete absence of any threat to it, experiences which are inconsistent with the self-structure may be perceived, and examined, and the structure of the self revised to assimilate and include experiences.

18. When the individual perceives and accepts into one consistent and integrated system all her/his sensory and visceral experiences, then s/he is necessarily more understanding of others and is more accepting of others as separate individuals.

19. As the individual perceives and accepts into his self-structure more of her/his organic experiences, s/he finds that s/he is replacing her/his present value *system* — based so largely upon introjections which have been distortedly symbolised — with a continuing organismic valuing *process*.

99

In a creative contribution to the translation of these propositions into lay language, Harkness (1998) illustrates them by means of a story of the development of a car — Percy the Propositions Prototype; for further discussion see Merry (1999).

personality change 'change in the personality structure of the individual, at both surface and deeper levels, in a direction which clinicians would agree means greater INTEGRATION, less internal conflict, more energy utilizable for effective living' (Rogers, 1957, p. 95); synonymous with GROWTH.

personality disorder literally, some disorder or disintegration (dis-INTEGRATION) of the personality, causing subjective distress and/or impairing the person's abilities to function as a social being. The common psychiatric view of personality disorders (PDs) is based on a structural conception of personality; a fixed patterning — 'the essential feature of a Personality Disorder is an enduring pattern of inner experience and behavior that deviates markedly from the expectations of the individual's culture' (American Psychiatric Association, 1994, p. 630); and the view that PDs are 'untreatable' (to date, as a clinical category, they fall outside the Mental Health Acts in Britain) and often 'dangerous'. As with its approach to PSYCHOPATHOLOGY in general, PCP takes a view which focuses on PERSONALITY (and BEHAVIOUR) in *process*, in *context* and in *change* (see, for instance, Gendlin, 1964; Bohart, 1990; Saunders and Tudor, 2001); as Bohart (1990) asserts:

borderline symptomatology does not reflect an underlying disorder in the person: While the person may act in 'borderline' ways, the person is not borderline. Furthermore, because borderline behavior is not a manifestation of an underlying personality structure I would not expect 'borderline' individuals to behave borderline all the time (p. 611).

an expectation which is congruent with clinical observations (see also PERSON-CENTRED THEORY OF PERSONALITY, SELF).

personality, person-centred theory of the self-theory of personality that posits how a person develops a SELF-CONCEPT and then acts in the world in accordance with that self-concept; an important aspect of person-centred personality theory is that it sees the self-concept as fluid and dynamic and always open to change. The theory (see NINETEEN PROPOSITIONS OF PERSONALITY AND BEHAVIOUR) posits that infants enter the world in a state of full CONGRUENCE and that their EXPERIENCES of their new environment constitute REALITY for them; HUMAN NATURE is regarded as constructive and social; positive SELF-REGARD is viewed as a basic human need and people do the best they can under the prevailing circumstances to develop and protect themselves; in interacting with their environment, infants are motivated by the ACTUALISING TENDENCY, some experiences will be perceived as satisfying the process of actualisation, whereas others will not; experiences are valued either as positive or negative by an ORGANISMIC VALUING PROCESS and, as the experience of reality for each person will be different, each will develop their own internal FRAME OF REFERENCE that cannot be completely assumed by another. As the infant develops, so does the awareness of SELF, which is a part of the infant's total experience; the need for POSITIVE REGARD from others develops alongside the emergence of the SELF-CONCEPT, and the infant develops a sense of self-regard in accordance with her or his varied experience of life. Because the infant is dependent for survival on others, the organismic valuing process may be overridden by the need for positive regard from them; the infant will, therefore, begin to adopt VALUES from outside of her/himself and internalise them in an effort to maintain the support and nurturing needed; the infant's trust in her/his own experiencing and valuing is likely to become suppressed if it conflicts with the values and needs of other more powerful people; infants thus acquire CONDITIONS OF WORTH (see ACQUISITION OF PSYCHOLOGICAL DISTURBANCE).

personal power   see POWER, PERSONAL.

personal self   see SELF, PERSONAL.

personal therapy   viewed by many theoretical orientations, schools of training and professional bodies as an essential requirement of becoming and being a counsellor/psychotherapist (although, interestingly, not for being a psychologist); while Rogers (1951) comments that 'the experience of personal therapy is ... a valuable experience for the student' (p. 437), he goes on to say that 'it does not seem compatible with the whole viewpoint of client-centred therapy to *require* individual therapy of the trainee' (p. 438, our emphasis); it is this issue of requirement that has been — and is — the subject of considerable debate within the BRITISH ASSOCIATION FOR COUNSELLING and (now) PSYCHOTHERAPY, following its introduction (in 1998) of the requirement of 40 hours personal therapy for counsellors seeking individual accreditation (see TRAINING THERAPY). Given the emphasis in PCP and PCT on developing and deepening the personal ATTITUDES AND QUALITIES of the therapist, such PERSONAL DEVELOPMENT is viewed as an essential and integral part of the course and best conducted in a group setting.

Person-Centered Journal, The   an international journal, founded in 1992 and sponsored by the ASSOCIATION FOR THE DEVELOPMENT OF THE PERSON-CENTERED APPROACH, co-edited by Jerold Bozarth and Fred Zimmring (1992–94), and edited by Jerold Bozarth (1995–96), Jeanne Stubbs (1997), Laura Jeanne Maher (1998) and Jo Cohen Hamilton (1998–) (see Appendix 2).

Person-Centered Review   an international journal of research, theory and application, edited by David Cain and published quarterly (1986–90) until it become economically unprofitable (see PERSON-CENTERED JOURNAL).

person-centred approach   literally an *approach* to the PERSON, as Wood (1996) puts it:

> it is neither *a psychotherapy* nor a *psychology*. It is not a *school* ... itself, it is not a movement ... it is not a philosophy. Nor is it any number of other things frequently imagined. It is merely, as its name implies, an *approach*, nothing more, nothing less. It is a psychological posture, if you like, from which thought or action may arise and experience be organized. It is a 'WAY OF BEING' (pp. 168–9);

first used by Rogers in 1977 (see Rogers, 1978), the PCA is the current term used in favour of CLIENT-CENTRED THERAPY and, before that, NON-DIRECTIVE THERAPY and RELATIONSHIP THERAPY, terms which reflect and in many ways represent the historical development of the approach (see Wood, 1996; Barrett-Lennard, 1998); see also CRITICISMS OF THE PERSON-CENTRED APPROACH, MISCONCEPTIONS OF THE PERSON-CENTRED APPROACH, PRINCIPLES OF THE PERSON-CENTRED APPROACH, RESEARCH, PERSON-CENTRED APPROACH, STRUCTURE OF THE PERSON-CENTRED APPROACH.

person-centred approach, criticisms of the as with any approach to or 'school' of psychology and therapy, the approach is open to criticism which it needs to address; unfortunately, all to often, supposed criticisms are based on simple (and, it appears, wilful) misunderstandings and MISCONCEPTIONS of the approach — for the correction of some of which see Barrett-Lennard (1983); both Thorne (1992) and Wilkins (in preparation) address and rebut common criticisms of the approach, which include:

- its overly positive view of HUMAN NATURE (e.g. Skinner in Kirschenbaum and Henderson, 1990a; Wheeler in Wheeler and Mcleod, 1995) — for responses to which see Barrett-Lennard (1983), Thorne (1992) and Wilkins (in preparation);
- its overly optimistic belief in the ACTUALISING TENDENCY, and ORGANISMIC VALUING PROCESS (Quinn, 1993) — see DESTRUCTIVENESS and Ford (1994);
- its 'self-worship' (Buber in Kirschenbaum and Henderson,

1990a; Vitz, 1977) — see Thorne (1992);
- its monocultural roots (Holdstock, 1990, 1993; Laungani, 1999) — see CULTURE, Mearns and Thorne (2000) and Wilkins (in preparation);
- its modernism and in particular its 'pretension to universality', especially as regards REALITY, SELF-ACTUALISATION and the concept of the FULLY FUNCTIONING PERSON (Jones, 1996) — see Van Kalmthout (1995) and ECOPSYCHOLOGY.
- its paradigmatic disparity (Ellingham, 1997, 1999a);
- its misguided naivity, especially regarding POWER and the THERAPEUTIC RELATIONSHIP and the nature of EVIL (e.g. Buber in Kirschenbaum and Henderson, 1990a; Masson, 1989) — see Thorne (1992);
- its (and Rogers') benevolence (Masson, 1989) — see Thorne (1992) and Wilkins (in preparation);
- its (and Rogers') retreat from external principles (Holland, 1977);
- its lack of genuine MUTUALITY (e.g. Van Belle, 1980; Masson, 1989) — see Thorne (1992);
- its lack of a theory of HUMAN growth and DEVELOPMENT (Wheeler in Wheeler and Mcleod, 1995) — see Rogers (1959), Biermann-Ratjen (1998b) and Cooper (2000);
- its insufficient theory of PERSONALITY and PSYCHOPATHOLOGY (Cain, 1993) — see Raskin (1996a), Barrett-Lennard (1998), Wilkins (in preparation);
- its lack of rigour in RESEARCH (Watson, 1984) — see Thorne (1992);

- the lack of evidence for the NECESSITY AND SUFFICIENCY OF THE THERAPEUTIC CONDITIONS (e.g. Lazarus, 1993) — see Bozarth (1993) and Wilkins (in preparation);
- its reliance on EMPATHY (Nye, 1986) — see Thorne (1992);
- the insufficient importance given to TRANSFERENCE and the UNCONSCIOUS (e.g. Tobin, 1991) — see Thorne (1992), Coulson (1995), Wilkins (1997b) and Wilkins in preparation);
- its disregard for ASSESSMENT (Wheeler in Wheeler and McLeod, 1995) — see Cain (1989) and Wilkins (in preparation).

person-centred approach, development of the birth of client-centred therapy is dated as 11 December 1940 when Rogers gave a talk at the University of Minnesota, entitled 'Newer Concepts in Psychotherapy', the intensity of the reaction to which he was surprised him:

> I was totally unprepared for the furor the talk aroused. I was criticized, I was praised, I was attacked, I was looked on with puzzlement ... it really struck me that perhaps I was saying something new that came from *me*; that I was not just summarizing the viewpoint of therapists in general (quoted in Kirschenbaum, 1979, p. 113).

Only ten years later Rogers (1951) was reviewing developments in CCT, observing similar work taking place in other centres, principally deriving from the work of Otto Rank (see RANKIAN THERAPY), and noting the applications of the NON-DIRECTIVE approach to work with children (see PLAY THERAPY) and with GROUPS, and in EDUCATION. In their review of the history of the PCA, Zimring and Raskin (1992) divide the first 50 years into four major periods, comprising four decades from the 1940s to the 1970s: (1) the first beginning in 1940 with Rogers' talk at the University of Minnesota (subsequently published in Rogers, 1942) and characterised by the development of two aspects of the therapist's role: that of responding to feelings (as distinct from content) and the acceptance, recognition and clarification of positive, negative and ambivalent feelings; (2) the second decade beginning in the 1950s with the publication of *CLIENT-CENTERED THERAPY* (Rogers, 1951), in which time Rogers outlined the framework and structure of the client-centred approach (Rogers, 1959), his hypothesis for therapy and therapeutic change and, specifically, the NECESSARY AND SUFFICIENT CONDITIONS (Rogers, 1957, 1959); (3) the third period of the 1960s is marked by the publication of *ON BECOMING A PERSON* (Rogers, 1961), the title of which conveys the direction of Rogers' interest and thinking with its emphasis on EXPERIENCE and EXPERIENCING, BEING and BECOMING; the importance and the development of the concept of CONGRUENCE may be traced back to this period; (4) the fourth decade and phase is characterised by an increasing interest in and emphasis on the applications of the principles of client-centred *therapy* to other areas and arenas of life such EDUCATION (Rogers, 1969, 1983), GROUPS (Rogers 1970), CONFLICT resolution, etc. and the phrase PERSON-CENTRED APPROACH becomes more widely used. Lietaer (1990) suggests that the termination of the Wisconsin project (see *THE THERAPEUTIC RELATION-SHIP AND ITS IMPACT*) was a crucial moment in the history of the approach, subsequent to which four discernible 'factions' within or associated with the approach may be traced:

1. a group around Rogers, then based in the CENTER FOR THE STUDIES OF THE PERSON, and who continued to develop the philosophy and practice of the approach;

2. a group around Eugene Gendlin who developed FOCUSING and EXPERIENTIAL THERAPY in the European tradition of EXISTENTIAL philosophy;

3. a group around Charles Truax and Robert Carkhuff who developed an eclectic model of the helping relationship (see Truax and Carkhuff, 1967; Patterson, 1985);

4. a group around David Wexler and Laura Rice who chose COGNITIVE learning PSYCHOLOGY as a theoretical framework for their development of the PCA (see Wexler and Rice, 1974).

Such developments are controversial, welcomed by some and disputed and despaired of by others: 'each of the neo-Rogerian methods takes something away from the thorough-going belief in the self-directive capacities that is so central to client-centered philosophy' (Raskin, 1987, p. 460). Two further reviews summarise the theoretical developments of the PCA: Raskin (1996a) identifies 20 historical steps in the development of PCT and Mearns (1997) offers a comprehensive understanding of the theory of the approach. In his stock-taking, Raskin (1990) sees both strengths and weak-nesses in the person-centred movement and attempts to account for the decline in its popularity, especially in the United States. The comparative strength of the PCA, especially in Europe, is reflected in the number of books — ten — published in English in the past four years: Barrett-Lennard (1998), Rennie (1998), Thorne (1998a), Thorne and Lambers (1998), Fairhurst (1999), Lago and MacMillan (1999), Merry (1999), O'Leary (1999), Mearns and Thorne (2000), Marques-Teixeira (2000) and Wyatt (2001), in addition to which four books of reprinted papers have been published (Bozarth, 1998b; Patterson, 2000e; Gaylin, 2001; Natiello, 2001) and, to date, a further seven books are known to be in preparation. Mearns and Thorne (2000) argue that one reason for the establishment of the PCA, especially in institutional domains in Britain and mainland Europe, is its engagement with professionalism.

person-centred approach, misconceptions of the despite an impressive body of literature, including RESEARCH, widespread misunderstandings and misconceptions of the approach persist; reflecting on this Mearns and Thorne (2000) conclude that

> such misconceptions are not always the outcome of ignorance but in some cases, at least, have much deeper roots. It would seem that our approach has the strange capacity to threaten practitioners from other orientations so that they seek refuge in wilful ignorance or in condemnatory dismissiveness (p. x).

a criticism applicable equally to some *within* the approach (see Tudor,

2000). In a paper specifically addressing questions and misconceptions, Barrett-Lennard (1983) identifies and corrects a number of points, including: the simplicity of MIRRORING; the exclusivity of REFLECTION; the totality of therapist GENUINENESS or transparency; the equation of UNCONDITIONAL POSITIVE REGARD with ACCEPTANCE; the (classic and 'straw') misconception of the necessity and sufficiency of the CORE CONDITIONS; the naivety of a belief in the essential GOODNESS OF HUMAN NATURE and human beings; the inapplicability of the approach to work with PSYCHOTIC patients/clients (see CRITICISMS OF THE PERSON-CENTRED APPROACH).

person-centred approach, politics of the see POLITICS OF THE PERSON-CENTRED APPROACH.

person-centred approach, principles of the although much disputed, in part due to the anti-dogmatic nature of the approach, what are referred to by Sanders (2000) as its 'primary principles' are: the primacy of the ACTUALISING TENDENCY, the assertion of the necessity and sufficiency of the THERAPEUTIC CONDITIONS, and the primacy of the NON-DIRECTIVE attitude (at least in content but not necessarily process); Sanders distinguishes these from secondary principles such as AUTONOMY, equality and HOLISM.

person-centred approach, structure of the this refers to the general structure of the PCA or, as Rogers (1959) originally formulated it, the client-centred framework. It comprises:

1. a theory of therapy, including the nature of the human ORGANISM and the CONDITIONS, PROCESS and OUTCOMES of therapy;

2. a theory of PERSONALITY;

3. a theory of the FULLY FUNCTIONING PERSON;

4. a theory of interpersonal RELATIONSHIPS.

Rogers also identified a number of theoretical applications of the CCA, i.e.

5. FAMILY life;
6. EDUCATION/LEARNING;
7. GROUP LEADERSHIP; and
8. GROUP CONFLICT.

Regarding the structure of the approach, it is interesting to note that Rogers (1959) acknowledged that 'the possibility of magnification of error in the theory increases as one goes out from the center [i.e. the theory of therapy]' (p. 193).

Person-Centred Practice the journal of the BRITISH ASSOCIATION FOR THE PERSON CENTRED APPROACH, founded in 1993 and edited by Tony Merry (see Appendix 2).

person, emerging synonymous with, and a more accurate construct than, a the FULLY FUNCTIONING PERSON, the characteristics of which are: OPENNESS TO EXPERIENCE, a trust in one's ORGANISM, an INTERNAL LOCUS OF EVALUATION and a willingness to be a process (rather than a product or a goal); also akin to the PERSON OF TOMORROW (Rogers, 1980) (see also A WAY OF BEING, the POLITICAL PERSON).

person, fully functioning synonymous with optimal PSYCHOLOGICAL ADJUSTMENT, complete CONGRUENCE and complete EXTENSIONALITY, and characterised by: openness to experience, the ability to live in the present and be attentive to each moment, and trust in organismic EXPERIENCING (that is, what *feels* right is a valid guide to BEHAVIOUR); the theoretical or ideal state of

105

optimal functioning in which a person's total potential for creative living has become fully ACTUALISED or MATURE (see Rogers, 1959), indeed, the concept of the fully functioning person developed from this concept of maturity, and is intended as an ideal state towards which a person grows or could grow throughout their life. Harman (1997) suggests that, in the last decade of his life, Rogers (1980a) broadened his conceptualisation of the fully functioning person to encompass new discoveries about the nature of human potentialities (see SPIRITUALITY).

person of tomorrow   akin to the EMERGING PERSON and the POLITICAL PERSON, Rogers (1980a) describes 12 qualities of such a person:

1. OPENNESS;
2. caring;
3. having a desire for AUTHENTICITY;
4. a scepticism regarding SCIENCE AND TECHNOLOGY;
5. a desire for WHOLENESS;
6. the wish for intimacy;
7. a closeness to and caring for nature;
8. an authority within;
9. a yearning for the SPIRITUAL;
10. being a PROCESS person;
11. being anti-institutional; and
12. being fundamentally indifferent to material things.

person, political   akin to the EMERGING PERSON and the PERSON OF TOMORROW; Rogers (1978) talks about 'a new political figure' gaining influence and fostering an EMERGING CULTURE; Frenzel and Przyborski (1983) discuss the significance of the POLITICAL implications of the PCA, and specifically on the evolutionary process of individual politicisation, which involves:

1. the recovery of a clear perception of the SELF;
2. the development of AUTONOMY and courage;
3. the development of hope and a positive vision;
4. the experience of relatedness and RESPONSIBILITY.

Person to Person: The Problem of Being Human   written by Rogers and Barry Stevens with contributions from Eugene Gendlin, John Shlien and Wilson Van Dusen and first published in 1967, the book interleaves papers written by Rogers and his associates with Stevens' personal 'warm, human reaction' to the papers; Rogers' own writings on VALUES, FREEDOM and the INTERPERSONAL RELATIONSHIP are followed by three contributions on work undertaken with people diagnosed as having SCHIZOPHRENIA.

phenomenal field   all that a person experiences (and, therefore, synonymous with 'experiential field'), 'whether or not these experiences are consciously perceived' (Rogers, 1951, p. 483); in this private world of experience only a small part of that experience is consciously experienced, although a large portion is *available* to CONSCIOUSNESS; those parts of EXPERIENCE that are available to consciousness, but not yet conscious (see PRECONSCIOUS and SUBCEPTION) may become so if the needs of the person cause them to become conscious 'because they are associated with the satisfaction of a need' (ibid., p. 483). This private world can be completely known only to the individual themselves, no other person can fully know how an experience was perceived by any other person: 'the world of experience is for each individual, in a very significant sense, a private world' (ibid., p. 484). Total familiarity with the world of experience remains only a potential; many impulses and sensations can be permitted into AWARENESS only under certain conditions: awareness and knowledge of the total phenomenal field is, therefore, limited.

phenomenology an approach to psychology (and other SCIENCES) based on the study of immediate experience; developed by Edmund Husserl, this form of analysis is concerned with how events are PERCEIVED, EXPERIENCED and given meaning; meaning, therefore, is derived from understanding individuals' relationships with and reactions to events (see EMPATHY). Although Rogers did not identify himself with phenomenology or phenomenologists (see EXISTENTIALISM and HUMANISM), his THEORY OF PERSONALITY is a phenomenological one as it is concerned with understanding individual perceptions of 'REALITY', indeed, Spinelli (1989) refers to the PCA as 'clinical phenomenology' (for a summary and synthesis of phenomenological psychology see Patterson, 1965, 2000d); also, the fact that EMPATHIC UNDERSTANDING has such a significant part in CCT and the PCA suggests that this tradition draws on the basic tenets of phenomenology; the relevance of a phenomenological attitude when working with PSYCHOTIC people is explored by Deleu and Van Werde (1998) (see also PRE-THERAPY).

play therapy used especially in working with children, a form of therapy which employs play as its primary (even exclusive) form of relationship, communication and understanding (or analysis); more commonly associated with the PSYCHOANALYTIC tradition (and the work of Melanie Klein, Anna Freud, Donald Winnicott and neo-Jungians), play therapy nonetheless also has humanistic roots (see Taft, 1933; Allen, 1942). In her first book Virginia Axline, one of Rogers' doctoral students at OHIO STATE UNIVERSITY and later a colleague at the UNIVERSITY OF CHICAGO COUNSELING CENTER, acknowledged the influence of Roge'rs NON-DIRECTIVE counselling on her own development of play therapy (Axline, 1947); she later wrote *Dibs — In Search of Self* (Axline, 1964/71), the story of an emotionally lost child (often referred to as autistic) and his personality development through play therapy; Rogers includes a chapter on play therapy (Dorfman, 1951) in his *CLIENT-CENTERED THERAPY*.

politics is concerned with '*power and control*': with the extent to which persons desire, attempt to obtain, possess, share or surrender power or control over others and/or themselves ... It has to do with the *locus of decision-making power*' (Rogers, 1978, p. 4) (see PERSONAL POWER, POLITICS OF THE PERSON-CENTRED APPROACH and POWER).

politics of the person-centred approach, the 'is a conscious renunciation and avoidance by the therapist of all control over, or decision-making for, the client. It is the facilitation of self-ownership by the client and the strategies by which this can be achieved; the placing of the locus of decision-making and responsibility for the effects of these decisions. It is politically centered in the client' (Rogers, 1978, p. 14). The openness of the approach, e.g. in recording and publishing transcribed therapeutic interviews and the demystification of the nature of therapy; the emphasis on the AUTHORITY of the client and the focus on *their* process; the MUTUALITY of the THERAPEUTIC RELATIONSHIP; and the application of the approach to resolving conflict at personal, micro as well as at social, macro levels — all represent and reflect the politics of the approach (see PERSONAL POWER; POLITICS, POWER; Rogers, 1978; Natiello, 1990, 1999a, 1999b, 2001; Tudor, 1997).

portrayal the tendency for a person, specifically a therapist in training, to 'portray' themselves as warm, empathic and acceptant. Mearns (1997) views this as working at a level of SURFACE RELATIONAL COMPETENCE, a level which is challenged and deepened through training and PERSONAL DEVELOPMENT to a point where the therapist is working at RELATIONAL DEPTH.

positive regard technically, the positive difference in one person's perceptual field as a result of perceiving the self-experience of another; this may be unilateral (given or received) or reciprocal; Rogers (1959) cites Standal (1954) who argues that, as with SELF-REGARD and POSITIVE SELF REGARD, this is a secondary or learned need rather than an inherent or instinctive human need; he also suggests that the term 'positive regard' selects 'the significant psychological variable' from other, broader terms such as LOVE etc. (see UNCONDITIONAL POSITIVE REGARD). Rogers (1959) makes several points about positive regard:

1. The need for positive regard is universal, pervasive and persistent.

2. Its satisfaction is inevitably based on inferences regarding the experiential (or PHENOMENAL) FIELD of the other, i.e. whether it includes you or not — and thus its satisfaction is ambiguous.

3. It is associated with a wide range of the individual's experiences.

4. It is reciprocal in that in satisfying someone else's need for such regard, the instigator thereby satisfies their own need for positive regard.

5. It is potent in that it enhances the REGARD COMPLEX, so much so that a person's desire to positively regard another may become more compelling than their own ORGANISMIC VALUING PROCESS (see also CONDITIONS OF WORTH).

positive self-regard the term used to denote 'a positive regard satisfaction which has become associated with a particular self-experience or a group of self-experiences, in which this satisfaction is independent of positive regard transactions with social others' (Rogers, 1959, p. 209); the internal sense or experience of this appears at least initially dependent on others, although this results in a positive attitude towards the self which is sustainable independently of others (see SELF-REGARD) and in this sense the individual becomes her/his 'significant social other'.

postmodernism literally, 'after modernism', a term with many different meanings and nuances applied to and represented in a wide variety of fields and disciplines (philosophy, sociology, the arts, etc.); in psychology, the 'postmodern turn' has challenged many 'modernist' (pre)conceptions including notions of demonstrably valid (and universal) knowledge about a knowable world; parallel to discussions of its relevance and impact on other therapies and therapists, postmodernism is the subject of some debate within the PCA: Jones (1996) suggests that 'Rogers' theory is allied to the principles of modernist thought' (p. 19) and takes up the challenge of a post-modernist critique to offer an alternative description of person-centred practice; Ellingham (1998, 1999b) is critical of the 'porridge' of postmodernism; and Mearns and Thorne (2000) wonder whether person-centred therapists have a stake in the question of postmodernism 'for it could justifiably be claimed that we still remain faithful to a metanarrative even if that narrative insists on the uniqueness of subjective truth' (p. 9).

power   literally, the ability to do something, it has come to have a negative connotation in a number of fields including psychology and therapy of 'power over' as distinct from 'power to ...'; in PCP PERSONAL POWER is viewed as positive and desirable and based on the premise of 'man' as a trustworthy ORGANISM (see also POLITICS). Natiello (1990) talks in terms of an equality of power in relationship, describing co-operative or COLLABORATIVE POWER as characterised by:

1. openness (all information is fully shared);
2. responsiveness (all needs and ideas are carefully heard);
3. dignity (everyone is respected and considered);
4. personal empowerment (each person has both freedom and responsibility to participate fully);
5. alternating influence (the impact on process is shared);
6. co-operation rather than competition.

power, personal   'the ability to act effectively under one's own volition rather than under external control. It is a state wherein the individual is aware of and can act upon his or her own feelings, needs, and values rather than looking to others for direction' (Natiello, 1987, p. 210); see CARL ROGERS ON PERSONAL POWER (Rogers, 1978) and POWER.

preconscious   originally a Freudian concept of the CONSCIOUS–UNCONSCIOUS which describes that which is potentially available to our consciousness or AWARENESS; rather than giving it a name, Rogers refers to this simply and descriptively as that material which could at any time be called into consciousness, referring to the equivalent concept in GESTALT THERAPY of 'the ground' (as distinct from the conscious 'figure') (see Evans, 1975).

presence   in a paper published in 1986, Rogers described another characteristic in addition to the CORE CONDITIONS:

> when I am at my best, as a group facilitator or a therapist ... when I am closest to my inner, intuitive self, when I am somehow in touch with the unknown in me, when perhaps I am in a slightly altered state of consciousness in the relationship, then whatever I seem to do seems full of healing. Then simply my *presence* is releasing and helpful. There is nothing I can do to force this experience, but when I can relax and be close to the transcendental core of me ... at those moments it seems that my inner spirit has reached out and touched the inner spirit of the other (Rogers, 1986a, p. 137).

In describing this Rogers was aware of the mystical nature and reading of this account (see SPIRITUALITY); while this may be regarded as a quality, comparable to CONGRUENCE, UNCONDITIONAL POSITIVE REGARD and EMPATHIC UNDERSTANDING (see Thorne, 1992), it is certainly *not a condition* of the therapeutic process (see also MINISTRY and TENDERNESS).

pre-therapy literally a stage before therapy, defined and elaborated as a result of a concern that some groups of clients, e.g. those diagnosed or assessed as 'mentally retarded' or 'psychotic' are unable to form successful relationships with their therapists (Prouty, 1976); this results in the first of Rogers' six NECESSARY AND SUFFICIENT CONDITIONS OF THERAPEUTIC PERSONALITY CHANGE remaining unfulfilled, i.e. that client and therapist are not in psychological contact; indeed 'pre-therapy is a theory of psychological contact' (Prouty, 1994, p. 37). Extending person-centred theory and practice in this area, and drawing on the EXPERIENTIAL tradition of Eugene Gendlin, Prouty has concentrated on discovering ways in which clients could be helped to develop psychological contact with the World, Self and Other (Merleau-Ponty, 1962) (see also ANCHORAGE; Van Werde, 1998); Prouty describes contact on three levels:

1. first, reflections of concrete client behaviour and/or elements from the client's surroundings, by which the therapist makes contact with the client (see CONTACT REFLECTIONS);
2. the second level of contact is defined as a set of psychological functions called CONTACT FUNCTIONS necessary for therapy to begin — the contact reflections are designed to establish and enhance the client's three contact functions (reality, affect and communicative contact);
3. the third level of contact is described in terms of the behaviour of clients resulting from the development of contact functions (see CONTACT BEHAVIOURS), following the development of which clients are able to enter psychotherapy and are more likely to benefit from it.

Conceptually, pre-therapy may be regarded as located at stages 1 and 2 of Rogers' (1961) seven stages PROCESS CONCEPTION OF PSYCHOTHERAPY (see also Prouty, 1990; Van Werde, 1994). While widely viewed as a development of EXPERIENTIAL, if not person-centred method (see Prouty, 1994), pre-therapy and its techniques, especially contact reflections, are not without its critics and is the subject of some debate within PCP and the PCA in terms of the nature of CONTACT and RELATIONSHIP, its *pre*-therapeutic position, its guidelines or TECHNIQUES (see also NON-DIRECTIVE) and its preconceptions — see Bozarth (1998d) and Prouty (1999).

primary drives see DRIVES, PRIMARY.

principles of the person-centred approach see PERSON-CENTRED APPROACH, PRINCIPLES OF.

prizing used originally and synonymously with UNCONDITIONAL POSITIVE REGARD and CARING, prizing carries the emphasis of a non-judgemental warmth towards the individual: a prizing of the uniqueness of the individual, of the cluster of characteristics that comprise the particular person.

process used by Rogers to refer to the fluid and changing nature of organisms, including humans; similar to the concept of movement in PERSONAL CONSTRUCT PSYCHOLOGY, Rogers views 'being process' as a direction which describes 'that self which one truly is' (Rogers, 1961) and being a process person, someone who is keenly aware of the certainty of CHANGE, as one of the qualities of 'the person of tomorrow' (Rogers, 1980a) (see the EMERGING PERSON, SELF-ACTUALISATION and QUALITIES).

process conception of psychotherapy the process Rogers (1961) describes as moving from a point of FIXITY (or rigidity) to FLUIDITY, a flowing 'in motion' WAY OF BEING — a quality which Rogers acknowledged as a value: 'some people do not value fluidity. This will be one of the social value judgements which individuals and cultures will have to make' (p. 155). Although Rogers himself describes this *process* conception in *stages* (1 to 7), he identifies a number of distinct threads in his theory:

(a) FEELINGS — from remote and unowned to an individual 'living in the process of experiencing a continually changing flow of feelings (p. 156);

(b) the manner of EXPERIENCING — from remoteness and an inability to symbolise its meaning to living 'freely and acceptantly in a fluid process of experiencing, using it comfortably as a major reference for his BEHAVIOR' (p. 157);

(c) from INCONGRUENCE to CONGRUENCE;

(d) internal COMMUNICATION — from complete unwillingness to communicate self to self to 'a rich and changing awareness of internal experiencing' (p. 157);

(e) the cognitive maps of experiencing (see CONSTRUCTS) — 'from construing experience in rigid ways which are perceived as external facts ... toward developing changing, loosely held construings of meaning in experience, constructions are modifiable by each new experience' (p. 157);

(f) the individual's relationship to problems — from problems being unrecognised, with (therefore) no desire to change to living problems subjectively and responsibly;

(g) The individual's manner of relating — from AVOIDANCE of close relationships (which are often perceived as dangerous) to living openly and freely in relation to others, and in a way in which behaviour is guided by experiencing (and not the other way around).

As Barrett-Lennard (1998) has commented, 'the process conception evolved as the primary vehicle for study of client process in therapy' (p. 84) (see THERAPEUTIC RELATIONSHIP AND ITS IMPACT) with four scales representing the different component strands or threads. It was the 'scale for rating of experiencing' which informed the development of Gendlin's (1964) theory of personality change and his emphasis on the EXPERIENTIAL.

process identification the therapist's activity of drawing the client's attention to what they are doing, a process in which 'we shift our attention away from the meaning of clients' experience of meaning to the activity in which they are engaged *as* they experience that meaning' (Rennie, 1998,

111

p. 73) (see EXPERIENTIAL THERAPY and NON-DIRECTIVE THERAPY).

process of therapy the directions in which clients experience CHANGE in SELF-CONCEPT, feelings, ATTITUDES and BEHAVIOUR during successful therapy; Rogers (1959) postulated that if the client experiences the therapist's UNCONDITIONAL POSITIVE REGARD and EMPATHIC UNDERSTANDING and the CONDITIONS OF THERAPEUTIC PROCESS are met, then a process is set in motion which has 12 characteristic directions for the client:

1. increasing freedom to express feelings;
2. expressed feelings have increasing reference to the SELF;
3. increasing capacity to differentiate and discriminate the objects of feelings and perceptions;
4. expressed feelings increasingly refer to the incongruities between some experiences and self concept;
5. the threat of such INCONGRUENCE is experienced in awareness; in therapy this experience of threat is made possible by the therapist's unconditional positive regard, which is shown to the client's incongruence as much as to the client's CONGRUENCE and absence of ANXIETY;
6. feelings that have been denied to AWARENESS become fully experienced;
7. the client's self concept becomes reorganised to include experiences that have previously been DENIED to awareness or DISTORTED;
8. the client's self-concept becomes increasingly congruent with experience, and the self is able to include experiences which previ-

ously would have been too threatening; there are fewer distortions or denials because there are fewer experiences that are threatening, and defensiveness is decreased;

9. the client becomes increasingly able to experience the therapist's unconditional positive regard without such experience being threatening;
10. the client increasingly feels unconditional SELF-REGARD;
11. the client increasingly experiences themselves as the LOCUS OF EVALUATION;
12. the client reacts to experience more in terms of his or her ORGANISMIC VALUING PROCESS than in terms of his or her CONDITIONS OF WORTH.

Writing rather less formally, Rogers and Sanford (1984) describe the process as follows:

in a broad sense, the process may be described as the client's reciprocation of the therapist's attitudes. As he finds someone listening to him with consistent acceptance while he expresses his thoughts and feelings, the client, little by little, becomes increasingly able to listen to communications within himself ... Finally, as the client is able to listen to more of himself, he moves toward greater congruence, toward expressing more of himself more openly. He is, at last, free to change and grow in the directions that are natural to the maturing human organism (p. 1381).

For further discussion of this process see Rogers (1959) and PROCESS CONCEPTION OF PSYCHOTHERAPY.

process-oriented psychology an approach to psychology and life combining insights from mythology, Eastern philosophy and meditation, bodywork and Jungian psychology, which has been developed by Mindell (1982/90a, 1990b, 1992) and which emphasises AWARENESS of PROCESS through the development of METASKILLS; Mindell's (1990b) steps in awareness — channel perception, amplification, edges, altered states and dream and body work — have similarities to Gendlin's EXPERIENTIAL development of PCP, while his views on leadership (Mindell, 1992) parallel Rogers' on the role of the group FACILITATOR.

projection 1. the process by which a person ascribes their own traits, characteristics, emotions, thoughts, beliefs, etc. to another.

2. the perceiving of external events and stimuli in terms of one's own expectations, desires, characteristics, etc.

Originally formulated in psychoanalysis, this concept has become more widely used to describe both these processes and is found in PCP (in Rogers, 1942, 1987) (see also INTROJECTION).

psychoanalysis see PSYCHODYNAMIC THERAPY.

psychodiagnosis see DIAGNOSIS.

psychodrama a theory of therapy originating with the work of Jacob Moreno (who is acknowledged as one of the founding influences of HUMANISTIC PSYCHOLOGY); although generally both more structured and more directive than PCT, psychodrama has common philosophical roots with the PCA; Wilkins (1994) explores the common ground and practice between the two approaches, asking whether psychodrama can be 'person-centred' — a question which, more generally, echoes concerns about the INTEGRATION of different, and sometimes differing, theoretical orientations (see also ECLECTICISM).

psychodynamic therapy literally, therapy based on psychological theories which emphasise dynamic processes and in which motivation and drive are central concepts, often used synonymously with psychoanalysis, and based especially on theories developed by Sigmund Freud and Melanie Klein. There is some considerable debate as to the differences and similarities between PCT and psychodynamic therapy, which have serious implications for practice and TRAINING. It is argued that 'both focus on theories of unconscious causation, DEFENCES and unconscious processes of empathic perception' (Owen, 1999, p. 166), and they share similar values about the importance of the THERAPEUTIC RELATIONSHIP (although it is understood and conceptualised differently) and of therapeutic independence and NEUTRALITY. Differences centre on the different understanding of HUMAN NATURE and POWER and emphasis given to the UNCONSCIOUS, defences and TRANSFERENCE or 'transferential attitudes' (Rogers, 1951) and, from the person-centred perspective, the principle of non-directiveness and LEVELS OF INTERVENTIVENESS.

psychological adjustment 'congruence as viewed from a social point of view' (Rogers, 1959, p. 207); optimally, 'when the concept of the self is such that all experiences are or may be assimilated on a symbolic level into the gestalt of the self-structure' (ibid., p. 206).

psychological contact synonymous with CONTACT; although Bozarth (1996c) suggests that there is a significant difference between Rogers' 1957 and 1959 formulations of the necessary and sufficient conditions in which Rogers refers to psychological contact and contact, respectively, this does not account for the fact that the 1959 paper was actually written *before* the 1957 paper (see NECESSARY AND SUFFICIENT CONDITIONS) — the *psychological* of psychological contact appears, therefore, especially in the context of a paper written for a psychology journal, more emphatic than significant; the extended term 'psychological contact' is used more in the literature on PRE-THERAPY.

psychological disturbance, acquisition of the process by which a person's psychological functioning becomes impaired; one of the NINETEEN PROPOSITIONS (XIV) concerns itself directly with the acquisition of PSYCHOLOGICAL MALADJUSTMENT. In PCP, it is assumed that at the beginning of life an individual is fully CONGRUENT, i.e. able to admit all EXPERIENCING into AWARENESS without DISTORTION or DENIAL, and fully able to be expressive of such experiencing; later, the person encounters disapproval, rejection, or other threats and experiences ANXIETY in the face of the continuing need for POSITIVE REGARD. The formation of the person's SELF CONCEPT becomes conditioned by these negative experiences, external CONDITIONS OF WORTH become internalised, and the person looks for protection from further negative experiences; eventually, the conditioned self-concept may become so reinforced that the person becomes completely alienated from their 'TRUE' SELF. A condition of INCONGRUENCE now exists, and the person's psychological functioning is disturbed; Holdstock and Rogers (1977) express this process as follows:

> the continuing estrangement between self-concept and EXPERIENCE leads to increasingly rigid perceptions and behavior. If experiences are extremely INCONGRUENT with the self-concept, the DEFENCE system will be inadequate to prevent the experiences from intruding into and overwhelming the self-concept. When this happens the self-concept will break down, resulting in disorganization of behavior. This is conventionally classed as psychosis when the disorganisation is considerable (p. 136).

An alternative way of expressing the acquisition of disturbance is by reference to the ACTUALISING TENDENCY and its subsystem of SELF-ACTUALISATION; in other words, the person attempts to actualise the CONDITIONED SELF, which may run counter to the promptings of the actualising tendency (see also PERPETUATION OF PSYCHOLOGICAL DISTURBANCE).

psychological disturbance, perpetuation of the continuation of a high degree of reliance on the evaluations of others for a sense of SELF-WORTH or SELF-ESTEEM. People with an EXTERNAL LOCUS OF EVALUATION need to preserve a SELF-CONCEPT likely to attract approval or POSITIVE REGARD from others; ANXIETY, threat and confusion will be created whenever INCONGRUITY is experienced between the self-concept (with its internalised CONDITIONS OF WORTH) and actual experience; thus, whenever such anxiety arises (or is threatened), the person will tend to

DENY certain AWARENESSES or DISTORT certain perceptions.

psychological maladjustment occurs when the organism DENIES to awareness, DISTORTS or IGNORES significant experiences 'which consequently are not accurately symbolized and organized into the gestalt of the self-structure, thus creating an incongruence' (Rogers, 1959, p. 204); such adjustment or adaptation to the social environment is, in humanistic terms, the best the organism can do but is bad ('mal') in terms of the organism's INTERNAL VALUING PROCESS.

psychology, humanistic see HUMANISTIC PSYCHOLOGY.

psychopathology literally, the science or study of 'disease' of the psyche (soul or mind). Given its critical view of DIAGNOSIS, PCP has traditionally eschewed such study, preferring to frame its enquiry in terms of PERSONALITY and PSYCHOLOGICAL MALADJUSTMENT. However, in recent years, there has been an increasing interest in developing a PCA to health and illness — and mental health and illness — within which three strands may be discerned:

1. The first strand is represented by the interest in PRE-THERAPY work for those clients whose ability to make and maintain CONTACT is impaired (Prouty, 1994; Van Werde, 1994). This work has been undertaken and research with people diagnosed as having mental retardation, acute psychosis, chronic schizophrenia and multiple personalities.

2. The second is based on an expanded and developed concept of INCONGRUENCE (see Speierer, 1990; Lambers, 1994; Biermann-Ratjen, 1998a). Thus the more general NEUROSIS and PSYCHOSIS, as well as specific clinical 'disorders' (including those diagnosed in childhood) and personality disorders may be understood in and translated into the more descriptive concepts of PCP.

3. The third is based on Warner's work identifying three styles of *processing*: FRAGILE (Warner, 1991), DISSOCIATED (Warner, 1998) and psychotic.

psychosanology a neologism, inspired by Antonovsky's (1979) study of the origins of *health* (salutogenesis) rather than illness (pathogenesis), this term represents the study of the health of the psyche i.e. mental *health* (as distinct from PSYCHOPATHOLOGY) as reflected especially in Rogers' (1951) *THEORY OF PERSONALITY* and the concept of the FULLY FUNCTIONING PERSON (see also CREATIVITY, INTEGRATION; Gaylin, 1974; Seeman, 1984).

psychosis a disorganisation of BEHAVIOUR in response to breakdown in SELF-CONCEPT (see Holdstock and Rogers, 1977); from a person-centred perspective psychosis is more accurately *described* (than prescribed as in diagnostic and statistical manuals of mental illnesses and 'disorders') as an acute behaviour which is 'consistent with the DENIED aspects of experience rather than consistent with the self' (Rogers, 1959, p. 230). Once exhibited, the person adopts a *process* of DEFENCE in order to protect the organism against the painful awareness of such INCONGRUENCE (see NEUROSIS). Contrary to popular MISCONCEPTIONS, the subject of significant study and theoretical developments in the PCA (see Rogers *et al.*, 1967; Prouty, 1990,

1994; Teusch, 1990; see also SCHIZO-PHRENIA).

psychotherapy Rogers defined psychotherapy as providing a special kind of experience which enables the client to differentiate their phenomenal SELF, the tendency to maintain and enhance which is a NEED; he viewed psychotherapy as synonymous with COUNSELLING (see also CLIENT-CENTRED THERAPY).

Psychotherapy and Personality Change a book edited by Rogers and Rosalind F. Dymond with contributions by members or former members of staff of the UNIVERSITY OF CHICAGO'S COUNSELING CENTER, first published in 1954; the book's subtitle — *Co-ordinated research studies in the client-centered framework* — reflects its concern with RESEARCH, based primarily on using the (then) recently developed Q-SORT technique as a means of studying client changes through counselling; the elements of CHANGE investigated are: changes in the client's PERCEIVED SELF and the IDEAL SELF, PERSONALITY CHANGE, mental health status, SELF-AWARENESS, changes in attitudes towards others including ETHNOCENTRIC attitudes, MATURITY and MOTIVATION.

Q-sort a research tool developed by Stephenson (1953) as a means of providing some 'objective' evidence of an individual's perception of her/himself. The procedure is to give the subject a pack of cards on each one of which is written a statement or description of some personality characteristic. The subject is asked to sort the cards into a number of categories. Each category corresponds to a point on a continuum ranging from those characteristics that are least like the person to those that are most like her or him. The methodology requires the subject to sort the cards in accordance with a pre-determined distribution by placing a set number of cards in each category. This technique was used by Rogers and others (see PERSONALITY CHANGE) to show changes in the PERCEIVED SELF and the desired or IDEAL SELF during and after therapy (see also RESEARCH).

A detailed example of research which included use of the Q-sort technique is given in Rogers (1961). One hundred self-descriptive statements, each printed on a card, were given to clients. Examples of statements are: 'I am a submissive person', 'I don't trust my emotions', 'I usually like people', 'I am afraid of what other people think of me.' Clients were asked to sort the cards to represent themselves 'as of now' into nine piles from those most characteristic of themselves to those least characteristic. They were asked to place a certain number of cards into each pile to give an approximately normal distribution of the cards. The clients did this before receiving therapy, after therapy and again at a follow up point. Each time they sorted the cards they were also asked to do so in ways that represented the self they would most like to be, i.e. their IDEAL SELF. An 'objective' representation of clients' self-perception at various times was produced in this way, together with perceptions of their ideal self. The various sortings were then inter-correlated so that a high correlation between two sortings indicated a lack of change, and a low correlation indicated that change had taken place. Rogers was able to show, for example, that CCT results in changes to the SELF-CONCEPT, that

117

the perceived self becomes closer to the ideal self, and the self as perceived becomes more comfortable and adjusted.

The Q-sort technique has been criticised because it forces subjects to categorise statements about themselves with which they may not agree or which they feel do not apply to them as individuals. Others may feel that most of the statements do apply to them, yet they are unable to place them in what they feel to be the appropriate category because of the way they are required to sort the cards. Nevertheless, Rogers and his colleagues showed that reliable 'objective' evidence concerning the change process in psychotherapy was obtainable, and had been obtained for client-centred psychotherapy. Rogers also thought that the Q-sort and other similar methods could be used to research the processes involved in other therapeutic approaches. Whilst important in the history and development of PCP, this methodology is somewhat at odds with Rogers' later views about SCIENCE AND RESEARCH (see also HEURISTIC) and SUBJECTIVITY.

qualities synonymous with ATTITUDES, Rogers (1980a) describes the characteristic qualities of the person of tomorrow as involving: openness (see OPENNESS TO EXPERIENCE); desire for AUTHENTICITY; scepticism regarding science and technology; desire for wholeness; the wish for intimacy; being process persons or being in PROCESS; caring; caring and closeness towards nature; anti-institutional; trust in their own, inner authority; indifference to material comforts and rewards; yearning for the spiritual (see SELF-ACTUALISATION).

quantum theory a theory, originating in physics, which has a dynamic conception of the universe as an interconnected web of relations, it represents a paradigm shift from mechanistic to HOLISTIC conceptions of reality. The principles of this 'new paradigm' thinking include an emphasis on: relationships rather than parts, the inherent dynamics of relationships, PROCESS thinking, holistic thinking, SUBJECTIVITY, and AUTONOMY (see Capra, 1975). The three principles of 'self-organisation' identified by Capra (1982) — of self-renewal towards wholeness, of the human ORGANISM as dynamic system, and of self-renewal and self-transcendence — provide a framework for explaining life, behaviour and change which is familiar to therapists and which Bozarth (1991/98e) relates to the PCA which 'as a therapeutic paradigm [is] different from other therapy and growth-activating approaches' (p. 92) (see CHAOS THEORY, POSTMODERNISM).

questions person-centred therapists generally eschew asking clients questions for a number of reasons, the principal one of which is that, inevitably, questions are formulated from within the therapist's FRAME OF REFERENCE, e.g. being curious or being fact- or story-centred rather than person-centred. Also, by their very nature, questions are directive (see NON-DIRECTIVE) in that a client has to think to construct an answer (or to decide not to answer), even if the content of the answer is *about* feelings. From the therapist's perspective, at the moment of formulating and asking questions, the therapist is not listening and thus questions are one of the BLOCKS TO EMPATHIC UNDERSTANDING.

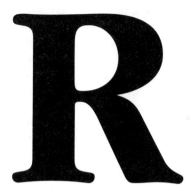

Rankian therapy a therapy, sometimes referred to as 'will therapy', based on the work of Otto Rank, the key principles of which are:

- that the person has creative powers or a will of their own;
- that a basic ambivalence e.g. between a will to health and a will to illness is an integral part of life;
- that the aim of therapy is an acceptance on the part of the client and the freeing of positive will through the elimination of blocks to CREATIVITY;
- that the patient is the central figure in the therapeutic process and is, in effect, their own therapist;
- that the therapist is in the role of ego helper or assistant ego;
- that the goals and therefore the focus of therapy is the experiencing of the present in the THERAPEUTIC RELATIONSHIP;
- that the end of therapy represents the growth towards independence and self-reliance.

deCarvalho (1999) discusses the influence on Rogers and the earliest formulations of the PCA (CCT) of Rank and 'the Philadelphia circle', one of whom was Jessie Taft, a student of Rank's, who later abandoned psychoanalytic interpretation and whose work was greatly influential on Rogers, especially during his years in the Child Study Department in Rochester, New York where she was a social worker and which Rogers directed. Although his knowledge of Rank's psychology was rudimentary, and he was not attracted to his 'theory' (Evans, 1975), Rogers was particularly influenced by Rank regarding individual integrity, the capacity for individual choice and a RELATIONSHIP THERAPY relying on the human QUALITIES of the therapist.

reading may be used as an aid to — even a form of — therapy (sometimes referred to as bibliotherapy), a process by which a therapist/librarian identifies books whose storyline may benefit the client; bibliotherapy dates back to the early years of the twentieth century and, along with its visual counterpart, cinematherapy, is enjoying something of a renaissance (see WRITING; Bentley, 2001).

real(ness) see CONGRUENCE.

reality that which is perceived — a perspective which places PCP within the PHENOMENOLOGICAL tradition.

reality contact one of three psychological CONTACT FUNCTIONS, identified within PRE-THERAPY as necessary for therapy to begin, consisting of clients' awareness of people, places and objects (see AFFECTIVE CONTACT and COMMUNICATIVE CONTACT).

real therapeutic relationship
see THERAPEUTIC RELATIONSHIP, REAL.

received empathy see EMPATHY CYCLE.

re-education a term used in many other approaches to therapy, in PCT it refers to 'sufficient practice in the application of new insights to build up the client's confidence and enable him to carry on in a healthy fashion without the support of the counselling relationship' (Rogers, 1942, p. 218). For Rogers, re-educative experiences are characteristic of the closing phases of counselling.

reflection, evocative a method, developed by Rice (1974) as part of the TECHNIQUE of REFLECTION OF FEELING, with the aim: 'to open up ... experience and provide the client with a process whereby he can form successively more accurate constructions of his own experience' (p. 290); viewed as a 'powerful tool', it is DIRECTIVE in terms of the quality of process (as distinct from the specific content) of the therapy, it has three characteristics of: particularity, SUBJECTIVITY, and its use of sensory, connotative language (see COGNITIVE PSYCHOLOGY).

reflection of feelings one of the processes in PCT of tentatively communicating the extent to which the therapist has empathically understood the feelings of the client, and specifically developed by those within the PCA who draw on COGNITIVE PSYCHOLOGY

as an example of EMPATHIC RESPONDING; Rogers expressed his unhappiness with the use of this term, though he admits to being partially responsible for its popularity. One concern was that 'reflection of feelings' had in some places been taught to trainee therapists as a technique 'and a fairly wooden one at that' (Rogers, 1986b, p. 375). A main objection to the term, however, resulted from Rogers explaining that, in fact, he was *not* trying to 'reflect feelings' but was

> trying to determine whether my understanding of the client's inner word is correct — whether I am seeing it as he or she is experiencing it at this moment. Each response of mine contains the unspoken question, 'Is this the way it is in you? Am I catching just the color and texture and flavor of the personal meaning you are experiencing right now? If not, I wish to bring my perception in line with yours' (pp. 375–6).

Terms preferred by Rogers were 'testing understandings' and 'checking perceptions'. However, another point of view is held by John Shlien who, in a letter to Rogers, defended the term:

> 'reflection' is unfairly damned. It was rightly criticized when you described the wooden mockery it could become in the hands of insensitive people, and you wrote beautifully on that point. But you neglected the other side. It is an instrument of artistic virtuosity in the hands of a sincere, intelligent, empathic listener. It made possible the development of client-centred

therapy, when the philosophy alone could not have. Undeserved denigration of the technique leads to fatuous alternatives in the name of 'CONGRUENCE' (quoted in Rogers, 1986b, p. 375).

A further problem is that the term tends to focus attention on only one aspect of a client's experiencing, i.e. feelings. Client-centred therapists try to understand and respond to the *totality* of a client's experiencing, i.e. everything within the client's present FRAME OF REFERENCE. This may include feelings but at different times it is likely to include thoughts, concepts, emotions, memories, fantasies and ideas, etc. To respond systematically only to feelings would be a form of directiveness, may not be particularly EMPATHIC, and would only ever give the client an incomplete sense of being understood; for another perspective, however, see EMPATHIC RESPONDING.

reflections, contact see CONTACT REFLECTIONS.

regard see UNCONDITIONAL POSITIVE REGARD (and CONDITIONAL POSITIVE REGARD, POSITIVE REGARD and POSITIVE SELF-REGARD).

regard complex as with POSITIVE REGARD, Rogers (1959) draws on Standal (1954) to define this as a construct which includes 'all those self-experiences, together with their interrelationships, which the individual discriminates as being related to the positive regard of a particular social other' (Rogers, 1959, p. 209). He continues: 'this construct is intended to emphasize the gestalt nature of transactions involving positive or negative regard, and their potency' (ibid., p. 209).

registration commonly, in the field of counselling and psychotherapy, the status given usually to qualified counsellors and psychotherapists (see UNITED KINGDOM REGISTER OF COUNSELLORS and UNITED KINGDOM COUNCIL FOR PSYCHOTHERAPY, respectively), following their fulfilment of sometimes additional criteria for registration and/or ACCREDITATION. Currently, such registration is voluntary, and moves towards statutory registration, have been heavily criticised (see Mowbray, 1995; House and Totton, 1997). In Britain, until recently with the introduction by Lord Allerdice of *The Psychotherapy Bill*, there appeared to be little political support for statutory registration and, generally, practitioners of the PCA take a critical and even sceptical view of moves towards the increasing professionalisation of helping activities.

reintegration describes a process, following BREAKDOWN and DISORGANISATION, 'which moves in the direction of increasing the *congruence* between SELF and EXPERIENCE' (Rogers, 1959, p. 230). Such reintegration or restoration of personality occurs only — and always — in the presence of THERAPEUTIC CONDITIONS in a variety of settings and intensity, i.e. in long-term or TIME-LIMITED THERAPY or relationships.

reiterative reflection see CONTACT REFLECTIONS.

relational depth a term coined by Mearns (1996, 1997) to describe the high and deep levels of PSYCHOLOGICAL CONTACT between the client and therapist, and contrasted with SURFACE RELATIONAL COMPETENCE. From the therapist's point of view, it is based on deep personal self-understanding (see CONGRUENCE and PERSONAL DEVELOPMENT) and a willingness to move to and to meet the client at deeper levels of contact and, from both the therapist's and the client's point of view, is characterised by subtle communication.

relationship the state of being related, usually with some implication of kinship; applied in the field of therapy to describe the condition or character of the contact between client and therapist — see THERAPEUTIC RELATIONSHIP/S.

relationship inventory designed by Godfrey (Goff) Barrett-Lennard, used to study the facilitative conditions present in relationships between therapists and clients, as well as in other relationships, e.g. between teacher and student. Results have provided some information on the extent to which relationship qualities affect other variables (Barrett-Lennard, 1962). Use of the relationship inventory is reported in Rogers (1961). Five variables were measured: the extent to which the client felt empathically understood; the level of regard or degree of liking of the client by the therapist; the unconditionality of the therapist's regard for the client; the CONGRUENCE or GENUINENESS of the therapist; and the therapist's psychological availability or willingness to be known. Results included conclusions that the more experienced therapists were perceived as having more of the first four qualities than the less experienced ones; in respect of 'willingness to be known', the reverse was true; in the more disturbed clients the first four measures were all significant in terms of the degree of personality change; EMPATHIC UNDERSTANDING was most significantly related to CHANGE; genuineness, level of regard and degree of unconditionality were associated with successful outcomes; willingness to be known was not found to be significant.

relationship, therapeutic see THERAPEUTIC RELATIONSHIP/S.

relationship therapy a term Rogers adopted from Jessie Taft and used, in the context of discussing traditional and older methods to describe 'a newer psychotherapy', referring to this as 'relationship therapy' (Rogers, 1942) (see RANKIAN THERAPY). He described basic aspects of this (new) therapeutic relationship as:

- warmth and responsiveness;
- permissiveness in regard to the expression of feeling;
- certain therapeutic limits, e.g. about time;
- freedom from pressure and coercion; and
- one in which the client has an increased ability to respond genuinely.

In this may be discerned the seeds of what Rogers later developed as the conditions of the therapeutic process which, in effect, describe and define the THERAPEUTIC RELATIONSHIP (see also Barrett-Lennard, 1998).

relationship, unspoken aspects of the psychotherapeutic relationship that are not referred to directly by either therapist or client. Mearns (1994) refers to the paradox that while CCT emphasises an open relationship, many thoughts and feelings (particularly those of the client about the relationship with the therapist) remain unspoken. Mearns also believes that it is those parts of the relationship which are the most difficult to access that may be the most therapeutically productive; see also Mearns and Dryden (1990).

relationships, functional the relationships between the several variables of Rogers' (1959) personality theory which Rogers described generally although not mathematically, equations for which he suggested would be a desirable development of the maturity of the theory. One example of such a relationship is 'the more actualizing the experience, the more adient the behavior' (p. 220).

relationships, law of interpersonal based on his theory of INTERPERSONAL RELATIONSHIPS, Rogers (1959) attempted to summarise this as one 'law':

> assuming a minimal mutual willingness to be in *contact* and to receive communications, we may say that the greater the communicated *congruence* of *experience*, *awareness* and behavior on the part of one individual, the more the ensuing relationship will involve a tendency toward reciprocal communication with the same qualities, mutually accurate understanding of the communications, improved *psychological adjustment* and functioning in both parties, and mutual satisfaction in the relationship. Conversely, the greater the communicated *incongruence of experience, awareness*, and behavior, the more the ensuing relationship will involve further communication with the same quality, disintegration of accurate understanding, lessened *psychological adjustment* in both parties, and mutual dissatisfaction in the relationship (p. 240).

relationships, theory of interpersonal describes the application of the PCA to all interpersonal relationships and communication. Rogers (1959) describes the conditions and process of a deteriorating relationship as well as those of an improving relationship principally in terms of the NECESSARY AND SUFFICIENT CONDITIONS, DEFENCES, SYMBOLISATION, etc. and elaborates the concept of incongruence or vulnerability *in the area related to communication*. Thus, a person may be congruent in other areas of their life but vulnerable and, to that extent, incongruent when communicating with people, or in a particular relationship, e.g. a couple or a family.

Renaissance the quarterly newsletter of the ASSOCIATION FOR THE DEVELOPMENT OF THE PERSON-CENTERED APPROACH.

research, person-centred approach to based on its approach to SCIENCE, person-centred research is characterised by a developing rather than pre-theorised mode of inquiry and is therefore generally HEURISTIC. Rogers himself was a great social scientist and PCP has a long and strong tradition of research which, indeed, is the basis of its original hypotheses which arose from the observation of work with clients. Rogers and his colleagues were the first psychologists to record client work. Rogers also used the Q-SORT method in order to describe and evaluate concepts and (Rogers, 1959) cites Chodorkoff's (1954) study approvingly in which Chodorkoff gives operational meaning to concepts such as SELF, EXPERIENCE, perceptual DEFENSIVENESS and personal adjustment. Rogers (1959) suggests a number of reasons why the client-centred approach is helpful in research terms:

1. that SCIENTIFIC study being a direction and not a fixed degree of

123

instrumentation means that such study can begin anywhere;

2. the constructs of the THEORY have been confined to those for which there are operational definitions; predictions can be made — and evaluated — in terms of these constructs, thus making the criteria of 'success' and 'failure' unnecessary;

3. The fact that these constructs have generality means that they can be studied in a wide variety of human contexts.

In 1956 Rogers himself was honoured by the American Psychological Association in receiving (along with Wolfang Kohler and Kenneth W. Spence) its first Distinguished Scientific Contribution Award; his citation included the reasons and acknowledgement for the award: 'for formulating a testable theory of psychotherapy, and for extensive systematic research to exhibit the value of the method and explore and test the implications of the theory' (cited in Kirschenbaum and Henderson, 1990b, p. 201). In the majority of its issues (from 1986 to 1990), the *PERSON-CENTERED REVIEW* carried articles on research, and devoted a special issue to 'Human Inquiry and the Person-Centered Approach' (Seeman, 1990).

resistance in traditional (psychoanalytic) therapy, any action that opposes the possibility of making CONSCIOUS that which is UNCONSCIOUS; in psychoanalysis, for example, resistance can include the tendency for a patient to oppose the analyst's interpretations. In CCT 'resistance' is thought to be a response to overzealous interpretation or intervention by the therapist, which is neither a desirable nor constructive part of therapy: 'resistance [is] an error of empathy on the therapist's side' (Speierer, 1990, p. 343) (see MOTIVATION).

responsibility the state or fact of being answerable or accountable to someone or some body (authority), a key concept in PCP in terms of its emphasis on people accepting responsibility for their own lives. This sense, as well as the practice of personal responsibility, extends to the SOCIAL and POLITICAL spheres (e.g. Rogers, 1982). From a person-centred perspective the THERAPEUTIC RELATIONSHIP is characterised by the experiencing of responsibility on the part of the client.

Rust Workshop, The a workshop on the theme of 'The Central American Challenge' which took place in Rust, Austria in November 1985, sponsored by the University for Peace and the CENTER FOR THE STUDIES OF THE PERSON (CSP), facilitated by Rogers and colleagues from the CSP (for a complete list of whom see Rogers, 1986e, p. 23, n), and comprising an invited group of fifty participants drawn from influential political, academic and other institutional spheres. The purposes, process and results of the workshop are well described by Rogers (1986e).

safety, psychological one of the two external conditions (the other being psychological FREEDOM) which Rogers (1961) proposed as a way of maximising the internal conditions which foster a constructive CREATIVITY; this, in turn, is established by three processes of: ACCEPTING the individual as of UNCONDITIONAL WORTH, providing a climate in which EXTERNAL (LOCUS OF) EVALUATION is absent, and understanding empathically.

schizophrenia a deep disturbance in relationship with other human beings. In diagnostic terms its symptoms include delusions, hallucinations, disorganised speech and grossly disorganised or catatonic behaviour (see American Psychiatric Association, 1994). People diagnosed with schizophrenia have been the subject of a number of research studies from a person-centred perspective (Shlein, 1961; Rogers, Gendlin, Kiesler and Truax, 1967; Teusch, 1990; Prouty, 1990, 1994) (see PSYCHOSIS and *THERAPEUTIC RELATIONSHIP AND ITS IMPACT: A STUDY OF PSYCHOTHERAPY WITH SCHIZOPHRENICS*).

science 'a *developing* mode of inquiry' (Rogers, 1959, p. 189) which, as a subject and a practice, moves towards more exact measurement, more rigorous theory and hypotheses, and findings which have greater validity and generality. Following Rogers, the PCP approach to science and scientific inquiry generally starts with EXPERIENCE, rather than pre-theorised constructs, and the observation of that experience, e.g. therapy, and then proceeds to hypotheses based on that observation (as was the case with practice which led to Rogers' hypothesis of the NECESSARY AND SUFFICIENT CONDITIONS OF THERAPY) (see also HEURISTIC). Given the emphasis in PCP and PCT on SUBJECTIVITY, and the view that we can never know objective truth (even if such a thing existed), it follows that there is no such thing as (objective) 'scientific KNOWLEDGE', 'only individual perceptions of what appears to each person to be such knowledge' (ibid., p. 192).

self a term which includes 'all of the individual perceptions of his organism, of his experience, and of the way in which those perceptions are related to other perceptions and objects in his environment and to the whole exterior world' (Evans, 1975, p. 16). This was Rogers' view of the self, in response to a question put by Evans who acknowledged Rogers to be one among the earliest group of individuals in psychology to emphasise the self. As in psychology in general, the term 'self' is used in a number of different ways in person-centred theory, in which three different aspects are discernible:

1.   The *emerging or developing self* — the self which is

> the organized, consistent conceptual gestalt composed of perceptions of the characteristics of the 'I' or 'me' and the perceptions of the characteristics of the 'I' or 'me' to others and to various aspects of life, together with the values attached to these perceptions. It is a gestalt which is available to awareness though not necessarily in awareness (Rogers, 1959, p. 200).

As an infant, experiencing is a relatively undifferentiated totality of sensations and perceptions that constitute reality for that infant. The development of the self essentially comprises this differentiation and the elaboration of the individual's being and functioning, through interaction with their environment, especially their significant others. The self is thus the inner, experiencing PERSON with reflective consciousness.

2.   *Self as self-concept*: interaction with significant others results in part of the infant's experiencing becoming differentiated into a self or SELF-CONCEPT. Perceptions become

discriminated as 'I' or 'me' or as being related to 'I' or 'me' — the PERSONAL SELF and SOCIAL SELF (Zimring, 1988) which Rogers termed SELF EXPERIENCES. According to Barrett-Lennard (1998), this is 'the self of construed personal identity, encompassing the self as observed (self-concept) and as desired' (SELF-IDEAL). Mearns and Thorne (2000) have developed an expanded concept of self which incorporates SUBCEIVED material (see EDGE OF AWARENESS) so that their definition of self is self = self concept + edge of awareness material. While they view this extended definition as important, they warn against the danger that distinguishing between the self and self concept 'could detract from the essentially phenomenological nature of person-centred therapy' (p. 175). At the same time, they believe that a widened concept of self enables an opportunity which

> lies in the tension which this difference creates between the client and therapist. The therapist has an eye not only to what the client is currently expressing as the contents of his Self but to those emerging elements not yet SYMBOLISED (P. 176).

Finally, Mearns and Thorne warn that in widening the person-centred concept of self, therapy could lose its discipline in holding to the edge of awareness and wander into the UN-CONSCIOUS ... an important and distinguishing feature of person-centred therapy is that it does not drift into the unconscious but works within the awareness and, we are suggesting, the *emerging* awareness of the client (p. 176).

3. The *self as agent* or *actor* — which symbolises the person's accumulated experience and acts on that, e.g. in adjusting behaviour; as an aspect of self theory this had more importance in Rogers' early work (e.g. Rogers, 1939).

In Western culture, the self connotes the individual; it has also become associated with an individualistic frame of reference and a self-centred 'me culture'. In response to this, Holdstock (1993) suggests revisioning and extending the person-centred concept of the self in a way which is (more) consistent with our global and postmodern society. Finally, while some person-centred theorists developed the notion of different selves, this did not have much meaning for Rogers himself. See also BEHAVIOUR, CHILD DEVELOPMENT, CONDITIONS OF WORTH, DEFENCE, INCONGRUENCE, POSITIVE REGARD, WE CONCEPT and other entries on SELF-. (*Note*: We are aware of the number of entries on and about aspects of the 'self' and, while wishing to represent PCP and PCT accurately, we do not wish to perpetuate an undue focus on the individual [see CRITICISMS OF THE PERSON-CENTRED APPROACH, CULTURE etc.]; as indicated in the Introduction, we view many of these entries as being equally applicable to phenomena beyond the individual such as couples, FAMILIES, GROUPS, ORGANISATIONS etc.)

self-actualisation 1. The motive to realise all of one's potentialities (originally introduced by the organismic theorist, Goldstein, 1940).

2. The final level of psychological development when the individual achieves actualisation (Maslow, 1954), although later Maslow (1967/93) came

to develop perspectives on the *process* of self-actualising. Maslow identifies eight ways in which one self-actualises:

1. *experiencing* 'fully, vividly, selflessly, with full concentration and total absorption' (p. 44);
2. making the choice for growth;
3. being discriminating;
4. being honest and taking responsibility;
5. listening to ourselves;
6. using one's intelligence;
7. allowing and recognising 'peak experiences';
8. exposing our psychopathology.

Often confused or conflated with the ACTUALISING TENDENCY, Ford (1991) makes the distinction clear: 'like the actualising tendency from which it is derived, the tendency towards self-actualisation is also motivationally invested in maintenance and enhancement; but its particular function is to maintain and enhance the SELF-STRUCTURE rather than the organism in general' (pp. 23–4). Seeman (1988) suggests reformulating self-actualisation so as to treat it as a metaphor (rather than as a concept) and to acknowledge it as a drive which stays within certain testable developmental laws or regularities (see ORGANISMIC SELF-REGULATION).

self-actualising tendency the conscious and unconscious tendency of (originally) the organism to maintain itself and to move to maturation. Rogers (1951) identifies the following directions of this movement:

- towards differentiation of organs and functions;
- towards expansion through growth and reproduction;

127

- towards greater independence and self-responsibility;
- towards increased self-government, self-regulation and autonomy (see also Rogers, 1978);
- towards socialisation.

See ACTUALISATION, ACTUALISING TENDENCY, SELF-ACTUALISATION.

self-awareness see SELF.

self-concept 'an organised configuration of perceptions of the self which are admissible to awareness, it is composed of such elements as the perceptions of one's characteristics and abilities; the percepts and concepts of the self in relation to the environment; the value qualities which are perceived as associated with experiences and objects; and goals and ideals which are perceived as having positive or negative value' (Rogers, 1951, pp. 136–7). In PCP this term is used mainly synonymously with SELF and SELF-STRUCTURE, although it is used to refer to the person's view of themselves, as distinct from SELF-STRUCTURE which refers more to how someone else views another (see also IDEAL SELF). In an interesting critique of Rogers, Holland (1977) explores Rogers' own self-concept, observing that throughout his life 'there is a clear direction here of retreat from external and religious principles into the self ... the theme of retreat is a constant one' (p. 71).

self, configurations of a term originally developed by Mearns (1999) to describe 'a number of elements which form a coherent pattern generally reflective of a dimension of existence within the Self' (p. 126). More recently, Mearns and Thorne (2000) have expanded this: a configuration 'is a hypothetical construct denoting a coherent pattern of feelings, thoughts and preferred behavioural responses symbolised or pre-symbolised by the person as reflective of a dimension of existence within the "Self"' (p. 102). This development of the self theory of PCP has conceptual similarities with OBJECT RELATIONS theory, to 'sub-personalities' (Rowan, 1990) and to ego state theory of TRANSACTIONAL ANALYSIS, and provides new ways of conceptualising the therapy process. Mearns and Thorne (2000) devote two chapters to a discussion of configurations of the self, demonstrating how this concept can be understood in a therapeutic context.

self-consistency while the SELF is not fixed, but is fluid and constantly changing in the light of new experiences, no matter how much change occurs, there remains within individuals a constant internal sense that they are still the same person at any given moment; thus there is a continuity of self over time: 'the very concept of selfhood hinges on the preservation of personal identity through time' (Davies, 1995, p. 16).

self-control internal, self-discipline; the free (constructive) use of power or 'power to the person' (see Rogers, 1978).

self-determination an aspect and quality of the ORGANISM, synonymous with AUTONOMY (see also EMERGING CULTURE).

self, development of see SELF.

self-disclosure the sharing or disclosure of some information a person has about themselves to another; in the context of therapy, usually on the part of the therapist to the client, it is sometimes confused with CONGRUENCE and SELF-EXPERIENCING, and overused; Kopp (1974), for instance, warns of 'indiscriminate frankness' (see SELF-INVOLVEMENT).

self-empathy see EMPATHY, SELF-.

self-esteem the value an individual has of her/himself which, in turn, relies on a SELF-CONCEPT to which to attach the value or esteem (see SELF-REGARD).

self-evaluation the giving of value by the subject her/himself, e.g. self-assessment by the student/trainee in student-centred learning (see ASSESSMENT).

self-experience 1. when experience is assimilated into the self-structure (Rogers, 1951); in general, these are the raw material of which the organised self-concept is formed;

2. the awareness of being and of functioning (Rogers, 1959).

self, false the conditioned self which develops in response to the internalisation of EXTERNAL CONDITIONS OF WORTH.

self, ideal 1. mainly synonymous with SELF-CONCEPT; the self-concept an individual would most like to possess and upon which they place the highest value.

2. the individual's projected view of their SELF-CONCEPT which has both realistic and unrealistic elements.

self-inconsistency the result of the individual admitting to awareness of values inconsistent with their SELF-STRUCTURE.

self-in-relationship a compound phrase which emphasises the context of the SELF and particularly that the self does not exist, differentiate or develop in isolation; this construct is widespread in the many collective cultures in the world.

self-insight 'the realistic acceptance of self and the realistic appraisal of the situation' (Rogers, 1990, p. 204) in which the individual finds her/himself, and synonymous with SELF-UNDERSTANDING.

self-involvement a term coined by Mearns and Thorne (1988) which distinguishes the appropriate communication of the therapist's self-awareness from SELF-DISCLOSURE (see CONGRUENCE).

self, organismic a term originally coined by Seeman (1983) and taken up by Mearns and Thorne (1988) which describes the 'real self' as distinct from the FALSE SELF, but one which generally and unhelpfully confuses and conflates the ORGANISM and the SELF.

self, personal the 'I' mode of the SELF which derives from the concept which one ('I') has about one's 'I' self (as distinct from the SOCIAL SELF); the self of agency (see Zimring, 1988).

self-psychology in general terms, any approach to psychology which places the SELF as the central concept. Fine (1986) describes self-psychology as constituting the fourth great wave in psychoanalysis (following object relations which succeeded ego psychology which, in turn, replaced Freudian drive theory). Self-psychology, as developed originally by Heinz Kohut, breaks from Freudian theory in arguing that archaic narcissism is not transformed into object-love but rather is a developmental driving force. Kohut postulated that if empathic responsiveness or attunement to the infant is provided by parents and/or significant others then the child transforms narcissistic experiences into a cohesive and dynamic self-structure, including healthy self-love. Self-psychology puts the self (rather than instinctual drives) at the centre of the psychological universe. In a personal perspective, Rogers

(1986c) himself commented on some similarities he saw between himself and Kohut (Rogers also included Milton Erickson in this comparative review).

One similarity Rogers identified with Kohut was their view of human nature as a constructive, assertive whole. Kohut's healthy re-reading and reclaiming of rage as a response to narcissistic injury (rather than an untamed aggressive drive) also finds resonance in Rogers' positive motivational psychology. While Rogers himself acknowledged that he shared with Kohut many common ideas about the self and the restructuring of the self through therapy, he criticises Kohut for (as Rogers viewed it) his lack of interest in the testability of his theories and specifically cites his theory of the 'grandiose self' and the 'idealised parent image' as an example of this, arguing specifically that we can never enter the infant's conceptual world to verify this and, as a more general critique of psychoanalytic theories, that they exist only in a speculative realm. However, Graf (1984) suggests that Kohut's self-psychology goes beyond Rogers', especially in his notions of creativity and healthy creative tension and idealising conceptual processes (guiding ideals and values) and concludes that a synthesis of Rogers and Kohut would 'create a more comprehensive humanistic theory of healthy self functioning' (p. 7). More recently, Tobin (1991) and Warner (2000b) offer articulations between PCT and self-psychology.

self-regard synonymous with SELF-ESTEEM (see also REGARD COMPLEX), viewed (arguably) as a secondary or learned need which, being experienced from others, results in a positive attitude towards oneself which then is no longer directly dependent on others (see POSITIVE SELF-REGARD and UNCONDITIONAL SELF-REGARD). A need for self-regard develops from the SELF-EXPERIENCE of the satisfaction or frustration of the need for POSITIVE REGARD. However, when a self-experience is sought only because it enhances or detracts from self-regard, the person is said to have acquired a CONDITION OF WORTH. Thus rebellion is the other side of compliance rather than freedom from it. When the individual comes to experience satisfaction/frustration independently, s/he becomes more her/his own 'significant social other'. Thus, the notion that someone is free from such conditions of worth when they do something *even though* their parents would approve, reflects an independent self-regard. As with positive regard, self-regard is communicated to and enhances the regard complex.

self-responsibility see RESPONSIBILITY.

self, socialised the 'me' mode of the SELF which derives from social — and socialised — experience which is then internalised; a recipient self (as distinct from the more active PERSONAL SELF) (see Zimring, 1988).

self-structure 'an organized, fluid, but consistent conceptual pattern of perceptions of characteristics and relationships of the "I" or the "me," together with values attached to these concepts' (Rogers, 1951, p. 498); mainly used synonymously with SELF and SELF-CONCEPT, although the term self-structure is generally used to refer to how someone else views another as distinct from the self-concept which refers to the person's view of themselves.

self-understanding synonymous with SELF-INSIGHT.

self-worth synonymous with SELF-ESTEEM.

seven stages of process see PROCESS CONCEPTION OF PSYCHOTHERAPY.

sexuality the quality of being sexual, and a subject notable by its absence from person-centred theory with the exception of a paper by Schmid (1996) in which he argues for an intentional sexuality (see CULTURAL PSYCHOLOGY) in the context of personality which 'in a person-centered sense does not mean ignoring sex, it means the congruent assignment of sexuality and personality' (p. 86); he goes on to develop a PCA to sexuality by discussing sexuality as ACTUALISATION; as ENCOUNTER; as variations of CONGRUENT and INCONGRUENT (alienated) sexuality; and the CONDITIONS for a fulfilled sexuality.

sharing-life therapy a term coined by Stamatiadis (1990) to describe a personal and extended way of being with clients in which the ways and means of working are developed from the process of therapy. These include what Stamatiadis refers to as verbal tools — the 'standard' therapeutic interview or meeting, taping sessions for the client and telephone calls; body tools — physical touching and holding, focusing, wrestling and walking; art tools — drawing and painting; dream work; and giving gifts. This takes place in a variety of time structures, including extended meetings and in a various settings outside the consulting room. The work is constantly negotiated with clear therapeutic limits, mainly to do with the therapist's commitment. It is a creative and intensive way of being and doing therapy and, judging by client reports, generally successful; it is also highly demanding of both client and therapist and, in the current defensive and litigious climate of therapy, challenging and rare.

situational reflections see CONTACT REFLECTIONS.

skill commonly viewed as practical knowledge in combination with ability, having a certain expertise, this also (and historically) refers to reason and the power of discrimination. In some circles in the field of counselling and psychotherapy, this is erroneously distinguished from 'THEORY' with the result that 'counselling skills' are viewed as separate and somehow separable from theory when actually such skills are based on and arise from the theory and philosophy of therapy. In PCP, 'skills' refer to the clear and AUTHENTIC communication of the therapist's POSITIVE REGARD and EMPATHIC UNDERSTANDING.

social development synonymous with socialisation (see SELF, SOCIALISED).

socialised self see SELF, SOCIALISED.

social issues there are clear social implications of the PCA which develop from its VALUES and especially OPENNESS and RESPONSIBILITY (see Rogers, 1960); in later life Rogers became more aware and more interested in the social and POLITICAL implications of the PCA and worked with GROUPS and LARGE GROUPS of people who were often in conflict and/or living in some of the world's 'hottest' areas of tension; see CROSS-CULTURAL COMMUNICATION WORKSHOPS, CULTURAL CONFLICT, RUST WORKSHOP (Rogers, 1986e), STEEL SHUTTER (McGaw, 1973).

spirituality that which has a spiritual character and, given that 'spirituality, especially its transcendent aspects, seemed to become more salient to

131

Rogers in his later life' (Menahem, 1996, p. 328), the subject of much debate within the PCA. As he himself acknowledged towards the end of his life, Rogers (1986a) discovered another 'characteristic' of a growth-promoting relationship:

> when I am closest to my inner, intuitive self, when I am somehow in touch with the unknown in me, when perhaps I am in a slightly altered state of consciousness in the relationship, then whatever I do seems to be full of healing. Then simply my *presence* is releasing and helpful (p. 198).

This concept of PRESENCE is akin to Thorne's (1985/91b) term TENDER-NESS. Thorne (1991a) identifies a number of parallels between the two concepts:

1. a high level of consciousness in the therapist;
2. a responsiveness to the intuitive;
3. an experience of relating at a new and deeper level;
4. an experience of the transcendent, in which there is
5. an overpowering sense of 'energy, well-being and healing' (p. 183).

Although both Thorne (1991b) and Menahem (1996) make the case that Rogers was equally aligned with the 'fourth' or transpersonal force in psychology, Thorne also acknowledges the suspicion that this characteristic — and Rogers' increasing interest in the transcendent, as well as reincarnation and cosmic consciousness (see Rogers, 1980a) — provokes. Proponents of the spiritual dimension in the PCT and the PCA include Arnold

(1984), Villas-Boas Bowen (1984), Thorne (1991b, 1998a), Morotomi (1998) and MacMillan (1999) while the sceptics include Van Belle (1990), Merry (1999) and Mearns in Mearns and Thorne (2000) (see EVIL). A number of practitioners have also discussed the relationship between the PCA and different spiritual and/or religious traditions, mostly drawing the conclusion that the basic tenets of the approach are highly compatible with beliefs and principles of a number of traditions: Buddhism (Harman, 1990, 1997; Brazier, 1995; Purton, 1996; Harman, 1997), Christianity (Thorne, 1998a), Taoism (Miller, 1998; Morotomi, 1998) and Sufi (MacMillan, 1999).

stages of process, seven see PROCESS CONCEPTION OF PSYCHOTHERAPY.

Steel Shutter, The a film, produced by William ('Bill') McGaw (1973), of an encounter group facilitated by Carl Rogers and Pat Rice, a psychologist, comprising four Catholic and five Protestant Irish men and women and one British soldier. The movement from bitterness, hatred, suspicion and mistrust to open, expressive communication and understanding is remarkable and touching — and controversial, as Rogers (1978) remarks: 'so rapid was the progress, so significant the changes, that some of the statements quoted ... had to be deleted from the film. To show such understanding of the opposition would have endangered the lives of the speakers' (p. 132) and, indeed, several original copies of the film were stolen (by, it is suspected, paramilitaries on both side of the 'divide'). After the film was completed, the group continued to meet and members of the group — one Catholic, one

Protestant — showed the film to a number of groups in their respective communities.

structure of the person-centred approach see PERSON-CENTRED APPROACH, STRUCTURE OF.

Studies of the Person the title of a series of books published from 1968 onwards and edited initially by Carl Rogers and William Coulson, a colleague of his at the WESTERN BEHAVORIAL SCIENCES INSTITUTE and co-editor of MAN AND THE SCIENCE OF MAN (Coulson and Rogers, 1968); Coulson continued as sole editor of the series after Rogers resigned in 1973.

subceive see SUBCEPTION.

subception a term Rogers adopted from McCleary and Lazarus (1949) to signify discrimination without awareness. In his discussion of PSYCHOLOGICAL CONTACT, the first of the six NECESSARY AND SUFFICIENT CONDITIONS, Rogers (1957) states that two people need to be to some degree in psychological contact such that each person makes a perceived difference in the experiential field of the other and that 'probably it is sufficient if each makes some "subceived" difference, even though the individual may not be consciously aware of this impact' (p. 96). This hypothesis is the basis for the various contact reflections of PRE-THERAPY work. For the practitioner working with clients who are in some way out of contact, e.g. catatonic, it may be useful to consider that her/his presence or her/his willingness to be present is, at some organic level, making a subceived difference to them.

subjectivity 1. 'the quality of dealing with objects and events as PHENOMENOLOGICAL, subjective experiences [and]

2. an approach to phenomena characterized by internal interpretation' (Reber, 1985, p. 742).

3. The emphasis in more recent philosophical and psychological debates is on the INTERSUBJECTIVE construction of the subjective as 'a pre-reflective opening out onto and engagement with alterity, rather than in an experience or objectification of it' (Crossley, 1996, p. 24).

supervision a forum and a relationship in which a therapist's work with clients is discussed with a more experienced colleague or with peers. Given the extent of literature about the philosophy and practice of, and learning in, CCT, PCT and PCP, comparatively and surprisingly little has been written about person-centred supervision. The following points summarise the PCA to supervision:

1. In CONDITIONS, PROCESS and OUTCOMES the supervisory relationship is essentially parallel to that which the supervisee (practitioner) is offering to the client in therapy (this is not the same as PARALLEL PROCESS); this both reflects the conditions and creates the growth-promoting climate in which the supervisee may freely explore their own feelings, issues, difficulties, etc. (see Rogers, 1956, p. 6).

2. Trust in the supervisee's capacity for SELF-DIRECTION and SELF-DETERMINATION is the basis of Villas-Boas Bowen's (1986) 'philosophy-of-life-oriented' supervision' (as distinct from a restrictive 'form-oriented' supervision) which emphasises the development of the INTERNAL LOCUS OF EVALUATION of the supervisee. On

the basis that the supervisee is a person in process and of trust in their potential for growth, Lambers (2000) emphasises and explores supervision as a relationship which supports the development of the therapist's CONGRUENCE in relation to their client.

3. Supervision focuses on the process and relationship dimensions of therapy, including the ATTITUDES and behaviour of the supervisee as therapist (see Rice, 1980; Villas-Boas Bowen, 1986) — and, in parallel, of supervision itself.

4. While person-centred supervisors do not DIRECT the supervisee as regards what they present for supervision, Patterson (1983) outlines three expectations he has of supervisees (trainee therapists) in their preparation for supervision: listening to taped interviews/sessions, making notes of particular sections they wish to play during supervision and of questions/problems they wish to raise; and, more recently, Conradi (1996) describes a procedure in supervision whereby the supervisee first describes the session in question from the perspective of the client's experience.

5. Similarly, person-centred supervisors generally do not assume or take as much RESPONSIBILITY for the supervisee's work as supervisors from other theoretical orientations, preferring to encourage responsibility in all parties and challenge traditional POWER dynamics, especially regarding authority and knowledge; nevertheless, indeed, *because* of

this perspective, supervisors need to be aware of any accountability and/or public/legal liability for the supervisee's work, the context of the work, and the supervisory contract (including any three-handed contracts whereby the supervisor may be accountable to a training institute or may be paid by an agency to supervise the practitioner); the issue of 'clinical responsibility' is a complex one, especially for supervisors and practitioners in the private/independent sector (see King and Wheeler, 1999).

6. There is a difference between providing a facilitative environment in which supervision takes place and the therapeutic effects of supervision, and offering therapy to the supervisee which, according to Patterson (1964) would be 'to impose counseling on a captive client' (p. 49) — and, in any case, is a dual role which is eschewed by most professional codes of ethics and practice for therapists; nevertheless, one purpose of supervision is to explore the effect of the practitioner's personal attitudes, VALUES and behaviours in enhancing or impeding the client in their growth or the course of the therapy (see THERAPEUTIC RELATIONSHIP).

7. Similarly, supervision is not the same as training, although it has an educative function, especially with regard to therapists in training (see Patterson, 1983).

8. While Patterson (1983, 1997), among others, asserts that it is necessary for the supervisee to be operating from the same theoretical base as the supervisor (and,

again, this is especially so in the case of therapists in training), supervision is also viewed as a meta-activity which may be applied across theoretical orientations and disciplines.

9. Merry (1999) regards person-centred supervision as a form of new paradigm research or 'collaborative enquiry' in which supervisor and supervisee participate as equals in an exploration of meaning derived from clinical experience (see CO-OPERATIVE ENQUIRY, INTERPERSONAL PROCESS RECALL).

supportive therapy one of the common misconceptions of PCP and PCT is that it is or offers (just or only) 'support' or 'supportive therapy'. While CCT may be experienced as supportive — Rogers (1951) characterises it as 'an island of constancy in a sea of chaotic difficulty' (p. 71) — it is not supportive or approving in the superficial sense in which this is often meant. In a philosophical sense, PCP is based on supporting the SELF and the person's INTERNAL VALUING PROCESS, a process which at times may well be experienced as unsupportive, for instance, of the SELF-CONCEPT.

surface relational competencies a term developed by Mearns (1997) to describe a number of competencies — partial or even accurate empathy, warmth, attention and communication of understanding — which are developed to a surface level (and which equate to competencies identified by National Vocational Qualifications and Scottish Vocational Qualifications) (see PORTRAYAL).

Sylvia a client with whom Rogers worked five times during different workshops; their fifth session was filmed and transcribed (Farber, Brink and Raskin, 1996). Uniquely, both Rogers and Sylvia reviewed their work together, their comments being incorporated into the final filmed version (Rogers, 1980b), further commentaries have been made by Cain (1996) and O'Hara (1996).

symbolisation the process whereby individuals make sense or meaning of their AWARENESS or CONSCIOUSNESS (terms with which it is synonymous). Accurate symbolisation is when the symbols which constitute our awareness correspond to REALITY (see PERCEPTION). Otherwise, symbols may be denied to awareness, distorted or ignored (see Rogers, 1951).

syntropy the opposite of ENTROPY, a term Rogers (1980a) used, acknowledging its source in the writing of Szent-Gyoergyi (1974), describing it as 'the ever operating trend toward increased order and interrelated complexity evident at both the inorganic and the organic level. The universe is always building and creating as well as deteriorating. This process is evident in the human being too' (Rogers, 1980a, p. 126).

technique the mechanical part of an art or science; SKILL or ability; while many within PCP and the PCA recognise that there are skills, abilities and even competencies to working as a psychologist or therapist (see THERAPEUTIC RELATIONSHIP), most place the emphasis on the person's ATTITUDES and eschew technique/s as such — for discussions of which see Rogers (1957), Bozarth (1996b) and Brodley and Brody (1996). Rogers himself identified client-centred techniques (as distinct from counsellor-centred techniques) as being appropriate and desirable: REFLECTION OF FEELINGS, simple ACCEPTANCE, structuring (regarding the THERAPEUTIC RELATIONSHIP), and giving NONDIRECTIVE lead (i.e. an initial open question) (Rogers and Wallen, 1946). In the context of his integrative statement about the NECESSARY AND SUFFICIENT CONDITIONS OF THERAPEUTIC PERSONALITY CHANGE, Rogers (1957) comments that: 'the techniques of the various therapies are relatively unimportant except to the extent that they serve as channels for fulfilling one of the conditions' (p. 102); on REFLECTING FEELINGS as a technique, he goes on to acknowledge that 'to the extent ... that it provides a channel by which the therapist communicates a sensitive empathy and an unconditional positive regard, then it may serve as a technical channel by which the essential conditions of therapy are fulfilled' (p.102); while viewing no value in techniques such as interpretation, free association, etc. in themselves, Rogers acknowledges that they *may* be 'channels' for these conditions — a comment which has led to much debate about the desirability (or otherwise) of incorporating techniques from other approaches (see ECLECTICISM and INTEGRATION); equally, such techniques 'may communicate attitudes and experiences sharply contradictory to the hypothesized conditions of therapy' (p. 103) (see LEVELS OF INTERVENTIVENESS, PRINCIPLES OF THE PERSON-CENTRED APPROACH).

tenderness a holistic quality, akin to PRESENCE, which Thorne (1985/91b) describes as irradiating the total person; communicating that suffering and healing are interwoven; which demonstrates a preparedness and ability to move between physical, emotional, cognitive and mystical worlds; which is without shame; and which, whilst transcending gender, is nourished by attraction. When this rare 'fourth quality' is present in a therapeutic relationship, Thorne suggests, 'something qualitatively different may occur' (p. 74). Although he does not view it as a fourth 'CORE CONDITION', Thorne considers its absence as indicative of some inadequacy in the offering of the three core therapeutic conditions. It becomes a possibility 'at the moment when two human persons meet and are able to give way to the liberating urge to trust without anxiety' (p. 81); see SPIRITUALITY.

tension see ANXIETY.

t-group a training group (hence 't'-group), initially established by Kurt Lewin, comprising volunteers (not clients) for the purposes of studying the qualities of the group — what he referred to as 'group dynamics'. This formed a part of his field theory (Lewin, 1952) whereby psychological relationships were viewed in terms of their surrounding field, in this case, the group which was understood as an entity in itself. Following Lewin's death some of his associates founded the National Training Laboratory (NTL) in Bethel, Maine, in which the t-group formed the basic instrument of education (see Gottschalk, 1966). Rogers recognised that the NTL did the real pioneering in the ENCOUNTER GROUP movement.

theory originally from words meaning *contemplation*, *speculation* and the *base of*, a mental view, a conception or scheme of something, held as an explanation, and often contrasted with SKILL/S. In his paper detailing his *theory* of therapy, personality and interpersonal relationships, as developed in the client-centred framework (Rogers, 1959), Rogers makes a plea for theory as 'a fallible, changing attempt to construct a network of gossamer threads which will contain the solid facts — then a theory would serve, as it should, as a stimulus to further creative thinking' (p. 191). Mearns (1997) asserts that in PCT

> there is no attempt to use theory to predict the behavior of an individual client. However, theory can be used by the person-centred counsellor to begin to understand the client's experience as reported by the client. The theory will not give a detailed understanding — only empathy can do that (p. 146).

therapeutic conditions see NECESSARY AND SUFFICIENT CONDITIONS OF THERAPEUTIC PERSONALITY CHANGE.

therapeutic process, characteristic steps in twelve characteristic steps or processes in therapy identified by Rogers (1942):

1. The individual comes for help.
2. The helping situation is usually defined.
3. The counsellor encourages free expression of feelings in regard to the problem.
4. The counsellor accepts, recognises and clarifies these negative feelings.
5. When these have been fully expressed, faint and tentative expressions of positive impulses follow.
6. The counsellor accepts and recognises these positive feelings.
7. Insight, understanding and acceptance of the self.

8. A process of clarification of possible decisions and courses of action.
9. The initiation of minute, highly significant, positive actions.
10. The development of further insight: more complete and accurate self-understanding.
11. Increasingly integrated positive action.
12 A feeling of decreasing need for help and a recognition on the part of the client that the relationship must end.

In a paper discussing these steps with regard to related process research studies, Barrett-Lennard (1990) reduces these to five broader stages:

A. Beginning: The entry phase (combining Rogers' steps 1–3).
B. Forging a personal-working alliance (the passage from woundedness to hope) (steps 4–6).
C. Trust development (the quest for self) (steps 6–8).
D. Synchronous engagement (the becoming self in action) (steps 9–11).
E. Termination phase: ending and entry (step 12).

See also PROCESS CONCEPTION OF THERAPY and PROCESS OF THERAPY.

therapeutic relationship the relationship usually between client and therapist and, according to a number of research studies, the single most important factor in determining the effectiveness of therapy (and a more important factor in counselling and psychotherapy than the practitioner's theoretical orientation) (see Lambert, 1992; Duncan and Moynihan, 1994; Kahn, 1997). Given the centrality of the relationship to person-centred therapy — or RELATIONSHIP THERAPY, as Rogers first referred to his newer psychotherapy (Rogers, 1942) — this places PCP at the centre of debates about the nature of the therapeutic relationship (see also RANKIAN THERAPY). A number of strands may be discerned in the development of the understanding of the therapeutic relationship from a person-centred perspective:

1. First, Rogers (1942) identified four positive qualities of the therapeutic relationship:

   • warmth and responsiveness on the part of the counsellor;
   • permissiveness in regard to the expression of feelings;
   • certain limits to action such as holding to agreed time and safety boundaries;
   • freedom from any type of coercion or pressure.

2. Later (Rogers, 1951), he characterised a particular counsellor–client relationship as 'im'-personal in that the counsellor's own evaluations and reactions are absent, and secure in that it is based on a thoroughly consistent acceptance.

3. Rogers' (1957, 1959) formulations of the NECESSARY AND SUFFICIENT CONDITIONS also describe the qualities of the therapeutic relationship and the attitudinal requirements on the therapist:

   • to be in psychological contact;
   • to be genuine;
   • to be unconditional in their positive regard and empathic in their understanding, and to communicate these attitudes.

4. Around the same time (Rogers, 1958/90e) he described a number of characteristics of a helping relationship which he formulated as a series of (ten) questions which his study and experience raised for him and which may be taken as a series of reflections or meditations:

    - Can I be trustworthy?
    - Can I communicate myself unambiguously?
    - Can I let myself experience positive attitudes towards this person?
    - Can I be strong enough to be separate (from the other) — and am I secure enough to permit them their separateness?
    - Can I let myself enter fully into the world of their feelings and meanings and understand these as they do?
    - Can I be acceptant of each facet of this other person?
    - Can I act with sufficient sensitivity in the relationship that my behaviour will not be perceived as a threat — and can I free them from the threat of external evaluation?
    - Can I meet this person as a person in the process of becoming (or will I be bound by their and my own past)?

5. It is within this real relationship that the therapist can work at 'relational depth' (Mearns, 1996), a depth of relationship which is dependent on the fostering over time of the trainee/therapist's congruence.

6. In a chapter on the therapeutic relationship as experienced by the client, Rogers (1951) identifies six elements of such experience:

    - the experiencing of responsibility;
    - the experience of exploration;
    - the discovery of denied attitudes;
    - the experience of reorganising the self;
    - the experiencing of progress;
    - the experience of ending.

Finally, it is important to note that Rogers viewed the therapeutic relationship as (but) one instance of all relationships and that the same 'lawfulness' — of genuine acceptance, understanding and a communication of that understanding — governs *all* relationships (Rogers and Dymond, 1954).

therapeutic relationship, real   Gelso and Carter (1985) distinguish this therapeutic relationship from the 'unreal' transferential relationship and suggest that it is more rooted in humanistic (as distinct from analytic) conceptions of therapy. The features of this relationship are not only therapist GENUINENESS, AUTHENTICITY and CONGRUENCE but also both participants' genuine and realistic perceptions, reactions and expectations of each other — and thus this relationship has a quality of MUTUALITY.

therapeutic relationship, transferential   the 'unreal' or, more accurately, past relationship which is projected usually, but by no means exclusively, by the client on to the therapist in present time. Rogers did not deny that transference feelings or 'attitudes' existed but thought that *all* feelings directed towards the therapist should be accepted as part of the therapeutic relationship, and that thus TRANSFERENTIAL ATTITUDES should not be seen as a special case (see

139

TRANSFERENCE and COUNTERTHEORY OF TRANSFERENCE). The transference relationship is perpetuated only when there is a lack of understanding or empathy on the part of the therapist or when the therapist retains the POWER in the relationship (e.g. power of knowledge and/or definition):

> a true transference relationship is perhaps more likely to occur when the client is experiencing considerable threat to the organization of self ... [and] when the client experiences another as having a more effective understanding of his own self than he himself possesses (Rogers, 1951, p. 218).

In CCT, however, this 'involved and persistent dependent transference relationship does not tend to develop' (p. 201), essentially, because it is not fostered:

> to deal with transference feelings as a very special part of therapy, making their handling the very core of therapy, is to my mind a grave mistake. Such an approach fosters dependence and lengthens therapy. It creates a whole new problem, the only purpose of which appears to be the intellectual satisfaction of the therapist — showing the elaborateness of his or her technique. I deplore it (Rogers, 1987, p. 184).

Therapeutic Relationship and Its Impact: A Study of Psychotherapy with Schizophrenics, The
the report of a comparative study of 48 subjects, comprising 16 'chronic schizophrenics', 16 'acute schizophrenics' and 16 'normal' volunteer adults, edited by Rogers with the collaboration

of Gendlin, Kiesler and Truax, colleagues in the research, and published, after much stress, conflict and crisis, in 1967 (Rogers *et al.*, 1967). In order to measure the process of therapy, new scales for congruence (Kiesler) and for unconditional positive regard and accurate empathy (Truax) were developed, and Rogers himself, influenced by Gendlin, went on to develop his seven stages PROCESS CONCEPTION OF PSYCHOTHERAPY (Rogers, 1961). On the whole the results were mixed, with no significant differences between the therapy group and the control group. However, high therapist conditions of congruence and empathy did correlate with successful outcomes to therapy and these were confirmed in a follow up study by Truax and Mitchell (1971) (see SCHIZOPHRENIA).

therapy the generic term used to refer to healing activity whether COUNSELLING, PSYCHOTHERAPY or PSYCHOLOGICAL COUNSELLING (see CLIENT-CENTRED THERAPY, DIALOGIC THERAPY, EXISTENTIAL THERAPY, EXPERIENTIAL THERAPY, EXPRESSIVE THERAPY, FAMILY-CENTRED THERAPY, GAY AFFIRMATIVE THERAPY, GESTALT THERAPY, GROUP THERAPY, INTEGRATIVE THERAPY, INTERPERSONAL THERAPY, PLAY THERAPY, PSYCHODYNAMIC THERAPY, RANKIAN THERAPY, SHARING LIFE THERAPY, TRANSACTIONAL ANALYSIS).

threat 'the state which exists when an experience is perceived or anticipated ... as incongruent with the structure of self' (Rogers, 1959, p. 204). From an external view it corresponds to an internal anxiety. One of Rogers' (1958/90e) questions as to how to create a helping relationship is 'Can I free [the client] from the threat of external evaluation?' (p. 123).

Three Approaches to Psychotherapy
a film, produced by Shostrom (1964), often (and still) used in therapy training, showing three demonstration therapy sessions with the same client, GLORIA, conducted by Rogers (CCT), Fritz Perls (GESTALT THERAPY) and Albert Ellis (rational emotive therapy).

Tilden, Mary Jane a client of Carl Rogers whose work with whom (over eleven meetings) he wrote up and published (Rogers, 1947), the case has been commented on by Dingman (1996) and Geller and Gould (1996).

time-limited therapy an arrangement and CONTRACT in which the number of therapy sessions is fixed and or agreed in advance. A number of counselling agencies or contexts (e.g. Employee Assistance Programmes, General Practice, University Counselling Services) restrict the number of sessions with any one client to a specific number (e.g. four, six or twelve). Often there is an understanding that client and counsellor may negotiate further sessions, but there is no expectation that the counselling will be 'open-ended'. Person-centred counsellors often feel at a disadvantage when working with such arrangements because, it is argued, establishing a strong relationship with a client based on the client's experiencing of the NECESSARY AND SUFFICIENT CONDITIONS often takes more time than just, say, six sessions allow.

Some therapeutic approaches appear at first sight more suited to time-limited arrangements than others (such as the PCA), especially those that tend to focus on specific problems or tasks and their solution — a partial focus which is fundamentally antithetical to the whole *person*-centred nature of the PCA. This said, it is also the case that clients experience profound change in one session or within a session (see OUTCOMES OF THERAPY) and thus PCT may be viewed equally (alongside other theoretical orientations) as an effective therapy in a time-limited framework or context in which resources are limited; O'Hara (1999) talks about 'moments of eternity' in such contexts 'within which the self-organizing formative tendency in nature can become manifest and effective on the world' (p. 67). Furthermore, as Taft (1933) observes:

> time represents more vividly than any other category the necessity of accepting limitation as well as the inability to do so, and symbolizes therefore the whole problem of living. The reaction of each individual to limited or unlimited time betrays his deepest and fundamental life pattern, his relation to the growth process itself, to beginnings and endings, to being born and to dying (p. 12).

Commenting on this passage, Barrett-Lennard (1998) suggests that 'for therapists, accepting limitations in and of time brings a certain transcendence of these limits' (p. 124). Rogers himself writes about two cases of time-limited client-centred psychotherapy (Rogers, Lewis and Shlien, 1959) and Merry (1999) offers some ideas and useful guidelines to those working in a time-limited context.

touch contact between two people and, specifically in the context of therapy, physical contact between client and therapist; in the context of different therapeutic approaches to such contact, institutionalised taboos against touch, childhood sexual abuse and therapist abuse, a controversial issue in therapy (for a thorough discussion of which see Hunter and Struve, 1998). From a person-centred perspective which values REALNESS and spontaneity and eschews the pathologising of clients' needs and desires, person-centred therapists generally may be more inclined to respond to clients with some appropriate physical contact (see Rogers, 1970); however, in the context of an increasingly litigious social culture and a defensive therapeutic culture and its codification of behaviour, therapists may limit such spontaneous responses.

training Rogers (1951) identified some significant trends in the training of counsellors and therapists: away from technique/s and towards 'attitudinal orientation' (see ATTITUDES); towards giving the student an experience of therapy themselves, primarily with a view to increasing the student's sensitivity and empathy; and providing the opportunity for the practice of therapy. He then made the following tentative suggestions as to the desirable preparation for training as a therapist:

- experiential knowledge of the human being in their cultural setting;
- empathic experiencing;
- consideration and formulation of personal basic philosophy;
- the experience of PERSONAL THERAPY;
- a deep knowledge of the dynamics of personality;
- a knowledge of research design, scientific methodology and psychological theory.

Person-centred 'training' — or, more accurately, education (literally, *educare*, to lead out) — has traditionally focused more on selection and preparation of trainees/students and then, and as a parallel to the therapeutic process, on providing the conditions under which the trainee/student develops their facilitative attitudes, rather than specifying course content. As far as training/education courses themselves, PCP and the PCA encourages self-direction on courses (see Blomfield, 1997). Mearns (1997) identifies four dynamics central to person-centred counselling training:

- the 'responsibility dynamic', i.e. the trainer's responsibility to course members, not for them;
- the development of self-acceptance;
- individualisation of the curriculum;
- individualisation of assessment.

Another emphasis in person-centred training/education is on PERSONAL DEVELOPMENT (see also PERSONAL THERAPY and TRAINING THERAPY). While there is some debate within the PCA about the value of ACCREDITATION, REGISTRATION and VALIDATION, as regards both individual practitioners and counselling courses, a number of person-centred counselling courses are accredited by the BACP. According to the BACP's courses accreditation scheme (BAC, 1997a), courses have to demonstrate a core theoretical model. While some courses are consistently person-centred in that their process, organisation and content is congruent with the philosophy of the approach, others view the PCA as a core model on to which they add or graft other models — which is clearly at odds with the necessity and sufficiency of the therapeutic conditions and the universal applicability of the approach.

training therapy the concept and practice, originally formulated in psychoanalytic training, of therapy for the trainee/student which forms an integral part of training. Within PCP and PCT this process is, more commonly, viewed as PERSONAL DEVELOPMENT, although Keil (1996) claims that PERSONAL THERAPY in the context of a training programme should, properly, be regarded as a training therapy and as such is essentially pedagogic rather than therapeutic, with the purpose of giving the trainee/student an experiential conviction of the CENTRAL HYPOTHESIS of the approach and its therapeutic qualities, and is, as a therapy, thus necessarily 'terminable' or incomplete. At present, in the context of ACCREDITATION and REGISTRATION, both the BACP and the UKCP require counsellors and psychotherapists in training to be in therapy (the BACP for 40 hours and the UKCP for the duration of a minimum of three years' training). Given PCP's emphasis on AUTONOMY, SELF-ACTUALISATION and NON-DIRECTIVENESS, such 'requirements' are controversial.

transactional analysis another humanistic/existential approach to psychology and therapy, founded by Eric Berne and based on the principles that people are 'OK' (positive and mutual respect), that everyone has the capacity to think (a belief in self-responsibility), and that people decide their own destiny (a belief in personal responsibility and autonomy) (see Tudor, 1999b). Although both living and working in California — Berne from 1947 until his death in 1970 and Rogers from 1964 until his death in 1987 — there is no evidence that these 'founding fathers' met or that either read or acknowledged each other's work. Nevertheless Rogers (1959) refers to the infant's relationship to their environment as 'transactional' and Seeman (1984) describes organismic INTEGRATION as a transactional process. Similarities and differences between transactional analysis (TA) and the PCA are discussed by Tudor (1999a, 1999c).

transference the displacement of an emotion or attitude from one person to another person. In psychoanalysis and other forms of psychodynamic therapy, transference most often refers to the displacement of feelings towards parents or siblings, etc. on to the therapist. In these cases, transference can be either positive or negative depending on whether the client (or patient) develops positive or negative attitudes towards the therapist (see THERAPEUTIC RELATIONSHIP, TRANSFERENTIAL). A key feature of these 'transferences' is that they are largely UNCONSCIOUS. According to Rogers (1951), while some *attitudes* of a transferential nature exist in most cases, strong attitudes of this kind occur only in a relatively small number of cases. It is one of the popular misconceptions of the PCA (from without and within) that person-centred practitioners do not 'believe' in transference and do not take it seriously enough. These are misrepresentations and misconceptions (see PERSON-CENTRED APPROACH, CRITICISMS). It is not a question of belief or seriousness, it *is* a difference of perception and definition (see TRANSFERENTIAL ATTITUDE) and of philosophy and therapeutic practice (see TRANSFERENCE,

COUNTERTHEORY OF). In psychoanalysis, transference attitudes are thought of as expressions and indicators of present-day conflicts, and working through them an essential part of analysis or psychodynamic therapy (see also CO-TRANSFERENCE).

transference, countertheory of the theory, originally put forward by Shlien (1984) which, from a client-centred viewpoint, questions the importance of TRANSFERENCE in psychotherapy and, indeed, its very existence. Beginning with the provocative statement, '"transference" is a fiction, invented and maintained by the therapist to protect himself from the consequences of his own behavior' (p. 153), the paper caused much controversy. Shlien built his case against transference in part by identifying 'the illogical assumption that any response that duplicates a prior similar response is necessarily replicating it ... In the first instance, the original love of the child for the parent is not transferred. There was no earlier instance' (p. 174). He goes on to say that:

> any therapist has an active and response-arousing set of roles and behaviors. He is loved for what makes him lovable, hated for what makes him hateful, and all shades in between. *This should be the first hypothesis* ... understanding and misunderstanding will, I believe, account for the major affects of love and hate (p. 174).

In 1987 one issue of the *PERSON-CENTERED REVIEW* 2(2) carried articles from therapists of different traditions discussing Shlien's theory. For example, Arnold Lazarus commented, 'in my case Shlien's article was merely

preaching to a longtime convert ... Shlien has deftly documented the manner in which two prudish, sexist, chauvinistic gentlemen, Bruer and Freud, generalised way beyond their anecdotal observations' (Lazarus, 1987, p. 168). Lazarus does not go all the way with Shlien, however:

> while I agree that 'transference' as embroidered by the Freudians and neo-Freudians is a fiction, one might enquire whether there is any substance to the central notion. The essence of the concept of transference is that human beings are capable of behaving towards people in the present as they once behaved towards significant others in their past. This important insight, if left at that, could be considered a pivotal psychological truth (Lazarus, 1987, pp. 168–9).

Maddi (1987) goes further, concluding that while therapists need to develop mechanisms for effecting client change, transference seems an unwise choice because it is 'logically implausible'. Maddi states that transference is not restricted to the therapeutic situation only, but that it is supposed to occur in all relationships:

> it is a very dangerous influence. If you cannot trust your reactions to things in the present, then you have no decision-making grounds to stand on. You also have no basis for taking the present seriously. This major thrust of psychoanalytic theory is toward skepticism, self-preoccupation, inertia, nihilism and finally, meaninglessness (p. 179).

In opposition to Shlien, Greenwald (1987) remarks:

> there is a charming naivety in Shlien's assumption that understanding and misunderstanding lead to love and hate respectively ... The existence of transference makes it possible for the therapist to understand the patient's earlier conflicts in the 'here and now' of the interview (pp. 165–6).

transferential attitudes 'emotionalized attitudes which existed in some other relationship, and which are inappropriately directed to the therapist' (Rogers, 1951, p. 218) which, with understanding and acceptance on the part of therapist and then client become accepted and recognised as perceptions. For Rogers, the focus in working through these attitudes was on AWARENESS rather than on the object of them (as in psychoanalytic therapy).

transparency the appearance to another of a person's GENUINENESS and that their external behaviour is consistent or congruent (integrated) with their inner experiencing and AWARENESS; as with CONGRUENCE, it is not something which one (i.e. a therapist) can *do*, rather it is something one *is* — or is not; indeed, Kopp (1974) claims that this is a process requiring active and continuing choice: 'my own free decision to be transparent is a commitment to a never-ending struggle' (p. 18) (see APPARENCY). In a book on transparency, Jourard (1971) equates this with Rogers' condition of congruence (see also Thorne, 1996b).

trust an attitude of faith, confidence and reliance on someone or something. In PCP and the PCA, this often refers to trusting the client to know what they NEED, a trust in the ACTUALISING TENDENCY and to trusting, prioritising and giving attention to the PROCESS between people, for instance, in a relationship, group or community. However, the humanistic principle (almost a mantra) 'trust the process' should be mediated and contextualised by the complementary completion 'and process the trust' (M. Worrall, personal communication, 1997).

unconditional confidence see CONFI-
DENCE, UNCONDITIONAL.

unconditional positive regard (UPR) a
consistent ACCEPTANCE of each aspect
of a person's experience. An essential
aspect is the lack of *conditions* of acceptance, i.e. no sense of 'I feel positive towards you on condition that
your behaviour conforms to certain
standards'. UPR is one of the CORE
CONDITIONS of effective CCT and all
helping relationships. It involves feelings of acceptance for both so-called
'positive' and 'negative' aspects of a
person, and can also be expressed as
non-possessive caring for a person as
a separate individual. Rogers (1957)
thought that the term itself might be a
little unfortunate as it had an absolute, 'all-or-nothing' ring to it. Other
terms used from time to time include
WARMTH, RESPECT, PRIZING and even
LOVE. UPR, like EMPATHY and CONGRU-
ENCE, cannot be considered simply as
a SKILL or part of a therapist's reper-
toire of TECHNIQUES. It is part of a person's system of values and an integrated aspect of that person, not
something that can be adopted tem-

porarily in order to 'fulfil' the core
conditions.

It is also necessary to make the
clear distinction between unconditional positive regard and excessive
friendliness or 'niceness'. Adopting
an overly warm or overly friendly attitude towards clients in therapy
might have at least two unintended
and deleterious effects: first, it might
make it difficult for clients to express
angry, hostile or other 'negative'
emotions towards their therapists or
about themselves; second, if UPR is
perceived by a client as implying uncritical approval of destructive behaviour, or implicit support for the
client remaining as s/he is, i.e. not
moving towards becoming more
fully functioning, this may actually
impede therapeutic progress.
Ideally, clients should experience
UPR as a quality exhibited by their
therapist that makes it possible for
them to express any part of themselves and their experience without
the fear that they will be judged as
persons. While it is not helpful to
pick out one of the three core conditions as being the most important,

there is a developing view among some person-centred practitioners that the empathy and congruence experienced by therapists may be the 'ways of being' that enable them to develop feelings of UPR (see Bozarth, 1998e; Wilkins, 2000). In terms of the development of UPR, Rogers (1959) postulated the following as a hypothetical and possible chain of events — and therefore important from a theoretical point of view:

> if an individual should *experience* only *unconditional positive regard*, then no CONDITIONS OF WORTH would develop, SELF-REGARD would be unconditional, the needs for POSITIVE REGARD and *self-regard* would never be at variance with ORGANISMIC EVALUATION, and the individual would continue to be PSYCHOLOGICALLY ADJUSTED, and would be FULLY FUNCTIONING (P. 224).

unconditional self-regard an attitude towards oneself whereby 'the individual perceives himself in such a way that no self-experience can be discriminated as more or less worthy of positive regard than any other' (Rogers, 1959, p. 209): the person ACCEPTS all of who they are and what they are experiencing from moment to moment.

unconscious generally, a state characterised by a lack of AWARENESS or CONSCIOUSNESS and/or a lack of awareness of internal processes such as material which is significantly inconsistent with the SELF-CONCEPT and, therefore, DENIED or DISTORTED; in PCP, those organic processes such as self-regulation of body heat which are aspects of the ORGANISM's ACTUALISING

TENDENCY. It is a third usage of the term, particularly in DEPTH PSYCHOLOGIES, in which the unconscious is viewed as a domain of the psyche which encompasses repressed functions and so-called 'primitive' desires from which PCP parts company, preferring to conceptualise and understand these as 'experiences that are not integrated with the self or available to awareness, yet are powerful in affecting one's feelings, perceptions, and behavior' (Villas-Boas Bowen, 1986, p. 300). In a discussion about the nature of SCIENCE Rogers (1968) suggests that our experiencing is both conscious and unconscious and emphasises the value of the ORGANISMIC process of soaking up *all* EXPERIENCING, out of which immersion we may discern some pattern, rhythm or relationship, especially as our conscious mind is full of fixed CONSTRUCTS: 'it appears that the discoverer of knowledge feels a trust in *all* his avenues of knowing: unconscious, intuitive and conscious' (p. 64,) (see SUBCEPTION) (see Coulson, 1995; Wilkins, 1997b).

understanding the degree or quality of comprehending which, in PCP, is the vehicle for change; as Rogers (1961) puts it:

> to understand is enriching in a double way. I find when I am working with clients in distress, that to understand the bizarre world of a psychotic individual, or to understand and sense the attitudes of a person who feels that life is too tragic to bear, or to understand a man who feels that he is a worthless and inferior individual — each of these understandings somehow enriches me ... Even more import-

ant perhaps, is the fact that my understanding of these individuals permits them to change ... to accept their own fears ... (pp. 18–19).

Rogers distinguishes between (this) EMPATHIC UNDERSTANDING and the more common *evaluative* understanding such as 'O, yes, I understand what's wrong with you.'

United Kingdom Council for Psychotherapy (UKCP) a federal umbrella organisation of member and accrediting organisations which operates the British national register of psychotherapists. Despite its large Humanistic and Integrative Psychotherapy Section, to date there are no member organisations offering a person-centred psychotherapy training and, therefore, no person-centred psychotherapists registered *as such* with the UKCP, although individuals may apply for full membership of the ASSOCIATION OF HUMANISTIC PSYCHOLOGY PRACTITIONERS as person-centred psychotherapists (see Appendix 2).

University of Chicago Counseling Center the Centre which Rogers founded in 1945 with others from OHIO STATE UNIVERSITY, including Virginia Axline (see ACCEPTANCE, PLAY THERAPY). His twelve years there are viewed as the most productive and growthful period of his career and for the development of the person-centred approach (see Kirschenbaum, 1979; Thorne, 1992). The Center currently operates in part as a group practice and in part as a training centre focusing mostly on graduate students; the Center offers a practicum in client-centred psychotherapy, public lectures and workshops on client-centred therapy to advocates and service providers in the Chicago area.

University of Wisconsin at which Rogers held a joint appointment in the Departments of Psychology and Psychiatry from 1957 to 1963, and the centre of the major research project on schizophrenia (Rogers, Gendlin, Kiesler and Truax, 1967); see *THERAPEUTIC RELATIONSHIP AND ITS IMPACT*.

unspoken relationship see RELATIONSHIP, UNSPOKEN.

unspoken shield the set of assumptions established about others which 'interprets the other's behaviour and protects us from the reality of that behaviour which may be inconsistent with our assumptions' (Mearns, 1994, p. 67).

valuing process a process whereby a person expresses a preference and values such choice on the basis of experiences which maintain, enhance or ACTUALISE the ORGANISM; this process is often and certainly in developmental terms only inferred by others from a person/infant's behaviour. When this process is flexible and changing it may be described as an ORGANISMIC VALUING PROCESS; when a person introjects the value judgements of (significant) others, then that person develops internalised CONDITIONS OF WORTH (or value).

valuing process, organismic 'an ongoing process in which VALUES are never fixed or rigid, but EXPERIENCES are being accurately symbolized and continually and freshly valued' (Rogers, 1959, p. 210) with the ACTUALISING TENDENCY as the criterion for such evaluation.

values the tendency of any ORGANISM to show preference; drawing on the work of Morris (1956), Rogers distinguishes between CONCEIVED VALUES and OPERATIVE VALUES and comments on a third category of OBJECTIVE VALUES.

values, conceived 'the preference of the individual for a symbolized object' (Rogers, 1964/90g, p. 160), e.g. choosing that 'Honesty is the best policy'.

values, objective literally, what is objectively preferable, whether or not it is sensed or conceived as desirable, a concept about which, unsurprisingly, Rogers had little to say.

values, operative the value choice indicated by the organism behaviourally.

values, professional in addition to specific 'ATTITUDINAL values' which are consistent with and, indeed, embody the PCA, Boy and Pine (1982) identify a number of professional values which they conceive as 'commitments', including: careful selection of the work setting; identification with colleagues who are, in turn, committed and concerned; to organisational involvement; and to ongoing self-assessment as well as periodic evaluation.

vulnerability 'the state of INCONGRUENCE between self and experience, when it is desired to emphasize the potentialities of this state for creating psychological disorganization' (Rogers, 1959, pp. 203–4), and the most general state of incongruence (see Singh and Tudor, 1997). Identifying incongruence as the second of the NECESSARY AND SUFFICIENT CONDITIONS of therapy, Rogers (1957, 1959) refers to the client being in a state of incongruence, being *vulnerable* or anxious.

way of being, a a psychological posture from which one lives and is in the world, a phrase which encapsulates the person-centred approach — see A WAY OF BEING (Rogers, 1980) — the elements of which Wood (1996) describes as entailing:

1. a belief in a FORMATIVE directional TENDENCY;
2. a will to help;
3. an intention to be effective in one's objectives;
4. having compassion for the individual and respect for her/his AUTONOMY and dignity;
5. a flexibility in thought and action;
6. an openness to new discoveries. a 'learning posture';
7. 'an *ability* to intensely concentrate and clearly grasp the linear, piece by piece, appearance of reality as well as perceiving it holistically or all-at-once' (p. 169);
8. a tolerance for uncertainty or ambiguity;
9. a sense of humour, humility and curiosity.

See also EMERGING PERSON.

Way of Being, A a book by Rogers, published in 1980 and bringing together diverse material, some of which had been previously published in various journals. The contents — organised into four parts covering 'Personal Experiences and Perspectives, Aspects of the PCA, The Process of Education and Its Future, and Looking Ahead: A Person-Centered Scenario' — encompass the changes that took place in the 1970s. Thus this book, together with CLIENT-CENTERED THERAPY (Rogers, 1951) and ON BECOMING A PERSON (Rogers, 1961), may be regarded as forming a trilogy of books which, reflecting advances and developments in the previous decades, describe the fundamental philosophy and applications of PCP.

'we' concept a term coined by Nobles (1973), writing about black psychology, to refer to views and concepts of identity which are wider and more communal than the individualism implied by the SELF-CONCEPT.

West, Ellen a 'case', first reported in 1944, in which two psychiatrists and psychoanalysts were involved, and the subject of an interdisciplinary symposium organised by Rollo May which included Rogers as one of two psychologists (see May, Angel and Ellenberger, 1958). From his reading, Rogers focused on the sense of Ellen West's loneliness, both in terms of estrangement or alienation and of lack of relationship. In his commentary on her life and death (from suicide), Rogers identifies 'mistakes' made in her treatment, presents the dynamics of the interactions (as he sees them) and speculates on the different dynamics from his way of working. An expanded version of his original contribution appears in Rogers (1980a) (and in Kirschenbaum and Henderson, 1990b).

Western Behavioral Sciences Institute founded in 1959 to engage in action research in the behavioural and social sciences, Rogers joined it in 1964 where he was a Resident Fellow until 1968 when he resigned over issues of organisational hierarchy and, with others, set up the CENTER FOR STUDIES OF THE PERSON.

will 'volition is simply the subjective following of a harmonious balance of organismic direction' (Rogers, 1961, p. 158).

will therapy see RANKIAN THERAPY.

wholeness a word often used in humanistic psychology in general to describe the whole or totality of a person's experience and experiencing. Rogers (1951) talks about the organism reacting to the phenomenal field as an organised whole and uses the word synonymously with the term GESTALT (see also HOLISM and INTEGRATIVE).

word-for-word reflections see CONTACT REFLECTIONS.

working alliance the one of three components of counselling relationships first identified within the psychoanalytic tradition by Greenson (1967) and later hypothesised as existing in all therapeutic relationships by Gelso and Carter (1985) (see THERAPEUTIC RELATIONSHIP, REAL and THERAPEUTIC RELATIONSHIP, TRANSFERENTIAL). Conceptualised by Bordin (1975) as having three characteristics: an emotional bond, and agreements about the goals and tasks of counselling, Gelso and Carter suggest that the CORE CONDITIONS are both central in developing this alliance and that they have their primary impact through the alliance they foster.

World Association for Person-Centred and Experiential Psychotherapy and Counselling (WAPCEPC) this Association developed out of discussions following the first World Conference on Psychotherapy (held in Austria in July 1996), at which the PCA and PCT were under-represented; following an open letter circulated among the international person-centred community and further meetings at the INTERNATIONAL CONFERENCE ON CLIENT-CENTERED AND EXPERIENTIAL PSYCHOTHERAPY (held in Lisbon), a core group (Provisional Executive Board) was formed — and thus the incipient Association was founded on 8 July 1997 — to work on a more detailed proposal and, at a meeting at the fifth International Conference on Client-Centered and Experiential Psychotherapy (held in Chicago, June 200), the principles, goals and structure of the Association were agreed and a Board elected to serve for three years (until the next International Conference in The Netherlands, 2003) (see also NETWORK OF THE EUROPEAN ASSOCIATIONS FOR PERSON-CENTRED AND EXPERIENTIAL PSYCHOTHERAPY AND COUNSELLING; Appendix 2).

worth, conditions of see CONDITIONS OF WORTH.

writing a therapeutic process in which writers make contact with their own inner reality and VALUES. The act of writing gives the writer the freedom to experience his or her own feelings without being threatened in doing so; the process of writing involves the writer's experiencing becoming more and more available to her as she is able 'to live more and more freely in the process of ... feelings' (Rogers, 1990g, p. 177) and, through this process, reach and value her inner intuitive self, thus enabling her to move towards being herself, being her real feelings and being what she is. The close connection between writing and therapy may be illustrated with reference to elements of the seven stages of process. Rogers (1961) refers to the 'experience of being received' as a key element in the process of 'loosening and flowing of symbolic expression' (p. 133). A writer creates the experience of being received for herself through the writing process.

From a starting point where feelings exist but are disorganised and un-owned, the writer moves to a description and differentiation of feelings and towards seeking the 'exactness of symbolisation' (ibid., p. 138) and the 'exactness in differentiation of feelings and meanings' (ibid., p. 142). The finished work represents an *'immediacy of experiencing, and the feelings which constitute its content, [being] accepted'* (ibid., p. 146). The process of editing and completing a piece of writing can then open awareness to new feelings and insights. Just as guided READING may be therapeutic, in therapeutic writing groups personal exploration and self-exploration lead to an increase in self-esteem, self-confidence and self-awareness in the participants; a person-centred approach on the part of the FACILITATOR in such groups is crucial in order to create 'an atmosphere of realness, of caring and of understanding listening' (Rogers, 1983, p. 73) (SS).

Appendix I:

The 'cases' of Carl Rogers

Client	Date	Context	Tape (audio, video, film)	Transcript	Summary	Commentaries	Other discussions
Herbert Bryan	pre-1942	Client (Total: 8 sessions)	n/a	Rogers (1942)		Rogers (1942)	Thorne (1992)
Mary Jane Tilden	1946	Client (Total: 11 sessions)	n/a	(of first interview) Rogers (1947)	Rogers (1947)	Geller & Gould (1996)	
Mrs Oakpre	pre 1954	Client (Total: 40 sessions)	n/a	n/a	Research analysis Rogers (1954b)	Rogers (1989)	
Mr Bebb	pre 1954	Client (Total: 9 sessions)	n/a		Rogers (1954a)		
Mr Lin	1955	filmed	Rogers & Segel (1955a)	n/a			
Miss Mun	1955	filmed	Rogers & Segel (1955b)	n/a			Bozarth (1990)
Ellen West	1958	Case discussion	n/a	n/a		Rogers (1961/90b)	
Loretta	1958	Single session, audiotaped conference demonstration, AAP (1958) inpatient		Temaner & Raskin (1996) in Farber et al. (1996)		Raskin (1996)	
Jim Brown aka Mr Vac	1962	Client (Total: 166 sessions), inpatient	n/a	n/a	Rogers (1967)	Bozarth (1996a), Greenberg (1996)	Rogers (1967), Truax et al. (1967)
Gloria	1964	Single session, filmed demonstration	Shostrom (1965)	Rogers & Wood (1974)	Rosenzweig (1996)	Zimring (1996)	Rogers (1984), Bozarth (1990), Weinrach (1990), Thorne (1992)
Kathy	1975	Single session, filmed demonstration	Shostrom (1975)	n/a			Bozarth (1984, 1990)
Sylvia	1976	5th interview, filmed workshop demonstration	Rogers (1980b)	Farber et al. (1996)		Cain (1996), O'Hara (1996)	

Client	Date	Context	Tape (audio, video, film)	Transcript	Summary	Commentaries	Other discussions
'Anger & Hurt'	1977	1st interview, filmed demonstration	Whiteley (1977b)	n/a			
'Anger & Hurt'	1977	2nd interview, filmed demonstration	Whiteley (1977a)	n/a	Brink & Rosenzweig (1996)	Brodley (1996), Menahem (1996)	
Jan	1982	Single session, large workshop taped demonstration	n/a	Rogers (1986a)		Rogers (1986a)	Thorne (1992), Spinelli (1989)
Mark	1982	Single session, small group demonstration	n/a	Rogers (1986d), Farber et al. (1996)		Hayes & Goldfried (1996), Seeman (1996)	
Jill	1983	Single sesson, workshop demonstration	n/a	Farber et al (1996)		Villas-Boas Bowen (1996)	
Ms G	1983	Single session, demonstration, PCAI Training Programme	n/a	Merry (1995)			
Mary	1986	Single session, Expressive Therapy Training Program	n/a	Farber et al. (1996)		Natiello (1996)	
Louise	1986	single sessoin, demonstration, Expressive Therapy Training Program	n/a	Farber et al. (1996)		Natiello (1996)	

Carl Rogers in groups

Group	Date	Context	Tape	Transcript	Summary	Commentaries	Other discussion
Encounter group	1968	Filmed group	McGaw (1969)	n/a			Kirschenbaum (1979)
Encounter group	1972	Filmed group, comprising Catholics and Protestants in the Six Counties/Northern Ireland	McGaw (1973)	n/a	Rogers (1978)	Rogers (1978)	Merry (1995)
Multi-racial encounter group	1982	Multi-racial conference, Johannesburg	n/a	Sanford (1984)			Merry (1995), Sanford (1999)
The Rust workshop on 'The Central American Challenge'	1985	Invited group participant, Rust, Austria	n/a	n/a	Rogers (1986e)	Rogers (1986e)	Wood (1994), Merry (1995)

Appendix 2: Contacts

Association for the Development of the Person-Centered Approach (ADPCA)
c/o Julia Rabin, PO Box 396, Orange, MA 01364, USA
Tel: +001 (978) 544-6512
e-mail: jlrabin@aol.com
website: http://www.adpca.org

Association for Humanistic Psychology (Britain) (AHP[B])
BM 3582, London WC1N 3XX

Association of Humanistic Psychology Practitioners (AHPP)
BCM AHPP, London WC1N 3XX
Tel. (08457) 660326

British Association for the Person-Centred Approach (BAPCA)
BM BAPCA, London WC1N 3XX
Tel. (01989) 770948
e-mail: enquiries@pccsbks.globalnet.co.uk
website: www.bapca.org.uk

Carl Rogers Memorial Library
Department of Special Collections, Davidson Library, University of California Santa
Barbara, Santa Barbara, CA 93106
Tel: +001 (805) 893-3062
Fax: +001 (805) 893 5749
e-mail: special@library.ucsb.edu
websites: http://www.library.ucsb.edu/speccoll/speccoll.html
http://www.oac.cdlib.org/dyaweb/ead/ucsb/rogers/

Center for the Studies of the Person (CSP)
450 Silverado Suite 112, La Jolla, CA 92037, USA
Tel: +001 (858) 459-3861
e-mail: stillwell@meinet.cc
website: http://www.centerfortheperson.org

Community Building Network (in Britain)
c/o Anthony Kirke, 125 Greenham Road, Newbury, Berkshire RG14 7JE

Foundation for Community Encouragement
website: http://www.fce-community.org/

International Archives of the Person-Centered Approach
Department of Education and Human Development/
Archivos Internacionales del Enfoque Centrado en la Persona, Departamento de
Educación y Desarrollo Humano, Universidad Iberoamericana, Prolonganción
Paseo de la reforma 880, 01210 México, D.F., México
Tel: +525 2674149

Living Now Workshops
c/o Gay Leah Barfield
e-mail: okika@aloha.net

Network of the European Associations for Person-Centred and Experiential
Psychotherapy and Counselling (NEAPCEPC)
c/o SGGT Office, Schoffelgasse 7, CH-8001, Zurich
Tel: +0041 1 2516080
Fax: +0041 1 2516084
e-mail: sggtspcp@access.ch
website: www.pfs.kabelnet.at

Person-Centered Expressive Therapy Institute
PO Box 6518, Santa Rosa, California, CA 95406, USA
Tel: +001 (707) 795-6713
e-mail: Exartspc@aol.com

Person Centred Expressive Therapy Institute Europe (PCETIE)
c/o 3, Brook Road, Fallowfield, Manchester M14 6UJ

The Person-Centered Journal
Jo Cohen, Editor, Department of Counseling, Kutztown University, Kutztown,
PA 19508, USA
Tel: +001 (610) 683-4211
e-mail: cohen@kutztown.edu

Person-Centred Practice
Tony Merry, Editor, The Old Post Office, Llangarron, Herefordshire HR9 6PA
Tel: (01989) 770327
e-mail: awmerry@aol.com

Renaissance
Jody Deridder, Editor, 1227 Luttrell Street, Knoxville, TN 37917, USA
Tel: +001 (423) 546-2973
e-mail: davidnjody@icx.net

World Association for Person-Centred and Experiential Psychotherapy and
Counselling (WAPCEPC)
c/o SGGT Office, Schoffelgasse 7, CH-8001, Zurich
Tel: +0041 1 2516080
Fax: +0041 1 2516084
e-mail: sggtspcp@access.ch
website: www.pfs.kabelnet.at

References

Allen FH (1942) Psychotherapy with children. New York: W.W. Norton.

Allport GW (1961) Pattern and Growth in Personality. New York: Holt, Rinehart & Winston.

American Academy of Psychotherapists (1958) Tape No. 1. Orlando, Fla: AAP.

American Psychiatric Association (1994) Diagnostic and Statistical Manual of Mental Disorders (4th edn). Washington, DC: APA.

Andersen H, Swim S (1993) Learning as collaborative conversation: combining the student's and the teacher's expertise, Human Systems: The Journal of Systemic Consultation and Management 4(3–4): 145–53.

Anderson R, Cissna K (1997) The Martin Buber – Carl Rogers dialogue: A New Transcript with Commentary. Albany, NY: Suny Press.

Anderson WJ, Cain DJ, Ellinwood C (eds) (1989) Person-centered approaches with families [Special Issue]. Person-Centered Review 4(3).

Angyal A (1941) Foundations for a Science of Personality. New York: Commonwealth Fund.

Antonovsky A (1979) Health, Stress and Coping: New Perspectives on Mental and Physical Well-Being. San Francisco, Calif: Jossey-Bass.

Arnett RC (1989) What is dialogic communication? Friedman's contribution and clarification, Person-Centered Review 4(1): 42–60.

Arnold L (1984) The person centered approach and spiritual development. In AS Segrera (ed.), Proceedings of the First International Forum on the Person-Centered Approach. Oaxrepec, Moreles, Mexico: Universidad Iberamericana.

Association of Humanistic Psychology Practitioners (1998) Statement of core beliefs, Self & Society 26(3): 3–6.

Axline V (1947) Play Therapy. Boston: Houghton Mifflin.

Axline V (1964) Dibs: In Search of Self. Harmondsworth: Penguin.

Baldwin M (1987) Interview with Carl Rogers on the use of self in therapy. In M Baldwin, V Satir (eds), The Use of Self in Therapy (pp. 45–52). New York: Howarth Press.

Barkham J (1999) The FDI (Britain) workshops. In C Lago, M MacMillan (eds), Experiences in Relatedness: Groupwork and the Person-Centred Approach (pp. 123–35). Llangarron: PCCS Books.

Barrett-Lennard GT (1962) Dimensions of therapist response as causal factors in therapeutic change, Psychological Monographs 76 (43, Whole No. 562).

Barrett-Lennard GT (1979) A new model of communicational-relational systems in intensive groups, Human Relations 32: 841–9.

Barrett-Lennard GT (1981) The empathy cycle, Journal of Counseling Psychology 28: 91–100.

Barrett-Lennard GT (1983) Understanding the person-centered approach to therapy: a reply to questions and misconceptions. In E McIlduff, D Coghlan (eds), The Person-Centered Approach and Cross-Cultural Communication: An International Review, Volume I (pp. 99–113). Dublin: Center for Cross-Cultural Communication.

Barrett-Lennard GT (1990) The therapy pathway reformulated. In G Lietaer, J Rombauts, R Van Balen (eds), Client-Centered and Experiential Psychotherapy in the Nineties (pp. 123–53). Leuven: Leuven University Press.

Barrett-Lennard GT (1994) Toward a person-centred theory of community, Journal of Humanistic Psychology 34(3): 62–86.

Barrett-Lennard GT (1997) The recovery of empathy – towards others and self. In AC Bohart, LS Greenberg (eds), Empathy Reconsidered: New Directions in Psychotherapy (pp. 103–21). Washington, DC: American Psychological Association.

Barrett-Lennard GT (1998) Carl Rogers' Helping System. London: Sage.

Bentley P (2001) Medicine for the soul: The healing power of fiction, ipnosis 2: 8–9.

Biermann-Ratjen E-M (1998a) Incongruence and psychopathology. In B Thorne, E Lambers (eds), Person-Centred Therapy (pp. 119–30). London: Sage.

Biermann-Ratjen E-M (1998b) On the development of the person in relationship. In B Thorne, E Lambers (eds), Person-Centred Therapy (pp. 106–18). London: Sage.

Blomfield V (1997) Practitioner development through self-direction: the South West London College counselling courses. In R House, N Totton (eds), Implausible professions: Arguments for pluralism and autonomy in psychotherapy and counselling (pp. 255–70). Llangarron: PCCS Books.

Bohart AC (1990) A cognitive client-centered perspective on borderline personality development. In G Lietaer, J Rombauts, R Van Balen (eds), Client-Centered and Experiential Psychotherapy in the Nineties (pp. 599–622). Leuven: Leuven University Press.

Bohart AC, Greenberg LS (eds) (1997) Empathy Reconsidered: New Directions in Psychotherapy. Washington, DC: American Psychological Association.

Bordin ES (1975) The generalizability of the psychoanalytic concept of the working alliance, Psychotherapy: Theory, Research and Practice 16: 252–60.

Boy AV, Pine GJ (1982) Client-Centered Counseling: A Renewal. Boston: Allyn & Bacon.

Bozarth J (1981) The person-centered approach in the large community group. In G Gazda (ed.), Innovations to Group Psychotherapy (2nd edn) (pp. 36–42). Springfield, Ill: Thomas.

Bozarth J (1984) Beyond empathy: emergent modes of empathy. In R Levant, J Shlien (eds), Client-Centered Therapy and the Person-Centered Approach: New Directions in Theory, Research and Practice (pp. 59–75). New York: Praeger.

Bozarth J (1990) The evolution of Carl Rogers as a therapist, Person-Centered Review 5(4): 387–93.

Bozarth J (1993) Not necessarily necessary, but always sufficient. In D Brazier (ed.), Beyond Carl Rogers (pp. 92–105). London: Constable.

Bozarth J (1996a) A silent young man: the case of Jim Brown. In BA Farber, DC Brink, PM Raskin (eds), The Psychotherapy of Carl Rogers (pp. 240–50). New York: The Guilford Press.

Bozarth J (1996b) Client-centered therapy and techniques. In R Hutterer, G Pawlowsky, PF Schmid, R Stipsits (eds), Client-Centered and Experiential Psychotherapy: A Paradigm in Motion (pp. 363–8). Frankfurt am Main: Peter Lang.

Bozarth J (1996c) The integrative statement of Carl Rogers. In R Hutterer, G Pawlowsky, PF Schmid, R Stipsits (eds), Client-Centered and Experiential Psychotherapy: A Paradigm in Motion (pp. 25–34). Frankfurt am Main: Peter Lang.

Bozarth J (1998a) Person-centered assessment. In J Bozarth, Person-Centered Therapy: A Revolutionary Paradigm (pp. 125–31). Llangarron: PCCS Books. (Original work published 1991.)

Bozarth J (1998b) Person-Centered Therapy: A Revolutionary Paradigm. Llangarron: PCCS Books.

Bozarth J (1998c) Quantum theory and the person-centered approach. In J Bozarth, Person-Centered Therapy: A Revolutionary Paradigm (pp. 89–94). Llangarron: PCCS Books. (Original work published 1991.)

Bozarth J (1998d) Remembering Eleanor: a different way of contact. The Person-Centered Journal 5(1): 36–8.

Bozarth J (1998e) Unconditional positive regard. In J. Bozarth, Person-Centered Therapy: A Revolutionary Paradigm (pp. 83–8). Llangarron: PCCS Books. (Original work published 1991.)

Brazier D (1993a) Beyond Carl Rogers. London: Constable.

Brazier D (1993b) Congruence. Occasional Paper No.28. Available from Eigenwelt Interskill, 53 Grosvenor Place, Newcastle upon Tyne, NE2 2RD.

Brazier D (1993c) The necessary condition is love: going beyond self in the person-centred approach. In D Brazier (ed.), Beyond Carl Rogers (pp.72–91). London: Constable.

Brazier D (1995) Zen Therapy. London: Constable.

Brink DC, Rosenzweig D (1996) The case of 'Anger and Hurt': summary. In BA Farber, DC Brink, PM Raskin (eds), The Psychotherapy of Carl Rogers (pp. 301–9). New York: The Guilford Press.

British Association for Counselling (1997a) Counselling Accreditation: Accreditation Criteria. Leaflet. Rugby: BAC.

British Association for Counselling. (1997b) Recognition of Training Courses. Booklet. Rugby: BAC.

British Association for Counselling (1998) Code of Ethics and Practice for Counsellors. Rugby: BAC.

Brodley BT (1990) Client-centered and experiential: two different therapies. In G Lietaer, J Rombauts, R Van Balen (eds), Client-Centered and Experiential Psychotherapy in the Nineties (pp. 87–107). Leuven: Leuven University Press.

Brodley BT (1996) Uncharacteristic directiveness: Rogers and the 'Anger and Hurt' client. In BA Farber, DC Brink, PM Raskin (eds), The Psychotherapy of Carl Rogers (pp. 310–21). New York: The Guilford Press.

Brodley BT (1999) About the nondirective attitude, Person-Centred Practice, 7(2): 79–82.

Brodley BT, Brody A (1996) Can one use techniques and still be client-centered? In R Hutterer, G Pawlowsky, PF Schmid, R Stipsits (eds), Client-Centered and Experiential Psychotherapy: A Paradigm in Motion (pp. 369–74). Frankfurt am Main: Peter Lang.

Buber M (1937) I and thou (RG Smith transl.). Edinburgh: T & T Clark.

Burrell G, Morgan G (1979) Sociological Paradigms and Organisational Analysis. London: Heinemann.

Cain DJ (ed.) (1989) Symposium on psychodiagnosis [Special Issue]. Person-Centered Review, 4(2).

Cain DJ (1993) The uncertain future of client-centered counselling, Journal of Humanistic Education and Development 31: 133–9.

Cain DJ (1996) Rogers and Sylvia: an intimate and affirming encounter. In BA Farber, DC Brink, PM Raskin (eds), The Psychotherapy of Carl Rogers (pp. 275–83). New York: The Guilford Press.

Capra F (1975) The Tao of Physics. Boulder, Colo: Shambala.

Capra F (1982) The Turning Point. New York: Simon & Schuster.

Carter RT (1995) The Influence of Race and Racial Identity in Psychotherapy. New York: John Wiley.

Cartwright D (1957) Annotated bibliography of research and theory construction in client-centred therapy, Journal of Consulting Psychology 4: 82.

Chodorkoff B (1954) Self-perception, perceptual defense, and adjustment, Journal of Abnormal Social Psychology, 49(4): 196–205.

Clarke P (1997) Interpersonal process recall in supervision. In G Shipton (ed.), Supervision of Psychotherapy and Counselling: Making a Place to Think (pp. 93–104). Buckingham: Open University Press.

Cochrane CT, Holloway AJ (1974) Client-centered therapy and gestalt therapy: in search of merger. In DA Wexler, LN Rice (eds), Innovations in Client-Centered Therapy (pp. 259–87). New York: Wiley.

Coghlan D, McIlduff E (1990) Structuring and non directiveness in group facilitation, Person-Centered Review 5: 13–29.

Coghlan D, McIlduff E (1999) Facilitating change in organizations, The Person-Centered Journal 6(1): 48–58.

Conradi P (1996) Person-centred therapy. In M Jacobs (ed.), In Search of Supervision (pp. 53–74). Buckingham: Open University Press.

Cooper M (2000) Person-centred developmental theory: reflections and revisions, Person-Centred Practice, 8(2): 87–94.

Coulson A (1995) The person-centred approach and the re-instatement of the unconscious, Person-Centred Practice 3(2): 7–16.

Coulson WR, Rogers CR (eds) (1968) Man and the Science of Man. Columbus, Ohio: Charles Merrill.

Crossley N (1996) Intersubjectivity: The Fabric of Social Becoming. London: Sage.

Davies D (1998) Gay affirmative therapy, The Person-Centered Journal, 5(2): 111–24.

Davies D, Neal C (eds) (1996) Pink Therapy: A Guide for Counsellors and Therapists Working with Lesbian, Gay and Bisexual Clients. Buckingham: Open University Press.

Davies P (1995) About Time: Einstein's Unfinished Revolution. Harmondsworth: Penguin.

deCarvalho RJ (1999) Otto Rank, the Rankian circle in Philadelphia, and the origins of Carl Rogers' person-centred psychotherapy, History of Psychology 2(2): 132–48.

Deleu C, Van Werde D (1998) The relevance of a phenomenological attitude when working with psychotic people. In B Thorne, E Lambers (eds), Person-Centred Therapy (pp.206–15). London: Sage.

Devonshire CM (1991) The person-centered approach and cross-cultural communication. In E McIlduff, D Coghlan (eds), The Person-Centered Approach and Cross-Cultural Communication: An International Review, Volume I (pp. 15–42). Dublin: Center for Cross-Cultural Communication.

Dingman RE (1996) Client-centered therapy and undivided attention: the case of Mary Jane Tilden. In BA Farber, DC Brink, PM Raskin (eds), The Psychotherapy of Carl Rogers (pp. 200–10). New York: The Guilford Press.

Doerhman MJG (1976) Parallel process in supervision and psychotherapy, Bulletin of the Menninger Clinic 10(1): 9–105.

Dolliver RH (1995) Carl Rogers's emphasis on his own direct experience, Journal of Humanistic Psychology, 35(4): 129–39.

Dorfman E (1951) Play therapy. In CR Rogers. Client-Centered Therapy (pp. 235–77). London: Constable.

Dorpat T (1985) Denial and Defense in the Therapeutic Situation. New York: Jason Aronson.

Duncan BL, Moynihan DW (1994) Applying outcome research: intentional utilization of the client's frame of reference, Psychotherapy 31: 294–301.

Ekstein R, Wallerstein RS (1958) The teaching and learning of psychotherapy. New York: International Universities Press.

Ellingham I (1997) On the quest for a person-centred paradigm, Counselling 8(1): 52–5.

Ellingham I (1998) Person-centred porridge, Person-Centred Practice 6(2): 110–12.

Ellingham I (1999a) Carl Rogers' 'congruence' as an organismic; not a Freudian concept, Person-Centered Journal 6(2): 121–40.

Ellingham I (1999b) On transcending person-centred postmodernist porridge, Person-Centred Practice 7(2): 62–78.

Ellingham I (2000) Foundation for a Person-Centred, Humanistic Psychology – and Beyond: The Nature and Logic of Carl Rogers' 'Formative Tendency'. Unpublished manuscript.

Evans RI (1975) Carl Rogers: The Man and His Ideas. New York: Dutton.

Fairhurst I (1999) Empathy at the core of the client-centred therapeutic relationship: contaminations of empathic understanding. In I Fairhurst (ed.), Women Writing in the Person-Centred Approach (pp. 19–35). Llangarron: PCCS Books.

Fairhurst I, Merry T (1999) Groupwork in client-centred counselling training. In C Lago, M MacMillan (eds), Experiences in Relatedness: Groupwork and the Person-Centred Approach (pp. 49–61). Llangarron: PCCS Books.

Farber BA, Brink DC, Raskin PM (eds) (1996) The Psychotherapy of Carl Rogers. New York: The Guilford Press.

Feltham C, Dryden W (1994) Developing Counsellor Supervision. London: Sage.

Fine R (1986) Narcissism, the Self and Society. New York: Columbia University Press.

Finke J (1990) Dream work in client-centered psychotherapy. In G Lietaer, J Rombauts, R Van Balen (eds), Client-Centered and Experiential Psychotherapy in the Nineties (pp. 503–10). Leuven: Leuven University Press.

Fischer CT (1989) The life-centered approach to psychodiagnostics: attending to lifeworld, ambiguity and possibility, Person-Centered Review 4(2): 163–70.

Ford JG (1991) Rogerian self-actualization: a clarification of meaning, Journal of Humanistic Psychology 31(2): 101–11.

Ford JG (1994) Extending Rogers's thoughts on human destructiveness, Person-Centered Journal 1(3): 33–42.

Fransella F, Dalton P (1990) Personal Construct Psychology in Action. London: Sage.

Freire P (1976) Education: The Practice of Freedom. London: Writers and Readers Publishing Cooperative. (Original work published 1967.)

Freire P (1972) Pedagogy of the Oppressed. Harmondsworth: Penguin.

Frenzel P, Przyborski A (1983) Becoming a political person: a person-centered view. In E McIlduff, D Coghlan (eds), The Person-Centered Approach and Cross-Cultural Communication: An International Review, Volume I (pp. 114–22). Dublin: Center for Cross-Cultural Communication.

Friedlander S (1918) Schöpferische Indifferenz (Creative Indifference). Munich: Georg Müller.

Friedman M (1996) Reflections on the Buber-Rogers dialogue: thirty years after. In M Friedman (ed.), Martin Buber and the Human Sciences (pp. 357–69). Albany, NY: State University of New York Press.

Fromm E (1962) The Art of Loving. London: Unwin.

Fromm E (1986) Psychoanalysis and Zen Buddhism. London: Unwin.

Gaylin N (1974) On creativeness and a psychology of well-being. In DA Wexler, LN Rice (eds), Innovations in Client-Centered Therapy (pp. 339–65). New York: Wiley.

Gaylin N (1990) Family-centered therapy. In G Lietaer, J Rombauts, R Van Balen (eds), Client-Centered and Experiential Psychotherapy in the Nineties (pp. 813–28). Leuven: Leuven University Press.

Gaylin N (1993) Person-centred family therapy. In D Brazier (ed.), Beyond Carl Rogers (pp. 181–200). London: Constable.

Gaylin N (2001) Family, self and psychotherapy: a person-centred perspective. Llangarron: PCCS Books.

Geller JD, Gould E (1996) A contemporary psychoanalytic perspective: Rogers' brief psychotherapy with Mary Jane Tilden. In BA Farber, DC Brink, PM Raskin (eds), The Psychotherapy of Carl Rogers (pp. 211–30). New York: The Guilford Press.

Gelso CJ, Carter JA (1985) The relationship in counseling and psychotherapy: components, consequences, and theoretical antecedents, The Counseling Psychologist 13, 159–234.

Gendlin ET (1961) Experiencing: a variable in the process of therapeutic change, American Journal of Psychotherapy 15: 233–45.

Gendlin ET (1964) A theory of personality change. In P Worchal, D Byrne (eds), Personality Change (pp. 206–47). New York: Wiley.

Gendlin ET (1981) Focusing (rev. edn). New York: Bantam.

Gendlin ET (1984) The client's client: the edge of awareness. In R Levant, J Shlien (eds), Client-Centered Therapy and the Person-Centered Approach: New Directions in Theory, Research and Practice (pp. 76–107). New York: Praeger.

Gendlin ET (1986) Let Your Body Interpret Your Dreams. Wilmette, Ill: Chiron.

Giesekus U, Mente A (1986) Client empathic understanding in client-centered therapy, Person-Centered Review 1: 163–71.

Gilbert TF (1978) Human Competence: Engineering Worthy Performance. New York: McGraw-Hill.

Gleick J (1987) Chaos: The Making of a New Science. New York: Viking Penguin.

Goldstein K (1940) Human Nature in the Light of Psychopathology. Cambridge, Mass: Harvard University Press.

Goodrich S, Bekerian D (2000) Recovered memories of sexual abuse: theoretical and practical issues. In C Feltham, I Horton (eds), Handbook of Counselling and Psychotherapy (pp. 567–9). London: Sage.

Gordon T (1951) Group-centered leadership and administration. In CR Rogers, Client-Centered Therapy (pp. 320–83). London: Constable.

Gottschalk LA (1966) Psychoanalytic notes on T-groups at the Human Relations Laboratory, Bethel, Maine, Comprehensive Psychiatry 7: 472–87.

Graf CL (1984) A comparison of Carl Rogers' and Heinz Kohut's humanistic theories of the fully functioning person. In AS Segrera (ed.), Proceedings of the First International Forum on the Person-Centered Approach. Oaxrepec, Moreles, Mexico: Universidad Iberamericana.

Greenberg LS (1996) The power of empathic exploration: a process-experiential/gestalt perspective on the case of Jim Brown. In BA Farber, DC Brink, PM Raskin (eds), The Psychotherapy of Carl Rogers (pp. 251–60). New York: The Guilford Press.

Greenberg LS, Elliot R (1997) Varieties of empathic responding. In AC Bohart, LS Greenberg (eds), Empathy Reconsidered: New Directions in Psychotherapy (pp. 167–86). Washington, DC: American Psychological Association.

Greenson RR (1967) The Technique and Practice of Psychoanalysis (Vol.1). New York: International Universities Press.

Greenwald H (1987) Yes, John, there is a transference, Person-Centered Review 2(2): 165–7.

Gurman AS (1977) The patient's perception of the therapeutic relationship. In AS Gurman, AM Razin (eds), Effective Psychotherapy: A Handbook of Research (pp. 503–43). Oxford: Pergamon.

Hall C, Lindzey G (1957) Theories of Personality. New York: Wiley.

Harkness M (1998) The story of Percy the propositions prototype (or the Mini with motivation), Person-Centred Practice 6(2): 104–9.

Harman JI (1990) Unconditional confidence as a facilitative precondition. In G Lietaer, J Rombauts, R Van Balen (eds), Client-Centered and Experiential Psychotherapy in the Nineties (pp. 251–68). Leuven: Leuven University Press.

Harman JI (1997) Rogers' late conceptualization of the fully functioning individual: correspondences and contrasts with Buddhist psychology, The Person-Centered Journal 4(2): 23–31.

Haugh S (1998) Congruence: a confusion of language, Person-Centred Practice 6(1): 44–50.

Hayes AM, Goldfried MR (1996) Rogers' work with Mark: an empirical analysis and cognitive-behavioral perspective. In BA Farber, DC Brink, PM Raskin (eds), The Psychotherapy of Carl Rogers (pp. 357–73). New York: The Guilford Press.

Heron J (1996) Co-operative Inquiry: Research into the Human Condition. London: Sage.

Heron J (1998) Sacred Science: Person-Centred Inquiry into the Spiritual and the Subtle. Llangarron: PCCS Books.

Hobbs N (1951) Group-centered psychotherapy. In CR Rogers, Client-Centered Therapy (pp. 278–319). London: Constable.

Holdstock L (1990) Can client-centered therapy transcend its monocultural roots? In G Lietaer, J Rombauts, R Van Balen (eds), Client-Centered and Experiential Psychotherapy in the nineties (pp. 109–21). Leuven: Leuven University Press.

Holdstock L (1993) Can we afford not to revision the person-centred concept of self? In D Brazier (ed.), Beyond Carl Rogers (pp. 229–52). London: Constable.

Holdstock TL, Rogers CR (1977) Person-centered theory. In RJ Corsini (ed.), Current Personality Theories (pp. 125–51). Itasca, Ill: Peacock.

Holland R (1977) Self in Social Context. London: Macmillan.

Holt J (1967a) How Children Fail. New York: Pitman.

Holt J (1967b) How Children Learn. New York: Pitman.

Homans P (1974) Carl Rogers' psychology and the theory of mass society. In DA Wexler, LN Rice (eds), Innovations in Client-Centered Therapy (pp. 319–37). New York: Wiley.

House R, Totton N (eds) (1997) Implausible Professions: Arguments for Pluralism and Autonomy in Psychotherapy and Counselling. Llangarron: PCCS Books.

Hulme P (1999) Collaborative conversation. In C Newnes, G Holmes, C Dunn (eds), This is Madness: A Critical Look at Psychiatry and the Future of Mental Health Services (pp. 165–78). Llangarron: PCCS Books.

Hunter M, Struve J (1998) The Ethical Use of Touch in Psychotherapy. Thousand Oaks, Calif: Sage.

Hutterer R (1993) Eclecticism: an identity crisis for person-centred therapists. In D Brazier (ed.), Beyond Carl Rogers (pp. 274–84). London: Constable.

Hutterer R, Pawlowsky G, Schmid PF, Stipsits R (eds) (1996) Client-Centered and Experiential Psychotherapy: A Paradigm in Motion. Frankfurt am Main: Peter Lang.

Hycner, R. (1993) Between Person and Person: Toward a Dialogical Psychotherapy. Highland, NY: The Gestalt Journal Press.

Illich, I. (1973) Deschooling Society. Harmondsworth: Penguin.

Jenkins P (1997) Counselling, Psychotherapy and the Law. London: Sage.

Jennings JL (1986) The dream is the dream is the dream, Person-Centered Review 1(3): 310–33.

Jones M (1996) Person-centred theory and the post-modern turn, Person-Centred Practice 4(2): 19–26.

Jourard S (1971) The Transparent Self (2nd edn). New York: Van Nostrand Reinhold Co.

Kahn M (1997) Between therapist and client: the new relationship (2nd edn). New York: W.H. Freeman.

Keil WW (1996) Training therapy in the client-centered approach. In R Hutterer, G Pawlowsky, PF Schmid, R Stipsits (eds), Client-Centered and Experiential Psychotherapy: A Paradigm in Motion (pp. 413–25). Frankfurt am Main: Peter Lang.

Kelly GA (1955) The Psychology of Personal Constructs. Vol.1. New York: W.W. Norton.

King D, Wheeler S (1999) The responsibilities of counsellor supervisors: a qualitative study, British Journal of Guidance and Counselling 27(2): 215–29.

Kirschenbaum H (1979) On becoming Carl Rogers. New York: Delacorte Press.

Kirschenbaum H, Henderson VL (eds) (1990a) Carl Rogers: Dialogues. London: Constable.

Kirschenbaum H, Henderson VL (eds) (1990b). The Carl Rogers Reader. London: Constable.

Kopp S (1974) If you Meet the Buddha on the Road, Kill Him! London: Sheldon Press.

Kreeger L (ed.) (1975) The Large Group: Dynamics and Therapy. London: Maresfield.

Lago C, MacMillan M (eds) (1999) Experiences in Relatedness: Groupwork and the Person-Centred Approach. Llangarron: PCCS Books.

Lambers E (1994) The person-centred perspective on psychopathology: the neurotic client. In D Mearns Developing Person-Centred Counselling (pp. 105–9). London: Sage.

Lambers E (2000) Supervision in person-centred therapy: facilitating congruence. In D Mearns, B Thorne, Person-Centred Therapy Today (pp.196–211). London: Sage.

Lambert MJ (1992) Psychotherapy outcome research: implications for integrative and eclectic therapists. In J Norcross, RM Goldfried (eds), Handbook of Psychotherapy Integration (pp. 94–129). New York: Basic Books.

Laungani P (1999) Client centred or culture centred counselling. In S Palmer, P Laungani (eds), Counselling in a Multicultural Society (pp. 133–52). London: Sage.

Lazarus AA (1987) A brief commentary on Shlien's countertheory, Person-Centered Review, 2(2): 168–70.

Lazarus AA (1993) Tailoring the therapeutic relationship or being an authentic chameleon, Psychotherapy 30(3): 404–7.

Lecky P (1945) Self-consistency: A theory of personality. New York: Island Press.

Lewin K (1952) Field Theory in Social Science. New York: Harper & Row.

Lieberman M, Yalom I, Miles M (1973) Encounter Groups: First Facts. New York: Basic Books.

Lietaer G (1990) The client-centered approach after the Wisconsin project: a personal view on its evolution. In G Lietaer, J Rombauts, R Van Balen (eds), Client-Centered and Experiential Psychotherapy in the Nineties. Leuven: Leuven University Press.

Lietaer G (1993) Authenticity, congruence and transparency. In D Brazier (ed.), Beyond Carl Rogers (pp.17–46). London: Constable.

Lietaer G, Dierick P (1996) Client-centered group psychotherapy in dialogue with other orientations: commonality and specificity. In R Hutterer, G Pawlowsky, PF Schmid, R Stipsits (eds), Client-Centered and Experiential Psychotherapy: A Paradigm in Motion (pp. 563–83). Frankfurt am Main: Peter Lang.

Lietaer G, Rombauts J, Van Balen R (1990) Client-Centered and Experiential Psychotherapy in the Nineties. Leuven: Leuven University Press.

Lindsay DS, Read, JD (1994) Psychotherapy and memories of childhood sexual abuse: a cognitive perspective, Applied Cognitive Psychology 8: 281–338.

Lindt MWJ (1988) Holding and the person-centered approach, Person-Centered Review 3(2): 229–40.

Lloyd Valentine J (2000) In search of the actualising organisation: an exploration of the person-centred approach to organisational development. Unpublished essay, Temenos, Sheffield.

McCleary RA, Lazarus RS (1949) Autonomic discrimination without awareness, Journal of Personality 18: 171–9.

McGaw W (prod., dir.) (1969) Journey into Self [film]. La Jolla, Calif: Center for Studies of the Person.

McGaw W (prod., dir.) (1973). The Steel Shutter [film]. La Jolla, Calif: Center for Studies of the Person.

McIlduff E, Coghlan D (1991) Dublin, 1985: perceptions of a cross-cultural communications workshop, The Person-Centered Approach and Cross-Cultural Communication: An International Review, Volume 1 (pp. 43–59). Dublin: Center for Cross-Cultural Communication.

McIlduff E, Coghlan D (1993) The cross-cultural communication workshops in Europe – reflections and review. In E McIlduff, D Coghlan (eds), The Person-Centered Approach and Cross-Cultural Communication: An International Review, Volume II (pp. 21–34). Dublin: Center for Cross-Cultural Communication.

MacMillan M (1999) In you there is a universe: person-centred counselling as a manifestation of the breath of the merciful. In I Fairhurst (ed.), Women Writing in the Person-Centred Approach (pp. 47–61). Llangarron: PCCS Books.

MacMillan M, Lago C. (1993) Large groups: critical reflections and some concerns, The Person-Centred Approach and Cross-Cultural Communication 2(1): 35–53.

Maddi SR (1987) On the importance of the present: reactions to John Shlien's article, Person-Centered Review 2(2): 171–81.

Marques-Teixeira J, Antones S (2000) Client-centred and experiential psychotherapy. Linda a Velha, Portugal: Vale & Vale.

Maslow AH (1943a) A theory of human motivation, Psychological Review 50: 370–96.

Maslow AH (1943b) Dynamics of personality organisation, Psychological Review 50: 514–39, 541–58.

Maslow AH (1954) Motivation and Personality. New York: Harper & Brothers.

Maslow AH (1993) Self-actualization and beyond. In The Farther Reaches of Human Nature (pp. 40–51). London: Arkana. (Original work published 1967.)

Masson J (1989) Against Therapy. London: Collins.

Masterson JF (1988) The Search for the Real Self: Unmasking the Personality Disorders of our Age. New York: The Free Press.

May R, Angel E, Ellenberger HF (eds) (1958). Existence: A New Dimension in Psychiatry and Psychology. New York: Basic Books.

Maylon A (1982). Psychotherapeutic implications of internalized homophobia in gay men. In J Gonsiorek (ed.), Homosexuality and Psychotherapy. New York: Haworth Press.

Mearns D (1993) Against indemnity insurance. In W Dryden (ed.), Questions and Answers on Counselling in Action (pp. 161–4). London: Sage.

Mearns D (1994) Developing Person-Centred Counselling. London: Sage.

Mearns D (1996) Working at relational depth with clients in person-centred therapy, Counselling 7(4): 306–11.

Mearns D (1997) Person-Centred Counselling Training. London: Sage.

Mearns D (1999) Person-centred therapy with configurations of the self, Counselling 10(2): 125–30.

Mearns D, Dryden W (eds) (1990). Experiences of Counselling in Action. London: Sage.

Mearns D, Lambers E (1976) Facilitator Development Institute, Self & Society 4(12): 9–12.

Mearns D, Thorne B (1988) Person-Centred Counselling in Action. London: Sage.

Mearns D, Thorne B (2000) Person-Centred Therapy Today: New Frontiers in Theory and Practice. London: Sage.

Menahem SE (1996) The case of 'Anger and Hurt': Rogers and the development of a spiritual psychotherapy. In BA Farber, DC Brink, PM Raskin (eds), The Psychotherapy of Carl Rogers (pp. 322–33). New York: The Guilford Press.

Merleau-Ponty M (1962) Phenomenology of Perception. New York: Routledge & Kegan Paul.

Merry T (1995) An Invitation to Person-Centred Psychology. London: Whurr.

Merry T (1999) Learning and Being in Person-Centred Counselling. Llangarron: PCCS Books.

Miller MJ (1998) Some comparisons between Taoism and person-centered therapy, The Person-Centered Journal 3(1): 12–14.

Mindell A (1990a) Dreambody: The Body's Role in Revealing the Self. London: Arcana. (Original work published 1982.)

Mindell A (1990b) Working on Yourself Alone. London: Arcana.

Mindell A (1992) The Leader as Martial Artist. New York: HarperCollins.

Mitchell KM, Bozarth JD, Krauft CC (1977) A reappraisal of the therapeutic effectiveness of accurate empathy, non-possessive warmth and genuineness. In AS Gurman, AM Razin (eds), Effective Psychotherapy: A Handbook of Research (pp. 482–502). New York: Pergamon Press.

Money M (1997) Defining mental health – what do we think we're doing? In M Money, L Buckley (eds), Positive Mental Health and Its Promotion (pp. 13–15). Institute for Health, John Moores University, Liverpool.

Morotomi Y (1998) Person-centred counselling from the viewpoint of Japanese spirituality, Person-Centred Practice 6(1): 28–32.

Morris CW (1956) Varieties of Human Value. Chicago: Chicago University Press.

Mothersole G (1999) Parallel process: a review, The Clinical Supervisor 18(2): 107–21.

Mowbray R (1995) The Case against Psychotherapy Registration: A Conservation Issue for the Human Potential Movement. London: Transmarginal Press.

Myers S (1999) Empathy: is that what I hear you saying?, Person-Centered Journal 6(2): 141–52.

Natiello P (1987) The person-centered approach: from theory to practice, Person-Centered Review 2: 203–16.

Natiello P (1990) The person-centered approach, collaborative power, and cultural transformation, Person-Centered Review 5(3): 268–86.

Natiello P (1996) On Mary and Louise: an argument for client self-determination. In BA Farber, DC Brink, PM Raskin (eds), The Psychotherapy of Carl Rogers (pp. 120–32). New York: The Guilford Press.

Natiello P (1999a) Sexism, gender dynamics and the person-centered approach. In C Lago, M MacMillan (eds), Experiences in Relatedness: Groupwork and the Person-Centred Approach (pp. 63–75). Llangarron: PCCS Books.

Natiello P (1999b) The person-centered approach: a solution to gender-splitting. In I Fairhurst (ed.), Women Writing in the Person-Centred Approach (pp. 163–71). Llangarron: PCCS Books.

Natiello P (2001) The Person-Centred Approach: A Passionate Presence. Llangarron: PCCS Books.

Neil AS (1968) Summerhill. Harmondsworth: Penguin.

Neville B (1996) Five kinds of empathy. In R Hutterer, G Pawlowsky, PF Schmid, R Stipsits (eds), Client-Centered and Experiential Psychotherapy: A Paradigm in Motion (pp. 439–53). Frankfurt am Main: Peter Lang.

Neville B (1999) The client-centered ecopsychologist, The Person-Centered Journal 6(1): 59–74.

Nobles WW (1973) Psychological research and the black self-concept: a critical review, Journal of Social Issues 29: 11–31.

Nye R (1986) Three Psychologies (3rd edn). Monterey, CA.: Brooks/Cole.

O'Hara M (1984) Person-centered gestalt: toward a holistic synthesis. In RS Levant, JM Shlien (eds), Client-Centered Therapy and the Person-Centered Approach (pp. 203–21). New York: Praeger.

O'Hara M (1986) Heuristic inquiry as psychotherapy: the client-centered approach, Person-Centered Review 1(2): 172–84.

O'Hara M (1989) Person-centered approach as conscientização: the works of Carl Rogers and Paulo Freire, Journal of Humanistic Psychology 29(1): 11–36.

O'Hara M (1996) Rogers and Sylvia: a feminist analysis. In BA Farber, DC Brink, PM Raskin (eds), The Psychotherapy of Carl Rogers (pp. 284–300). New York: The Guilford Press.

O'Hara M (1999) Moments of eternity: Carl Rogers and the contemporary demand for brief therapy. In I Fairhurst (ed.), Women Writing in the Person-Centred Approach (pp. 63–77). Llangarron: PCCS Books.

O'Leary E (1997) Towards integrating person centered and gestalt therapies, The Person-Centered Journal 4(2): 14–22.

O'Leary C (1999) Couple and Family Counselling: A Person-Centred Approach. London: Sage.

Owen IR (1999) Exploring the similarities and differences between person-centred and psychodynamic therapy, British Journal of Guidance and Counselling 27(2): 165–78.

Parloff MB, Waskow IE, Wolfe BE (1978) Research on therapist variables in relation to process and outcome. In SL Garfield, AE Bergin (eds), Handbook of Psychotherapy and Behaviour Change: An Empirical Analysis (2nd edn) (pp. 233–82). New York: John Wiley & Sons.

Patterson CH (1964) Supervising students in the counseling practicum, Journal of Counseling Psychology 11: 47–53.

Patterson CH (1983) A client-centered approach to supervision, The Counseling Psychologist 11(1), 21–5.

Patterson CH (1985) The Therapeutic Relationship. Belmont, Calif: Brooks/Cole.

Patterson CH (1997) Client-centered supervision. In CE Watkins (ed.), Handbook of Psychotherapy Supervision (pp. 134–46). New York: John Wiley.

Patterson CH (2000a) A unitary theory of motivation and its counseling implications. In CH Patterson, Understanding Psychotherapy: Fifty Years of Client-Centred Theory and Practice (pp. 10–21). Llangarron: PCCS Books. (Original work published 1964.)

Patterson CH (2000b) Empathy, warm and genuineness in psychotherapy: a review of reviews. In CH Patterson, Understanding Psychotherapy: Fifty Years of Client-Centred Theory and Practice (pp. 161–73). Llangarron: PCCS Books. (Original work published 1984.)

Patterson CH (2000c) On being non-directive. In CH Patterson, Understanding Psychotherapy: Fifty Years of Client-Centred Theory and Practice (pp. 181–4). Llangarron: PCCS Books.

Patterson CH (2000d) Phenomenological psychology. In CH Patterson, Understanding Psychotherapy: Fifty Years of Client-Centred Theory and Practice (pp. 143–53). Llangarron: PCCS Books. (Original work published 1965.)

Patterson CH (2000e) Understanding Psychotherapy: Fifty years of Client-Centred Theory and Practice. Llangarron: PCCS Books.

Pearson PH (1974) Conceptualizing and measuring openness to experience in the context of psychotherapy. In DA Wexler, LN Rice (eds), Innovations in Client-Centered Therapy (pp. 139–70). New York: Wiley.

Peck S (1987) A Different Drum. London: Rider & Co.

Perls F, Hefferline RF, Goodman P (1973) Gestalt Therapy: Excitement and Growth in the Human Personality. (Original work published 1951.)

Prouty GF (1976) Pre-therapy, a method of treating pre-expressive, psychotic and retarded patients. Psychotherapy: Theory, Research and Practice 13(3), 290–5.

Prouty GF (1990) Pre-therapy: a theoretical evolution in the person-centered/experiential psychotherapy of schizophrenia and retardation. In G Lietaer, J Rombauts, R Van Balen (eds), Client-Centered and Experiential Psychotherapy in the Nineties (pp. 645–58). Leuven: Leuven University Press.

Prouty GF (1994) Theoretical Evolutions in Person-Centered/Experiential Therapy: Applications to Schizophrenic and Retarded Psychoses. Westport, Conn: Praeger.

Prouty GF (1999) Pre-therapy: is it person-centred?: a reply to Jerold Bozarth, The Person-Centered Journal 6(1): 28–31.

Prouty GF, Cronwal M (1989) Psychotherapy with a depressed mentally retarded adult: an application of pre-therapy. In A Dozen, F Menolascino (eds), Depression in Mentally Retarded Children and Adults (pp. 281–93). Leiden: Logan Publications.

Purton C (1989) The person-centered Jungian, Person-Centered Review 4(4): 403–19.

Purton C (1996) The deep structure of the core conditions: a Buddhist perspective. In R Hutterer, G Pawlowsky, PF Schmid, R Stipsits (eds), Client-Centered and Experiential Psychotherapy: A Paradigm in Motion (pp. 455–67). Frankfurt am Main: Peter Lang.

Quinn R (1993) Confronting Carl Rogers: a developmental-interactional approach to person-centered therapy, Journal of Humanistic Psychology 33(1): 6–23.

Raskin NJ (1948) The development of non-directive psychotherapy, Journal of Consulting Psychology 13: 154–6.

Raskin NJ (1987) From spyglass to kaleidoscope [review of RF Levant, JM Shlien (eds), Client-centered therapy and the person-centered approach: new directions in theory, research and practice], Contemporary Psychology 32: 460–1.

Raskin NJ (1990) The First 50 Years and the Next 10, Person-Centered Review 5(4): 364–72.

Raskin NJ (1996a) Person centred psychotherapy: twenty historical steps. In W Dryden (ed.), Developments in Psychotherapy: Historical Perspectives. London: Sage.

Raskin NJ (1996b) The case of Loretta: a psychiatric inpatient. In BA Farber, DC Brink, PM Raskin (eds), The Psychotherapy of Carl Rogers (pp. 44–56). New York: The Guilford Press.

Reber AS (1985) The Penguin Dictionary of Psychology. Harmondsworth: Penguin.

Reich W (1975) The Mass Psychology of Fascism (VR Carfagno, trans) (3rd edn). Harmondsworth: Penguin.

Rennie DL (1998) Person-Centred Counselling: An Experiential Approach. London: Sage.

Rice LN (1974) The evocative function of the therapist. In DA Wexler, LN Rice (eds), Innovations in Client-Centered Therapy (pp. 289–311). New York: Wiley.

Rice LN (1980) A client-centered approach to the supervision of psychotherapy. In AK Hess (ed.), Psychotherapy Supervision: Theory, Research and Practice (pp. 136–47). New York: Wiley.

Rogers CR (1931) Measuring Personality Adjustment in Children Nine to Thirteen. New York: Teachers College, Columbia University, Bureau of Publications.

Rogers CR (1939) The Clinical Treatment of the Problem Child. Boston: Houghton Mifflin.

Rogers CR (1942) Counseling and Psychotherapy: Newer Concepts in Practice. Boston: Houghton Mifflin.

Rogers CR (1947) The case of Mary Jane Tilden. In WU Snyder (ed.), Casebook of Nondirective Counseling (pp. 127–203). Boston, Mass: Houghton Mifflin.

Rogers CR (1951) Client-Centered Therapy. London: Constable.

Rogers CR (1954a) The case of Mr. Bebb: the analysis of a failure case. In CR Rogers, RF Dymond (eds), Psychotherapy and Personality Change (pp. 349–409). Chicago: University of Chicago Press.

Rogers CR (1954b) The case of Mrs. Oak: a research analysis. In CR Rogers, RF Dymond (eds), Psychotherapy and Personality Change (pp. 259–348). Chicago: University of Chicago Press.

Rogers CR (1956a) Intellectualized psychotherapy. [Review of The Psychology of Personal Constructs]. Contemporary Psychology 1: 357–8.

Rogers CR (1956b) The essence of psychotherapy: Moments of movement. Paper given to the First Meeting of the American Academy of Psychotherapists. New York.

Rogers CR (1957) The necessary and sufficient conditions of therapeutic personality change, Journal of Consulting Psychology 21: 95–103.

Rogers CR (1959) A theory of therapy, personality and interpersonal relationships, as developed in the client-centred framework. In S Koch (ed.), Psychology: A study of science, Vol. 3: Formulation of the Person and the Social Context (pp. 184–256). New York: McGraw-Hill.

Rogers CR (1960) A Therapist's View of Personal Goals. Wallingford, Penn: Pendle Hill Pamphlet 108.

Rogers CR (1961) On Becoming a Person. London: Constable.

Rogers CR (1963) The actualizing tendency in relation to 'motive' and to consciousness. In M Jones (ed.), Nebraska Symposium on Motivation, 1963 (pp. 1–24). Lincoln, Neb: University of Nebraska Press.

Rogers CR (1965) Dealing with psychological tensions, Journal of Applied Behavioral Science 1: 6–24.

Rogers CR (1966) Client-centered therapy. In S Arieti (ed.), American Handbook of Psychiatry (pp. 183–200). New York: Basic Books.

Rogers CR (1967a) A silent young man. In CR Rogers, ET Gendlin, DJ Kiesler, CB Truax (eds), The Therapeutic Relationship and Its Impact: A Study of Psychotherapy with Schizophrenics (pp. 184–256). Madison, Wis: University of Wisconsin Press.

Rogers CR (1967b) Some learnings from a study of psychotherapy with schizophrenics. In CR Rogers, B Stevens, Person to Person: The Problem of Being Human (pp. 181–92). Moab, Utah: Real People Press. (Original work published 1962.)

Rogers CR (1968) Some thoughts regarding the current presuppositions of the behavioural sciences. In W Coulson, CR Rogers (eds), Man and the Science of Man (pp. 55–72). Columbus, Ohio: Charles E. Merrill.

Rogers CR (1969) Freedom to Learn. Columbus, Ohio: Charles E. Merrill.

Rogers CR (1970) Carl Rogers on Encounter Groups. New York: Harper & Row.

Rogers CR (1973) Becoming Partners. London: Constable.

Rogers CR (1978) Carl Rogers on Personal Power. London: Constable.

Rogers CR (1980a) A Way of Being. London: Constable.

Rogers CR (1980b) The Struggle for Acceptance. Interview with Sylvia [film]. University of California, Santa Barbara, Calif: Carl Rogers Memorial Library.

Rogers CR (1982) A psychologist looks at nuclear war, Journal of Humanistic Psychology 21(4): 9–20.

Rogers CR (1983) Freedom to Learn for the 80's. Columbus, Ohio: Charles E. Merrill.

Rogers CR (1984) Gloria – A historical note. In R Levant, J Shlien (eds), Client-Centered Therapy and the Person-Centered Approach: New Directions in Theory, Research and Practice (pp. 423–5). New York: Praeger.

Rogers CR (1986a) A client-centered/person-centered approach to therapy. In IL Kutash, A Wolf (eds), Psychotherapist's Casebook (pp. 197–208). San Francisco, Calif: Jossey-Bass.

Rogers CR (1986b) Reflection of feelings, Person-Centred Review 1(4): 375–7.

Rogers CR (1986c) Rogers, Kohut, and Erickson: a personal perspective on some similarities and differences, Person-Centred Review 1(2): 125–40.

Rogers CR (1986d) The dilemmas of a South African white, Person-Centred Review 1: 15–35.

Rogers CR (1986e) The Rust workshop, Journal of Humanistic Psychology 26(3): 23–45.

Rogers CR (1987) Transference, Person-Centred Review 2(2): 182–8.

Rogers CR (1989) The case of Mrs Oak. In D Wedding, JR Corsini (eds), Case Studies in Psychotherapy (pp. 63–85). Itasca, Ill: Peacock.

Rogers CR (1990a) A note on the 'Nature of Man'. In H Kirschenbaum, VL Henderson (eds), The Carl Rogers Reader (pp.401–8). London: Constable. (Original work published 1957.)

Rogers CR (1990b) Ellen West – and loneliness. In H Kirschenbaum, VL Henderson (eds), The Carl Rogers Reader (pp. 157–68). London: Constable. (Original work published 1961.)

Rogers CR (1990c) Notes on Rollo May. In H Kirschenbaum, VL Henderson (eds), Carl Rogers Dialogues (pp. 237–9). London: Constable. (Original work published 1981.)

Rogers CR (1990d) Some new challenges to the helping professions. In H Kirschenbaum, VL Henderson (eds), The Carl Rogers Reader (pp. 357–75). London: Constable. (Original work published 1961.)

Rogers CR (1990e) The characteristics of a helping relationship. In H Kirschenbaum, VL Henderson (eds), The Carl Rogers Reader (pp. 108–26). London: Constable. (Original work published 1958.)

Rogers CR (1990f) The use of electrically recorded interviews in improving psychotherapeutic techniques. In H Kirschenbaum, VL Henderson (eds), The Carl Rogers Reader (pp. 211–19). London: Constable. (Original work published 1942.)

Rogers CR (1990g) Toward a modern approach to values: the valuing process in the mature person. In H Kirschenbaum, VL Henderson (eds), The Carl Rogers Reader (pp. 168–85). London: Constable. (Original work published 1964.)

Rogers CR (1990h) Toward a more human science of the person. In H Kirschenbaum, VL Henderson (eds), The Carl Rogers Reader (pp. 279–95). London: Constable. (Original work published 1985.)

Rogers CR (1990i) What I learned from two research studies. In H Kirschenbaum, VL Henderson (eds), The Carl Rogers Reader (pp. 203–11). London: Constable. (Original work published 1986.)

Rogers CR (1991) An open letter to participants of European workshops. In E McIlduff, D Coghlan (eds), The Person-Centered Approach and Cross-Cultural Communication: An International Review, Volume 1 (pp. 11–13). Dublin: Center for Cross-Cultural Communication.

Rogers CR, Barfield G (1984) Behind the Iron Curtain. Carl Rogers speaking about a Hungarian workshop [Audi tape]. La Jolla, Calif: Center for the Studies of the Person.

Rogers CR, Dymond, RF (eds) (1954). Psychotherapy and Personality Change. Chicago: University of Chicago Press.

Rogers CR, Hart JT (eds) (1970) Looking back and ahead: A conversation with Carl Rogers. In JT Hart, TM Tomlinson (eds) New Directions in Client-Centered Therapy (pp. 502–33). Boston, Mass: Houghton Mifflin.

Rogers CR, Sanford R (1984) Client-centered psychotherapy. In H Kaplan, B Sadock, A Freeman (eds), Comprehensive Textbook of Psychiatry Vol. 3 (pp. 1374–88). Baltimore, Md: Williams & Wilkins.

Rogers CR, Segel RH (prods) (1955a) Client-centered therapy. Part I: Psychotherapy Begins: The Case of Mr. Lin [film]. Pittsburgh, Penn: Pennsylvania State University Psychological Cinema Register.

Rogers CR, Segel RH (pods) (1955b) Client-centered therapy. Part II: Psychotherapy in Process: The Case of Miss Mun [film]. Pittsburgh, Penn: Pennsylvania State University Psychological Cinema Register.

Rogers CR, Stevens B (1967) Person to Person: The Problem of Being Human. Moab, Utah: Real People Press.

Rogers CR, Wallen JL (1946) Counseling with Returned Servicemen. New York: McGraw-Hill.

Rogers CR, Wood JK (1974) The changing theory of client-centered therapy. In A Burton (ed.), Operational Theories of Personality (pp. 211–58). New York: Brunner/Mazel.

Rogers CR, Kell BL, McNeil H (1948) The role of self-understanding in the prediction of behavior, Journal of Consulting Psychology 12: 174–86.

Rogers CR, Lewis M, Shlien J (1959) Two cases of time-limited client-centered psychotherapy. In A Burton (ed.), Case studies of counseling and psychotherapy (pp. 309–52). New York: Prentice-Hall.

Rogers CR, Gendlin ET, Kiesler DJ, Truax CB (eds) (1967) The Therapeutic Relationship and Its Impact: A Study of Psychotherapy with Schizophrenics. Madison, Wis: University of Wisconsin Press.

Rogers N (1980) Emerging Woman: A Decade of Midlife Transitions. Point Reyes, Calif: Personal Press.

Rogers N (1993) The Creative Connection: Expressive Arts as Healing. Palo Alto, Calif: Science and Behavior Books.

Rosenzweig D (1996) The case of Gloria: Summary. In BA Farber, DC Brink, PM Raskin (eds), The Psychotherapy of Carl Rogers (pp. 57–64). New York: The Guilford Press.

Rowan J (1988) Ordinary Ecstasy: Humanistic Psychology in Action (2nd edn). London: Routledge.

Rowan J (1990) Subpersonalities. London: Routledge.

Rowan J (1994) A Guide to Humanistic Psychology (2nd edn). London: Association for Humanistic Psychology in Britain.

Sanders, P (2000) Mapping person-centred approaches to counselling and psychotherapy, Person-Centred Practice 8(2): 62–74.

Sanders P, Tudor K (2001) This is therapy: a person-centred critique of the contemporary psychiatric system. In C Newnes, G Holmes, C Dunn (eds), This is Madness Too: Critical Perspectives on Mental Health Services (pp. 147–60). Llangarron: PCCS Books.

Sandler J, Dare C, Holder A (1992) The Patient and the Analyst. London: Karnac Books.

Sanford R (1984) The beginning of a dialogue in South Africa. The Counselling Psychologist 12(3): 3–14.

Sanford R (1993) From Rogers to Gleick and back again. In D Brazier (ed.), Beyond Carl Rogers (pp. 253–73). London: Constable.

Sanford R (1999) Conversation with Ruth Sanford at the 5th Person-Centred International Forum at Terschelling, 1992. In I Fairhurst (ed.), Women Writing in the Person-Centred Approach (pp. 129–46). Llangarron: PCCS Books.

Sapriel L (1998) Can gestalt therapy, self-psychology and intersubjectivity theory be integrated? The British Gestalt Journal 7(1): 33–44.

Schmid PF (1996) Intimacy, tenderness and lust: a person-centered approach to sexuality. In R Hutterer, G Pawlowsky, PF Schmid, R Stipsits (eds), Client-Centered and Experiential Psychotherapy: A Paradigm in Motion (pp. 85–99). Frankfurt am Main: Peter Lang.

Schmid PF (1998a) 'Face to face' – the art of encounter. In B Thorne, E Lambers (eds), Person-Centred Therapy: A European Perspective (pp. 74–90). London: Sage.

Schmid PF (1998b) 'On becoming a person-centred approach': a person-centred understanding of the person. In B Thorne, E Lambers (eds), Person-Centred Therapy: A European Perspective (pp. 38–52). London: Sage.

Schneider C, Stiles W (1995) Women's experience of depression, The Person-Centered Journal 2(1): 67–77.

Schutz W (1973) Elements of Encounter. Big Sur, Calif: Joy Press.

Seeman J (1983) Personality Integration: Studies and Reflections. New York: Human Sciences Press.

Seeman J (1984) The fully functioning person: theory and research. In RF Levant, J Shlien (eds), Client-Centered Therapy and the Person-Centered Approach: New Directions in Theory, Research and Practice (pp. 131–52) New York: Praeger.

Seeman J (1988) Self-actualization: a reformulation, Person-Centered Review 3(3): 304–15

Seeman J (ed.) (1990) Human inquiry and the person-centered approach [Special Issue], Person-Centered Review 5(2).

Seeman J (1996) Rogers and Mark: the power of the brief encounter. In BA Farber, DC Brink, PM Raskin (eds), The Psychotherapy of Carl Rogers (pp. 350–6). New York: The Guilford Press.

Segrera AS (ed.) (1984) Proceedings of the First International Forum on the Person-Centered Approach. Oaxrepec, Moreles, Mexico: Universidad Iberamericana.

Senge PM (1990) The Fifth Discipline: The Art and Practice of the Learning Organisation. London: Doubleday.

Shlein J (1961) A client-centered approach to schizophrenia: first approximation. In A Burton (ed.), Psychotherapy of the Psychoses (pp. 404–16). New York: Basic Books.

Shlien J (1984) A countertheory of transference. In R Levant, J Shlien (eds), Client-Centered Therapy and the Person-Centered Approach: New Directions in Theory, Research and Practice (pp. 153–81). New York: Praeger.

Shlien J (1989) Boy's person-centered perspective on psychodiagnosis: a response, Person-Centered Review 4(2): 157–62.

Shostrom E (prod.) (1964) Three Approaches to Psychotherapy [film]. Santa Ana, Calif: Psychological Films.

Shostrom E (prod.) (1975) Three Approaches to Psychotherapy [film]. Santa Ana, Calif: Psychological Films.

Singh J, Tudor K (1997) Cultural conditions of therapy, The Person-Centered Journal 4(2): 32–46.

Smuts J (1926) Holism and Evolution. New York: Macmillan.

Snyder M (1994) The development of social intelligence in psychotherapy: empathic and dialogic processes, Journal of Humanistic Psychology 34(1): 84–108.

Snyder WU (1945) An investigation of the nature of non directive psychotherapy, Journal of General Psychology 33: 193–223.

Snygg D, Combs AW (1949) Individual Behavior: A New Frame of Reference for Psychology. New York: Harper & Bros.

Speierer G-W (1990) Toward a specific illness concept of client-centered therapy. In G Lietaer, J Rombauts, R Van Balen (eds), Client-Centered and Experiential Psychotherapy in the Nineties (pp. 337–59). Leuven: Leuven University Press.

Speierer G-W (1996) Client-centered psychotherapy according to the differential incongruence model (DIM). In R Hutterer, G Pawlowsky, PF Schmid, R Stipsits (eds), Client-Centered and Experiential Psychotherapy: A Paradigm in Motion (pp. 299–311). Frankfurt am Main: Peter Lang.

Spinelli E (1989) The Interpreted World. London: Sage.

Stamatiadis R (1990) Sharing life therapy, Person-Centered Review 5(3): 287-307.

Standal S (1954) The need for positive regard: a contribution to client-centered theory. Unpublished PhD thesis, Chicago, Mich: University of Chicago.

Stephenson W (1953) The Study of Behaviour: Q-Technique and Its Methodology. Chicago, Mich: University of Chicago Press.

Stern DN (1985) The Interpersonal World of the Infant. New York: Basic Books.

Stigler JW, Shweder RA, Herdt G (eds) (1990) Cultural Psychology. Cambridge: Cambridge University Press.

Sullivan HS (1945) Conceptions of Modern Psychiatry. Washington, DC: W.A. White Foundation.

Szent-Gyoergyi A (1974) Drive in living matter to perfect itself. Synthesis, Spring, 12–24.

Tajfel H (1972) Experiments in a vacuum. In J Israel, H Tajfel (eds), The Context of Social Psychology: A Critical Assessment. Spring London: Academic Press.

Taft J (1933) The Dynamics of Therapy in a Controlled Relationship. New York: Macmillan.

Temaner M, Raskin N (1996) The case of Loretta (1958). Transcript. In BA Farber, DC Brink, PM Raskin (eds), The Psychotherapy of Carl Rogers (pp. 33–43). New York: The Guilford Press.

Teusch L (1990) Positive effects and limitations of client-centered therapy with schizophrenic patients. In G Lietaer, J Rombauts, R Van Balen (eds), Client-Centered and Experiential Psychotherapy in the Nineties (pp. 637–44). Leuven: Leuven University Press.

Thorne B (1991a) Carl Rogers: the legacy and the challenge. In B Thorne, Person-Centred Counselling: Therapeutic and Spiritual Dimensions (pp. 178–89). London: Whurr.

Thorne B (1991b) Person-Centred Counselling: Therapeutic and Spiritual Dimensions. London: Whurr.

Thorne B (1991c) The quality of tenderness. In B Thorne, Person-Centred Counselling: Therapeutic and Spiritual Dimensions (pp. 73–81). London: Whurr. (Original work published 1985.)

Thorne B (1992) Carl Rogers. London: Sage.

Thorne B (1995) The accountable therapist: standards, experts and poisoning the well, Self & Society 23(4): pp. 31–8.

Thorne B (1996a) Person-centred therapy. In W Dryden (ed.), Handbook of Individual Therapy (pp. 121–46). London: Sage.

Thorne B (1996b) The cost of transparency, Person-Centred Practice 4(2): 2–11.

Thorne B (1998a) Person-Centred Counselling and Christian Spirituality: The Secular and the Holy. London: Whurr.

Thorne B (1998b) The two Carls – reflections on Jung and Rogers. In B Thorne, Person-Centred Counselling and Christian Spirituality: The Secular and the Holy (pp. 60–70). London: Whurr.

Thorne B, Lambers E (eds) (1998) Person-Centred Therapy: A European Perspective. London: Sage.

Tillich P (1952) The Courage to Be. London: Fontana.

Tobin SA (1991) A comparison of psychoanalytic self psychology and Carl Rogers' person-centered therapy, Journal of Humanistic Psychology 30: 9–33.

Tophoff M (1984) The dynamics of person-centered body work in a group setting. Paper presented at The VIIIth International Congress of Group Psychotherapy, Mexico City.

Totton N (1997) The Independent Practitioners Network: a new model of accountability. In R House, N Totton (eds), Implausible Professions: Arguments for Pluralism and Autonomy in Psychotherapy and Counselling (pp. 287–93). Llangarron: PCCS Books.

Truax CB, Carkhuff RR (1967) Toward effective counseling and psychotherapy: training and practice. Chicago, Mich: Aldine.

Truax CB, Mitchell KK (1971). Research on certain interpersonal skills in relation to process and outcome. In AE Bergin, SL Garfield (eds), Handbook of Psychotherapy and Behaviour Change: An Empirical Analysis (pp. 299–344). New York: Wiley & Sons.

Tscheulin D (1990) Confrontation and non-confrontation as differential techniques in differential client-centered therapy. In G Lietaer, J Rombauts, R Van Balen (eds), Client-Centered and Experiential Psychotherapy in the Nineties (pp. 327–36). Leuven: Leuven University Press.

Tudor K (ed.) (1997) The person-centred approach and the political sphere [Special Issue], Person Centred Practice, 5(2).

Tudor K (1998) Value for money, British Journal of Guidance & Counselling 26(4): 477–93.

Tudor K (1999a) Group Counselling. London: Sage.

Tudor K (1999b) 'I'm OK, you're OK – and they're OK': therapeutic relationships in transactional analysis. In C Feltham (ed.), Understanding the Counselling Relationship (pp. 909–19). London: Sage.

Tudor K (1999c) TA and the PCA – OK? Transactional analysis and the person-centred approach. In K Leach (ed.), Conference Papers of the Annual Conference of the Institute of Transactional Analysis. Edinburgh: ITA.

Tudor K (2000) The case of the lost conditions, Counselling 11(1): 33–7.

Tudor K, Worrall M (1994) Congruence reconsidered, British Journal of Guidance and Counselling 22(4): 197–206.

Tudor K, Worrall M (in press) The unspoken relationship: financial dynamics in freelance therapy. In J Clark (ed.), Freelance Counselling and Psychotherapy. London: Sage.

Van Belle HA (1980) Basic Intent and Therapeutic Approach of Carl R. Rogers. Toronto: Wedge Publishing Foundation.

Van Belle HA (1990). Rogers' later move towards mysticism: implications for client-centered therapy. In G Lietaer, J Rombauts, R Van Balen (eds), Client-Centered and Experiential Psychotherapy in the Nineties (pp. 47–57). Leuven: Leuven University Press.

van Deurzen-Smith E (1996) Existential therapy. In W Dryden (ed.), Handbook of Individual Therapy (pp. 166–93). London: Sage.

Van Kalmthout M (1995) Religious dimensions of Rogers's work, Journal of Humanistic Psychology 35(4): 23–39.

Van Werde D (1994) An introduction to client-centred pre-therapy. In D Mearns, Developing Person-Centred Counselling (pp. 121–5). London: Sage.

Van Werde D (1998) 'Anchorage' as a core concept in working with psychotic people. In B Thorne, E Lambers (eds), Person-Centred Therapy (pp. 195–205). London: Sage.

Villas-Boas Bowen M (1984) Spirituality and person-centered approach: interconnectedness in the universe and psychotherapy. In AS Segrera (ed.), Proceedings of the First International Forum on the Person-Centered Approach. Oaxrepec, Moreles, Mexico: Universidad Iberamericana.

Villas-Boas Bowen M (1986) Personality differences and person-centered supervision, Person-Centered Review 1(3): 291–309.

Villas-Boas Bowen M (1996) The myth of non directiveness: the case of Jill. In BA Farber, DC Brink, PM Raskin (eds), The Psychotherapy of Carl Rogers (pp. 84–94). New York: The Guilford Press.

Vitz P (1977) Psychology as Religion: The Cult of Self-Worship. Grand Rapids, Mich: William B. Eerdmans.

Vossen TJ (1990) Client-centered dream therapy. In G Lietaer, J Rombauts, R Van Balen (eds), Client-Centered and Experiential Psychotherapy in the Nineties (pp. 511–48). Leuven: Leuven University Press.

Warner MS (1991) Fragile process. In L Fusek (ed.), New Directions in Client-Centered Therapy: Practice with Difficult Client Populations (Monograph Series 1) (pp. 41–58). Chicago, Ill: Chicago Counseling and Psychotherapy Center.

Warner MS (1998) A client-centered approach to therapeutic work with disssociated and fragile process. In L Greenberg, J Watson, G Lietaer (eds), Handbook of Experiential Psychotherapy (pp. 368–87). New York: The Guilford Press.

Warner MS (2000a) Person-centered psychotherapy: one nation, many tribes, The Person-Centered Journal 7(1): 28–39.

Warner MS (2000b) Person-centred therapy at the difficult edge: a developmentally based model of fragile and dissociated process. In D Mearns, B Thorne, Person-Centred Therapy Today (pp. 144–71). London: Sage.

Watson J, Warner M, Goldman R (in preparation) Proceedings of the Fifth International Conference on Client-Centred and Experiential Psychotherapy. Llangarron: PCCS Books.

Watson N (1984) The empirical status of Rogers's hypotheses of the necessary and sufficient conditions for effective psychotherapy. In RF Levant, JM Shlien (eds), Client-Centered Therapy and the Person-Centered Approach: New Directions in Theory, Research and Practice (pp. 17–40). New York: Praeger.

Weinrach SG (1990) Rogers and Gloria: the controversial film and the enduring relationship, Psychotherapy 27, 282–90.

West W (1998) Developing practice in a context of religious faith: a study of psychotherapists who are Quakers, British Journal of Guidance & Counselling 26(3): 365–75.

Wexler DA (1974) A cognitive theory of experiencing, self-actualization and therapeutic process. In DA Wexler, LN Rice (eds), Innovations in Client-Centered Therapy (pp. 49–116). New York: Wiley.

Wexler DA, Rice LN (eds) (1974) Innovations in Client-Centered Therapy. New York: Wiley.

Wheatley MJ, Kellner-Rogers M (1996) A simpler way. San Francisco, Calif: Berret-Koehler Publishers.

Wheeler S, McLeod J (1995) Person-centred and psychodynamic counselling: a dialogue, Counselling 6(4): 283–7.

Whitely JM (prod.) (1977a) Carl Rogers Counsels an Individual on Anger and Hurt [film]. Washington, DC: Personnel and Guidance Association.

Whitely JM (prod.) (1977b) The Right to be Desperate [film]. Washington, DC: American Personnel and Guidance Association.

Wijngaarden HR (1990) Carl Rogers, Carl Jung and client-centered therapy. In G Lietaer, J Rombauts, R Van Balen (eds), Client-Centered and Experiential Psychotherapy in the Nineties (pp. 469–79). Leuven: Leuven University Press.

Wilkins P (1994) Can psychodrama be 'person-centred'? Person-Centred Practice, 2(2), 14–18.

Wilkins P (1997a) Congruence and countertransference: similarities and differences, Counselling, 8(1), 36-41.

Wilkins P (1997b) Towards a person-centred understanding of consciousness and the unconscious, Person-Centred Practice 5(1): 14–20.

Wilkins P (2000) Unconditional positive regard reconsidered, British Journal of Guidance and Counselling 28(1): 23–36.

Wilkins P (in preparation) Person-Centred Therapy in Question. London: Sage.

Winnicott DW (1985) The theory of the parent–infant relationship. In The Maturational Processes and the Facilitating Environment (pp. 37–55). London: Hogarth Press/The Institute of Psycho-Analysis. (Original work published 1960.)

Wolter-Gustafson C (1999) The power of the premise: reconstructing gender and human development with Rogers' theory. In I Fairhurst (ed.), Women Writing in the Person-Centred Approach (pp. 199–214). Llangarron: PCCS Books.

Wood JK (1984) Communities for learning: a person-centered approach. In RS Levant, JM Shlien (eds), Client-Centered Therapy and the Person-Centered Approach (pp. 297–316). New York: Praeger.

Wood JK (1994) The person-centered approach's greatest weakness: not using its strength. The Person-Centered Journal 1(2): 69–78.

Wood JK (1995) The person-centered approach to small groups: more than psychotherapy. Unpublished manuscript.

Wood JK (1996) The person-centered approach: towards an understanding of its implications. In R Hutterer, G Pawlowsky, PF Schmid, R Stipsits (eds), Client-Centered and Experiential Psychotherapy: A Paradigm in Motion (pp. 163–81). Frankfurt am Main: Peter Lang.

Wood JK (1999) Toward an understanding of large group dialogue and its implications. In C Lago, M MacMillan (eds), Experiences in Relatedness: Groupwork and the Person-Centred Approach (pp. 137–65). Llangarron: PCCS Books.

World Health Organization. (1991) The International Classification of Diseases (10th edn.). Geneva: WHO.

Worrall M (1997) Contracting within the person-centred approach. In C Sills (ed.), Contracts in Counselling (pp. 65–75). London: Sage.

Wyatt G (ed.) (2001) Congruence. Llangarron: PCCS Books.

Yalom I (1995) The Theory and Practice of Group Psychotherapy (4th edn). New York: Basic Books.

Zimring FM (1974) Theory and practice of client-centered therapy: a cognitive view. In DA Wexler, LN Rice (eds), Innovations in Client-Centered Therapy (pp. 117–37). New York: Wiley.

Zimring FM (1988) Attaining mastery: the shift from the 'me' to the 'I'. Person-Centered Review 3(2): 165–75.

Zimring FM (1996) Rogers and Gloria: the effects of meeting some, but not all, of the 'necessary and sufficient' conditions. In BA Farber, DC Brink, PM Raskin (eds), The Psychotherapy of Carl Rogers (pp. 65–73). New York: The Guilford Press.

Zimring FM, Raskin NJ (1992) Carl Rogers and client/person-centered therapy. In DK Freedheim (ed.), History of Psychotherapy: A Century of Change (pp. 629–56). Washington, DC: American Psychological Association.